CAT
Owner's Survival Manual

Claire Horton-Bussey and David Godfrey

BVetMed Cert SAD Cert SAM Dip A

DEDICATION

For Dodie, Tiggy (One and Two), Tabbie, Paddie, Suki, Lady, Nobbie, Schuey and Georgie, and all the cats that will share my life in the future.

VETERINARY CONTRIBUTIONS

DAVID GODFREY AND ROSIE ANDERSON: David and Rosie are partners at The Nine Lives Veterinary Practice for Cats, based in the West Midlands, UK. It was the first cat-only veterinary practice in England when founded in 1994, and sees first-opinion cases as well as referrals in internal medicine and dermatology. David is the only European vet who has passed the American further qualifications in feline practice (currently there is no European equivalent). Currently, he is performing research for a RCVS Fellowship on osteoarthritis in cats.

CAROLINE BLUNDELL: Caroline was Feline Fellow at Bristol Veterinary School for two years; since then she has been working with cats in both referral and first-opinion capacities. In 1997, Caroline was appointed Feline Fellow at Bristol, where she expanded her interest in clinical feline medicine. She gained the RCVS Certificate in Small-Animal Medicine in 2001, and is now a partner at the Oxfordshire Cat Clinic.

CHRIS DAY: Chris is a leading expert in veterinary homeopathy. He runs the Alternative Veterinary Medicine Centre in south Oxfordshire and is a founder member of the British Association for Veterinary Homeopathy. He gained Membership of the Faculty of Homeopathy in 1987, later becoming Veterinary Dean of the Faculty, and a Fellow. He is a founder member of the International Association for Veterinary Homeopathy, was its first president, and is currently serving another term in office.

TREVOR TURNER: After qualifying as a vet more than 40 years ago, Trevor started a small-animal practice, specialising primarily in cats and dogs. Together with his wife, Jean, he has bred and exhibited longhaired silver tabbies and Maine Coons. Jointly with Jean, he is overall editor of *Veterinary Notes For Cat Owners*, and writes regularly for the cat press. He acts as honorary veterinary surgeon at major cat shows in the UK, including the National and the Supreme.

ILLUSTRATIONS

Photos: Amanda Bulbeck and *Your Cat* magazine. Cover photography: Marc Henrie.
Cartoons: Russell Jones.

GENDER

Throughout this text, cats have been referred to as 'she' but no gender bias is intended.

Copyright © 2002 by Ringpress Books.
This edition published by Friedman/Fairfax, by arrangement with Ringpress Books,
a division of Interpet Ltd, Vincent Lane, Dorking, Surrey RH4 3YX

Designed by Rob Benson.

ISBN 1-58663-747-9

Printed and bound in Singapore

0 9 8 7 6 5 4 3 2 1

THE TEN-PART SURVIVAL GUIDE

Cat Owner's Survival Manual has been divided into ten parts so that you can find your way around with ease, learning as much as possible about your feline friend.

CONTENTS IN DETAIL

PART NINE: *BREEDING CATS*

PART TEN: *HEALTH CARE*

APPENDICES

Part I
Understanding Cats

Chapter I

From Ancient Times

"Even the smallest feline is a work of art" claimed celebrated artist Leonardo da Vinci, capturing the great appeal of the cat – her beauty. Whether lying Sphinx-like by the fire, stretching in the warm sun, or sitting by a window, statuesque and proud, watching the world go past, the cat is a joy to behold. She moves with stealth and gracefulness, speed and agility, combining power, athleticism, and elegance.

The cat isn't simply aesthetically pleasing. Her aura of natural wildness is both fascinating and appealing. Sharing your life with a cat is to invite a little of the wild outdoors into your home. An enigmatic and independent free spirit, the cat is a perfect balance between the wild and the domestic. Dozing on the sofa one moment, and stalking prey in the garden the next, the cat leads a dual life, and it is this untamed aspect that makes the cat so mysterious and captivating.

As a companion, the cat cannot be bettered. A puss makes a house a home. Another great artist, Stanley Spencer, said: "Wherever a cat sits, there shall happiness be found." Her warm, soft, silky coat makes her exceptionally strokable; her fastidious cleanliness makes her an ideal house-mate; she is independent when you cannot spend time with her; and her small size means she can nap on your lap without giving you cramp!

One of the best aspects of cat ownership is the responsiveness – there is nothing better than stroking a contented cat and hearing her warm, rhythmic purr. Knowing the cat enjoys our company, and that she lives with us out of choice and not necessity, is a huge compliment, and repays all the love and kindness we give to our pets.

PUSS'S PAST

The cat's history has been a turbulent one, reliant on her relationship with humans, who have oscillated between idolizing and persecuting her.

The story starts about 60 million years ago, when a group of animals called miacids developed. They had fairly long bodies, short legs, and fox-like, pointed faces. All carnivore mammals are believed to have descended from miacids, including the cat.

By 45 million years ago, creatures with some feline characteristics had emerged, and by 20 million years ago, cats remarkably similar to today's were roaming the earth, present in most parts of the world, except Australia, New Zealand and New Guinea, which were geographically isolated from other continents.

By 100,000 years ago, the cat family had developed three distinct groups:

• *Panthera* (big cats, such as lions and tigers)
• *Acinonyx* (cats that cannot retract their claws, such as cheetahs)
• *Felis* (smaller wildcats, such as lynx).

It is to this third group that the African wildcat, the father of the modern domestic cat, belonged.

HEART OF AFRICA

The African wildcat (*Felis sylvestrus libyaca*) is a solitary hunter. Considerably smaller than the big cats, she does not need to hunt in packs, because her food needs are not that great. She can adequately survive on small rodents and birds to satisfy her hunger, and such prey she is more than capable of catching alone.

Genetically, the African wildcat and the modern domestic cat are very similar, although there are a few key physical differences. As well as having much shorter intestines (to deal with a less varied diet), wildcats have a much larger brain – surviving in the wild, hunting for food and avoiding becoming food, required extra brain power that domestic cats no longer need.

Around 6,000 years ago, this increased intelligence also stood her in good stead for exploiting a valuable new opportunity that was about to come her way.

RODENT REVOLUTION

It has been the cat's good fortune to love mice. A supreme survivor, reliant on her keen senses and hunting skills to catch a meal, the wildcat rarely went hungry. The same could not be said for humans.

The agricultural revolution of the neolithic Stone Age meant that humans relied on the land for their survival, rather than hunting and gathering. Crops harvested once or twice a year had to feed villages all year round, so their safe storage was vital. Grain was the main crop that was produced, for milling into flour, but voracious swarms of rats and mice jeopardised the precious reserves.

Cats are great opportunists and it wouldn't have taken them long to see the potential that these granaries offered – why waste time and energy roaming, hunting for the odd rodent, when there were hundreds in one spot? As well as an abundance of easy prey, the grain stores offered protection from any wild predators, which were too fearful of hunting the cat so close to human settlements.

If cats are great opportunists, then humans certainly are too, and they would have welcomed the cats' help in eradicating the rodents. Over time, cats became less wary of people, realizing they offered no threat. In fact, cats were positively encouraged to hang around, because they were so useful at protecting the grain.

It is believed that some kind of genetic mutation took place, making the cats more docile. Selective breeding also played an important part in the cat's domestication: the granaries would have attracted bold cats that were not too fearful of humans. They would have mated with like-minded cats, raising their kittens in close proximity to people. Kittens that were too scared of people would have left the settlement, reverting back to life in the wild; with each generation that stayed and bred, so the domestic 'people-friendly' qualities would have been replicated and reinforced.

It wasn't long before the cat was invited into people's homes to keep rodents and poisonous snakes at bay. Here, the cat flourished. In addition to all their other skills, cats are fantastic manipulators – in the nicest possible way, of course! A friendly rub against the leg and a responsive, friendly purr, and the cat can win over the hardest of hearts. Useful at ratting, yet a warm, loving companion, the cat assured her place in our homes – somewhere she has been ever since.

EGYPTIAN ENIGMA

It was the cat's great mousing and ratting skills that made her so valuable in Egypt, a country that feared famine and was more reliant than most on agriculture. This nation understood the importance of storing food in good times to see it through the bad times.

The fertile flood-plains of the Nile usually yielded rich crops, and ensured the wealth for which Egypt was famed. Without safe storage, a good crop meant nothing. The ruling government, led by the pharaoh, therefore placed great value on the cat – without her, the nation could starve.

Laws were passed that forbade the harming of a cat. Killing a cat, even accidentally, was punishable by death. Historical accounts show that the punishment was not an idle threat – it was implemented without hesitation.

When a cat died of natural causes, the family was expected to observe a strict period of mourning as if a human member of the household had died. They would shave off their eyebrows, and organize for the cat to be embalmed, and sometimes elaborately decorated, before being interred. Food and milk for the cat to enjoy in the afterlife were often provided. People were frequently buried with their cats as a sign of their eternal respect and love.

The cat went beyond being a useful ratter, and became a symbol of fertility – a quality prized in a land that lived on a knife edge between barrenness and fertility, desert and flood-plain, life and death. Beautiful, fecund, and mysterious, the cat was an ideal candidate for deification.

The dual god of agriculture (i.e. life) and death, Osiris, was featured as a cat, and around 600 to 200 BC, the cat was particularly associated with Bastet (also called Pasht), the cat-headed goddess of fertility, and life and death. More than 300,000 cat mummies were buried at the luxurious Bast temple, located at Bubastis (meaning 'city of Bastet'), the scene of mass cat-worshipping ceremonies.

Unfortunately, when they were discovered in the 19th century, the mummified cats were not treated with the same respect that they commanded in their lifetimes. Many of the cats were sold to a company in Birmingham, England, where they were rendered into fertilizer. A sad, if ironic, end for animals that were intrinsically associated with agriculture and fertility.

CONQUERING THE WORLD

Because of the spiritual (and practical) importance of cats in Egypt, the authorities forbade their export. When the Greeks first got hold of the domestic cat, one Pharaoh sent out an army to recapture the precious 'hostages'. Gradually, however, the domestic cat found its way into neighboring countries, and, from there, was introduced around the world by traders and sailors.

In many of the countries she found herself in, the cat received a similarly reverential audience. In Thailand, the cat was considered the carrier of kings' souls. When a king died, a living cat was put into the tomb, and was later allowed to escape through a drilled hole. When the cat left the tomb, she was believed to have been imbued

GOOD MEWS

The Egyptians called their domestic cat 'mau', showing that cat language clearly hasn't changed in more than 4,000 years! Interestingly, mau also means 'to see', referring to the cat's all-seeing god-like status.

LESSON IN LATERAL THINKING

Egypt's enemies quickly learned of the country's deep respect for the cat, and used it to their advantage. When the Persians tried to capture the Egyptian city of Pelusium in 500 BC, they realized that force would get them nowhere. Instead, the canny Persians carried cats close to their bodies, knowing that this would render the Egyptians helpless, and took the city unchallenged!

with the spirit of the king, and was treated as such – she would attend court and be revered wherever she went. When the cat finally died, it was believed she would carry the king's soul to heaven.

In Japan, cats were called tama, meaning treasure or jewel, and were only kept by nobility. Until 1602, they were walked on leads, like dogs, until they were ordered to be released to save the silkworm industry that was being threatened by rodents.

FREE SPIRIT

The spiritual aspect of the cat was emphasized time and again in different cultures. Christianity embraced the cat as a symbol of fertility, with a cat often featuring in sculptures and paintings of the Virgin Mary, and, in Scandinavia, cats were believed to pull the chariot of Freya, the fertility goddess.

The prophet Mohammed was a cat lover, and was saved from being bitten by a deadly snake, thanks to a cat. He loved cats to such an extent that when he found his pet, Muezza, asleep on the sleeve of his coat, he cut the sleeve off, so the slumbering puss could continue to rest undisturbed. (A similar story is told of the poet W.B. Yeats, who, preparing to leave the Abbey Theatre in Dublin, found the theatre cat asleep on his coat.)

WHAT'S IN A NAME?

The name for the cat is recognizable in many different languages.

Chat	French	Kot	Polish
Chatul	Hebrew	Koshka	Russian
Cath	Welsh	Kotsur	Slovakian
Cattus	Latin	Gatto	Italian
Katze	German	Gato	Mexican/Spanish
Kat	Dutch	Mio	Chinese
Kate	Lithuanian	Mau	Egyptian
Kats	Yiddish	Maow	Cantonese
Katt	Swedish	Maa-oh	Thai
Kitt	Arabic	Pishi	Persian

The majority of languages use 'cat' or similar, and this derives from the cat fertility amulets worn by young women in ancient Egypt that were called 'utchats'. The word 'puss' is thought to come from 'Pasht', the alternative name for the goddess Bastet. There's no need to explain where the 'miaow'-type names come from!

Because of Mohammed's fondness for cats, they are still highly respected in Islam; they are free to come and go as they please in mosques and it is illegal in Islamic law to kill one.

CHANGE OF FORTUNE

Sadly, the love affair with the cat could not last forever. Perhaps it was the dual symbolism with which the cat was associated – life and death – that made her downfall inevitable.

The Catholic Church's Inquisition of the 13th century was the start of a long period of persecution for the cat. The church was determined to stamp out heresy. With the cat's links with numerous non-Catholic religions, including Islam, Hinduism and the Nordic religions, the cat was guilty by association. Pope Gregory IX believed the devil would transform himself into a black cat, when he would be worshipped by devil-idolizing heretics. Black cats, and then cats in general, were blamed if illness or bad luck hit a village.

Single women have been perceived as dangerous throughout history, and bore the brunt of the hysteria that swept Europe and North America (later culminating, in 1692, in the infamous Salem witch trials, in Massachusetts). Spinsters and widows were persecuted as witches if they owned cats – deemed their 'familiars'.

Mass ceremonies of cat burning, hanging and drowning entertained crowds of people, all brainwashed into thinking they were ridding themselves of evil spirits and the devil himself. Their owners often joined them at the stake. The cat's nocturnal life was proof enough, for some, of the cat's link with 'the dark side', and cat-lovers were guilty by association.

BLACK DEATH

Perhaps it was the cat's reduced numbers that enabled the Black Death to have such an impact when it reached Europe in 1347. Spread by rats (carrying fleas that transferred the disease to humans) in just five years, it was responsible for the death of 25 million people. Ironically, cats were blamed for disease, and the killings were increased. In England, the Lord Mayor of London decreed that all cats should be destroyed, unwittingly aiding the further spread of the disease.

RISE AGAIN

Eventually, the anti-cat fervor ran its course. With fewer cats, rodents were enjoying great freedom to breed unchecked in large numbers. So it was with a degree of relief that people welcomed the repeal of the witchcraft laws in 1736, and the Church's more relaxed attitude towards the misunderstood cat. Such was the Church's turnaround, in fact, that it wasn't long before Popes, previously responsible for millions of feline deaths, started to own cats themselves. No longer fearful of the consequences, ordinary people welcomed the feline back into their homes where she resumed her career in pest control and lap-warming!

Since then, the cat's history has been relatively steady, lacking the peaks and troughs of fortune that she has enjoyed and endured in the past.

Vestiges of irrational superstition still remain, however. Black cats are still considered unlucky in America, through their association with the devil, and comprise a high number of abandoned and stray cats in shelters and adoption agencies. Britain has a different perspective on the black cat, believing it is lucky if a black cat crosses your path, as it means the devil has passed you by.

Generally, the cat is considered a good omen, though, particularly in Japan, where manekineko, the figure of a cat with a paw raised, is a popular symbol of good fortune. The French perpetuated the concept of the matagot, a cat who, if treated well, bestows good luck on its carers. And, in theatres around the world, it is considered very good luck if a cat fouls backstage.

BREEDS APART

Compared with dogs, that have been domesticated over more than 20,000 years, the cat is a relative newcomer, sharing our lives for a quarter of this time. This explains why the cat has retained many of her wild instincts (see Chapter Two), which are much more to the fore than those of a dog.

It also explains why cats are all so similar to each other. Although there are many different breeds of cats (Chapter Four), incorporating different colors, coat types, and temperaments, cats are all roughly the same size and shape – they do not have the type of canine diversity illustrated by the towering Great Dane and the diminutive Chihuahua.

It is unlikely that we will ever see feline breeds as varied as canine ones, because dogs were bred for a wide variety of roles that required them to be different sizes and shapes. Primarily, cats are companions and ratters – jobs which do not require them to be any different from what they already are.

If change does come to the cat it will be because of the show world and changing fashion. Already, in just 50 years, selective breeding has noticeably altered breeds such as the Siamese (who has become much more angular and athletic) and the Persian (whose face is flatter and broader).

Both breeds are quite different to those of just a few decades ago, although breed clubs throughout the world are working to protect individual breeds from extreme

KINGLY CATASTROPHE
British king Charles I was so convinced that his black cat protected him from bad luck that he had puss guarded. It seems Charles's instincts were right – when the cat died from illness, Charles was arrested the next day, and later beheaded.

conformation standards that would potentially compromise the cat's health.

With another 15,000 years of breeding, perhaps cats *will* exhibit a similar diversity to that of their canine counterparts?

GOLDEN AGE

Just as they had been invaluable in the Agricultural Revolution, so cats came into their own with the Industrial Revolution of the 19th century. Warehouses and factories were mice magnets, and cats were used – and still are used – to keep rodents at bay. Some companies actually put cats on the payroll, making sure their feline staff were well provided for and adequately recompensed for their hard work!

As a pet, the cat is enjoying something of a return to a golden age at the moment. Pet ownership has changed considerably in the last few decades, with animals being viewed as integral family members rather than walking mouse-traps.

Modern living favors the cat, too. More adults are working full-time, making them unsuitable owners for the demanding needs of a dog. The cat, however, has filled the niche perfectly – independent when alone, and loving and affectionate when the owners return home from work. Some breeds of cat can adapt to living in flats and apartments too, and house-cats do not even require you to have a garden (although they do need space and stimulation within the home to keep them healthy and happy – see Chapter Eighteen).

The cat has adapted, just as she did thousands of years ago, and so has ensured her continued survival. She is now considerably more popular than the dog in many countries around the world (see below), and her popularity looks set to continue well into the 21st century and beyond.

BATTLE OF THE PETS

	CATS	DOGS
Australia	2.7	3.9
Canada	6.5	5.8
France	8.4	7.9
Germany	6.4	5.2
Italy	6.6	5.8
Japan	8	10.3
Russia	40	19
UK	8	6.5
US	75	59

* All figures expressed in millions

Chapter 2

The Panther In Our Home

One of the most appealing aspects of sharing your life with a cat is that, despite years of domestication, she is wild at heart. Witnessing a cat stalking a leaf in the garden is a joy to watch, and similarities with the big cats of Africa cannot be missed.

JEKYLL AND HYDE

Cats lead double lives. Indoors, puss is a lap-loving cuddle fiend; outdoors, she can be the feline equivalent of Terminator – hunting, chasing, and killing prey with great speed and skill. There are always exceptions, of course. Some cats couldn't catch a mouse if it came up and bit them on the tail, but such cases are very rare. If hungry, most cats could catch their supper, and many abandoned cats turn feral with ease.

Although a domestic habitat does not present the same perils as life in the wild, the cat never completely switches off from the environment around her, wherever she is. Built to react quickly to unexpected noises or sudden movements, the cat is ever alert, indoors or out. A cat can be asleep on the bottom of your bed one moment, and crunching a huge spider on your stairs the next. Her very survival over millennia has relied on her fast reflexes and vigilance, and her entire body is built to hunt (see Chapter Twenty-five).

STUDY OF A HUNTER

Cats hunt by sight; if they see something moving past quickly, they will automatically chase it – without even registering what it is.

If a cat spots something to hunt, her senses all go on red-alert – her pupils will dilate, to allow more light into the eyes, and her ears and whiskers will all face forwards, focused on the prey.

She will then crouch down so that her head and body are flat, ensuring she cannot easily be seen. If she can, she will move to a hunting post, somewhere sheltered where she can hide until she is ready to pounce. If nowhere is suitable, or if moving would jeopardize her chances of being discovered, she will remain where she is.

Next, she will creep forward slowly and silently, to get into the best position from which to pounce; all the time, her topline will remain immobile. She may swing her head from side to side, to double-check the precise location of the prey.

Finally, comes the cutest bit of all – the bottom wiggle – where the cat gears up her back legs, warming and preparing her muscles, ready for the big pounce.

Once on the prey, the cat will puncture the neck with her sharp incisors. It is thought that the cat's whiskers help to locate the best place to bite – studies have shown that cats with damaged whiskers are not as successful at delivering the 'death bite' as their full-whiskered counterparts.

Towser the mouser reputedly killed a staggering 28,899 mice in his lifetime. He worked at Glenturret whisky distillery in Scotland, where he died in 1987.

Alternatively, the cat will hold the prey in her mouth or front paws, and bring her back legs up to kick down at the prey's body. When she does this, she is trying to break the unfortunate creature's neck.

When the prey is dead or putting up no resistance, the cat will skulk away with it in her mouth to find somewhere quiet – and safe – to eat.

PLAYTHING

Pet cats often 'play' with their prey. Rather than killing it swiftly and eating it, they invariably torture the poor creature, tossing it around and flicking it up in the air with their paws so they can pounce on it once more. Eventually, the prey will be killed or the cat will lose interest and let the animal escape.

No one can really blame the cat for this behavior. It is entirely natural for a cat to hunt – the instincts are too strong for her to resist. The reason why she doesn't kill it swiftly is that she doesn't need to – she doesn't need to eat because she is fed regularly.

(There are many ways of preventing your cat from wreaking havoc on the wildlife population – see page 75.)

PREY

One of the downsides of cat ownership is dealing with the killed prey which your proud puss will bring home to you. A cat's idea of breakfast in bed is quite different to ours, and many a cat owner knows the 'joy' of realizing they are sharing a bed with a rat or bird corpse that the cat has kindly plonked on the bed from a successful night's hunting.

Tip: experienced cat owners always wear slippers around the house. This prevents early-morning 'ugh' moments when you unwittingly tread on one of your cat's victims. Once done, you'll never walk barefoot again…

The reason why your cat insists on bringing you such 'gifts' is that she has noticed what a hopeless hunter you are and doesn't want to see you go hungry. Kind, thoughtful puss is treating you as she would a kitten – bringing food back to the nest.

THE CAT'S MOTHER

This is a complete reversal to how a cat usually views the owner – as a parent-figure. A human does everything that the cat's mother would – providing food, play, warmth, and affection – and, because the cat never has to stand on her own four feet, she remains in a permanently juvenile state, as far as behavior is concerned.

Your cat displays kitten behavior in a number of ways. When you walk into a room, your cat is likely to greet you with her tail held high. She is very pleased to see you, and is holding up her tail so you can lick her bottom (something the mother cat would do to help the kittens to defecate!).

When you cuddle your cat, she is likely to dig her claws into your lap. This is known as 'milk-treading' and relates to when the kitten would knead the mother's teats to stimulate the milk flow. Often, this behavior is accompanied by the cat dribbling – in anticipation of the milk.

21

FERAL FELINES

Feral cats are those that live as wild cats. Some are born feral; others are lost or abandoned cats that have had to fend for themselves, reverting back to their wild ways to survive. They live in the shadows of our towns and villages, raiding bins or hunting for food. They are usually deeply mistrustful of humans, but their confidence can often be won.

Feral cats will tend to congregate where there is food. If meals are left out for them, they will return the next day to eat. Many people take on the responsibility for caring for local feral cats, a responsibility that should be taken as seriously as adopting a domestic pet.

The feeding duty is a daily one – seven days a week, 52 weeks of the year. If you go away on holiday, arrangements should be made to feed your new charges. By your regularly feeding the cats, they will abandon other food sources, so you will let them down badly if you suddenly stop their routine.

POPULATION CHECK

Simply feeding feral cats is not the solution, however. It is imperative that they are neutered (Chapter Twenty-three) to prevent burgeoning numbers.

The Feral Cat Coalition in San Diego, California, (see Useful Addresses, Appendix I) has estimated that a breeding pair, producing two litters a year (and many can produce three), is responsible for 420,000 offspring over a seven-year period. Around 50 per cent of kittens will not survive. Unvaccinated, and exposed to the elements and outside dangers, they often die of preventable cat diseases.

Those that survive their infancy go on to lead a difficult life. With unchecked hormones, the males will fight endlessly, and the females will become progressively weaker by producing litter after litter. Road deaths are common, as the cats roam for mates, and finding a meal is a struggle.

It is important, therefore, that feral cats are neutered, something many animal charities will support. Many are released back into the 'wild', but some can be rehabilitated as pets.

TAMING A FERAL

Kittens are the best candidates for rehabilitation. If they are taken into a domestic environment at a young enough age (5 to 7 weeks), they have a good chance of becoming fully tamed. However, the same process can be successful for adult ferals who were once domestic cats, or for those with more placid temperaments.

CAUTION

Firstly, never take any chances. Ferals should be handled with great care. They survive on their wits and can be fierce – even kittens are amazingly strong.

The kittens would have been raised by the mother in a quiet spot, away from danger – which, in a feral's eyes, means humans. The kittens would, therefore, have received no socialization or contact with people.

Research has shown that the critical period in a kitten's life for socialization and contact with people is seven weeks of age. Beyond this, it becomes much harder for them to be domesticated. Fearful, they will hiss and spit, and lash out with their claws and teeth if they feel threatened.

Unvaccinated and exposed to many other ferals, they could also be carrying disease (even rabies in some countries), so should be handled with care.

Always wear thick 'claw-proof' clothes when handling a feral, and, if you do get scratched, wash the affected area straight away with warm, soapy water and then seek medical advice.

VETERINARY ATTENTION

The feral cat should be checked over by a vet, and will need vaccinations, flea and worming programs, and treatment for any other conditions she may have. The vet will be able to talk to you about the incidence of rabies in your area, and the incubation period of the disease. You should also talk to your vet about neutering (Chapter Twenty-three).

CONFINEMENT

Once all the practicalities have been attended to, it's time to embark on a long process of trust-building with your kitten or adult cat.

Ferals are nervous of large open spaces, preferring small areas where they feel more protected. Keep your feral in a cat carrier, making sure all sides are covered, except the front. This 'cave-like' den will mean puss can keep an eye on what's going on around her, from the safety of her carrier.

Place the carrier in a small, quiet room. Make sure she has access to water (most carriers come with water bowls that fix on the front). Place newspaper at the bottom of the carrier, overlaid with an old jumper or any other piece of clothing which has your scent on and which makes comfortable bedding.

Leave the cat alone for a few hours, and then start to visit the room, sitting in the room, near the carrier, for just a few minutes every couple of hours. Whenever you are in the same room as the cat, move and talk slowly and calmly. When you put food into the cage, sit nearby so she associates you with the enjoyable experience of eating – to a feral, food is the ultimate reward.

If the carrier needs cleaning because of an accident, take another carrier and transfer the cat to it. There's no need to handle the cat during this process – just put the open door of the new carrier against the opening of the other one and tip it up slightly to encourage her to walk into the fresh new den.

LARGER SPACE

After a day or two, transfer the feral cat or kitten to a larger cage, and again make sure that all but the front is covered. This cage should still be in a quiet part of the house.

In a cage (available from pet stores – see page 66), there will be room for the cat to have a designated litter area, feeding area and sleeping area.

After a couple of days in her new cage, she should be less wary when you are near. She will be familiar with the sound of your voice and your smell, and your movements will be predictable to her. Now you can progress to handling.

HANDLING

Make sure the room you are in does not have any hiding places from which it will be difficult to retrieve her. Block up any hidey-holes or she will inevitably dive under the bed or behind a bookcase and stay there, refusing to come out. It won't help your early bonding if you have to move furniture to get to her – she will feel like trapped prey being hunted out.

- Make sure all windows and doors in the room are shut so she cannot escape.
- Place a thick towel over her, leaving her face free, and pick her up.
- Act calmly and confidently at all times, and reassure her with your voice.
- Put her back into her crate after a few moments, and feed her a tasty treat – preferably by hand, if she will accept it.
- The approach of a hand can be construed as a threatening gesture to a nervous cat, so don't worry if she won't be hand-fed – just place the treat down in front of her to take later.
- If she struggles to get free of you while you are holding her, don't get involved in a battle of strength or wills. Just calmly place her in her crate.

Over time, she will struggle less, and you will be able to hold her for longer periods. This may take around two to six weeks with a kitten, but can take longer. Some cats remain a little nervous and skittish throughout their lives, but the majority will bond closely with the person who persevered with them from the beginning.

BODY LANGUAGE

Once the cat is happy being handled by you, she can be exposed to more people. Each introduction should be calm and non-aggressive. Remember, even innocuous behavior can be interpreted as being threatening to a nervous cat.

Instead of standing up and stooping over her to pet her, kneel down so you are at the same level as her. If you want to stroke her head (which, with time, she will allow you to do), then make sure your hand is behind her head – if she sees a hand coming towards her face, she may be intimidated.

PLAY

One way of gaining your feral's trust and of giving her an opportunity to exercise and to have fun is to play together. Buy a long dangle toy that you can entice her out of her cage with, and that you can play with from a distance. These toys can also be used to get your feral used to the sensation of being touched gently. For example, a long feather can stroke her back and get her used to the sensation while you are safely out of claws' reach.

FURTHER HELP

Many ferals become fully domesticated over time – but it does take a lot of hard work and patience. If you would like more information or help, contact a specialist feral organization (see Useful Addresses, page 247), or a cat-welfare charity.

Part 2

Choosing A Cat

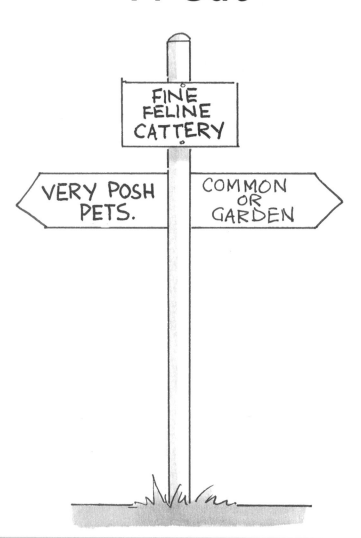

Chapter 3

Cat Compatibilty

Owning a cat is not a responsibility that should be taken on lightly. Yes, cats are independent – they don't need twice-daily walks as dogs do, and they are quite happy to amuse themselves while you go out to work – but they still require considerable care and company, and you should still think carefully about the commitment involved before you take the plunge.

CRY FREEDOM

Cats are free spirits, but the moment one moves into your home, so will your own freedom be curtailed! Owning a cat is a joy, but your life will lose a degree of spontaneity. You can't just throw a toothbrush and a change of clothes into a bag on a Friday night and shoot off for an unplanned weekend away once you have a feline house-mate. Everything needs planning well in advance. And, if the cattery is full or you can't find a trustworthy cat-sitter, then you'll have to make do with a weekend at home with your furry friend.

Planning a holiday is even more difficult. Where a neighbor might be happy to look in on the cat for a short weekend, feeding her, spending cuddle time with her, and changing her litter-tray, expecting someone to do this for two or three weeks is out of the question. Then, a complex rota system of friends and family has to be drawn up, with lots of keys cut and cat-instruction leaflets issued to all those press-ganged or bribed to help out. Or the services of a (costly) professional should be called upon (Chapter Ten).

With a feline, you are never footloose and fancy-free!

COSTLY CATS

Cats do not require any expensive specialist equipment, as an iguana would, for example, but the little bits and pieces that she does need do add up (Chapter Seven). A bed, collar, litter-tray, grooming equipment, scratching post, and cat-carrier will last for years, but the initial outlay is costly. More regular bills include a fairly regular flow of cat toys (a necessity, not a luxury!), food and cat-litter.

If you plan to have a longhaired or semi-longhaired breed, can you afford the professional grooming bills? Or will you undertake all the time-consuming, labor-intensive work yourself?

What arrangements will you make for your cat when you go away on holiday? Do you have cat-friendly family or friends that can move into your house while you are away, or will you have to pay for a professional cat-sitter or cattery?

Veterinary bills are the biggest expense. The initial cost of vaccinating, worming, neutering and microchipping your cat seriously damages your bank balance, but the health costs do not end there. Annual vaccinations, and regular worming and flea treatments should all be accounted for, and that is not forgetting the cost of unexpected fees for illnesses or accidents. Invariably, a cat will conspire to sprain a toe on a Sunday morning, when the call-out fee for a vet is astronomical! Remember, pet insurance (which is itself a monthly or annual outgoing) covers many veterinary costs, but never prophylactic treatment.

ROAD RAGE

You should also assess whether it is safe for you to have a cat. If you live near a busy road, you can only consider having a house-cat (Chapter Eighteen). This will limit your options to a kitten, to a breed or mixed-breed that is suitable for an exclusively indoor life (see Chapter Four), or to a shelter cat that previously lived as a house-cat. It isn't fair to take a cat that loves the outdoors and incarcerate her for the rest of her days (although some very old cats – in their high-teens – adapt well to indoor life).

PEDIGREE OR NON-PEDIGREE?

By far, the majority of cats are mixed-breed (known as moggies in the UK). In fact, around 90 per cent of cats are non-pedigree. Perhaps it is because all cats are essentially so similar that people do not feel the need to purchase an expensive purebred. Perhaps people are not fully aware of the different breeds and their range of appearances and characters. Or perhaps people simply prefer the mixed-breed.

Whatever the reason, we seem more than content with the average 'alleycat'. And so we should be – they are

HOUSE-WRECKERS
Most cats grow up to be well-behaved members of the family. Some, however, take great delight in scratching the sofa, the carpets, the doors, and anything else they can lay their claws on! Some prefer to chew their way through the house. Others, for creatures that are meant to be oh-so-agile, have a real clumsy streak and can topple ornaments and houseplants just by looking at them.
If you are seriously houseproud, it's best to consider a more sedate choice of pet.

generally healthier than purebred cats that have a smaller gene pool, and you can find huge diversity in non-pedigrees. They come in all coat types and colors, with personalities to match.

Most mixed-breed cats are taken from shelters or from friends or neighbors whose cat has had an 'accidental' litter. They are free or cheap, and you go home with the feel-good factor, knowing you are giving a future to an otherwise homeless puss.

There are some advantages to having a pedigree, however, the main one being that you know what you are getting. If you like the look of a certain breed, you know your kitten will turn out to be very similar and will have a known breed temperament too. For example, if you are desperate to have an outgoing, 'people' cat, a Siamese would be a good choice. With a mixed-breed kitten, the same character could not be guaranteed.

That said, although nature plays a part, nurture is very important – a calm, confident, outgoing owner can inspire the same sensible qualities in a kitten, and a neurotic Siamese owner can turn a promising kitten into a bag of nerves (though it is usually the other way around!).

CAT OR KITTEN?

Kittens are gorgeous. They have an irrepressible energy and *joie de vivre* that is infectious. It is impossible not to smile when you see a kitten in action; they invariably pretend to be grown-up big cats, hunting furniture tassels and anything else that moves, and yet they have none of the finesse of an adult, clumsily tripping over or misjudging their pounces and ending up in a collapsed fluffy heap.

However, kittens come at a price. They have none of the sense of an adult cat. If there's trouble to be had, they'll find it, and so they need constant supervision to stop them getting into danger or wrecking your home.

Then there's teaching them the house-rules and how to be toilet-trained, not forgetting their all-important socialization (page 52), and finally the expense of a kitten, particularly the neutering costs.

For many people, it's all too much bother. Why go through months of mayhem, when you can adopt a house-trained, well-adjusted adult who already knows that scratching the sofa is wrong, and who is crying out for some love? Most kittens are rehomed pretty quickly after reaching a shelter, but adult cats – particularly older ones – are usually harder to home, and many healthy, loving animals are destroyed every year because of this. In shelters that have a no-destruction policy, there are usually long-term residents that have been waiting for months, even years, for someone to take them home, but they are invariably overlooked in favor of a cute little kitty that everyone is clamoring to take home.

One often-quoted advantage of taking on a kitten is that you can mould the kitten to your family life – kitty can grow up around the dog, or kids, or whatever. However, there are so many stray and abandoned adult cats, you will have no difficulty finding one that will suit you perfectly. In many cases, the rescue shelter knows the background of each cat (dog-friendly, cat-friendly, child-friendly etc.), and can find one tailor-made for each prospective owner.

If you want an unusual purebred cat, your choice may be limited to a kitten, but the more common breeds, such as the Siamese or Persian, can often be found in rescue shelters, and you can adopt one at a fraction of the price. Alternatively, it may be worth contacting the welfare officer of a particular breed club, as they may know of a pedigree in need of a new home.

MALE OR FEMALE?

Provided they are neutered (as all pet cats should be, see Chapter Twenty-three), both males and females make superb pets. The key difference is size – male cats are almost always larger than their female counterparts. Character-wise, all cats are individual, and, as with humans, no generalizations can be made about each sex's 'personality'.

Your choice of sex may be determined by any cats you already have. For example, if you have a nervous boy, then he may feel intimidated by a boisterous adult male coming into his territory, so you may prefer to bring in a kitten or a calm adult female (or even male). It's a case of creating harmonies.

If you choose a pedigree kitten, there are often fewer females around (as they are kept for breeding) and so your choice may be limited to a male.

The breeder/shelter will identify the sex of the kittens for you (see also page 188).

MORE THAN ONE

If there's anything better than one cat, it's two cats, or three or four…! It's very easy to get carried away on a cat spree, though, and you should seriously consider whether you can cope with a multi-cat household.

If you are out at work all day, one cat (particularly a house-cat) can get terribly bored and lonely. Some cats, especially older ones, revel in the peace and quiet of being an only cat, and love having no rivals for their owner's affection. But other cats thrive in feline company – stalking house-mates, chasing each other up and down the stairs at great speed, and curling up together for a doubly-warm nap.

If you are intending to introduce a new cat to your existing puss, consider her personality. Is she well socialized with other cats, or does she attack anything that comes near her garden? Is she too old to cope with a mad-case kitten or would she prefer more sedate company? Once you've assessed her character and needs, then you can start looking for the ideal buddy (Part Three).

If you are catless, there should be no problems introducing two adult cats, two kittens, or one of each, as there will be few territorial issues at stake. Certainly, it's much kinder for kittens to have company, as they can incessantly play with each other while you cannot be with them.

Do remember, though, that two cats means double the mayhem, double the time and double the money. Are you sure you can afford two lots of vet fees and the increased feeding and cat-litter bills? If you plan to have two longhaired cats, do you have the time to groom them both? Also be prepared to wage an eternal war on fleas and parasites in a multi-cat house, as they tend to spread quickly from cat to cat. (De-fleaing several cats is a nightmare – as soon as one has been treated, word quickly gets out to the rest, and they disappear until it's 'safe' to return!)

Finally, you should ask yourself if you can honestly give each cat the individual love and attention she needs, particularly if you have more than two cats. If you can't promise that each cat will be treated as if she were your only one, then are you really doing your best for them?

Chapter 4

Top Cats

If you are interested in a purebred cat, there are lots of breeds from which to choose. Although cats do not have the same diversity as dog breeds, there is a considerable difference in looks and personalities between them, as the following profiles of the most popular cats show. This is far from a definitive list – check out the websites of your national cat registry for details of all the breeds recognized (see Useful Addresses).

 **PERSIAN LONGHAIR**

HISTORY

With her long, luxurious coat, the Persian is the real glamorpuss of the cat world. Although this breed takes her name from Persia (now Iran), she may not actually descend from there. Hieroglyphics dating from around 1680 BC describe a cat very similar to the Persian.

The first longhaired cats were known as Angoras, a name taken from Ankara, Turkey, the place where they were first discovered (not to be confused with the breed now known as the Angora). Travelers introduced these cats to Europe around the 16th century, at about the same time that cats from Persia also appeared. The two types were fairly similar in type and some were interbred. However, the early Persian cats had longer coats and became more popular than the Angora.

The Persian became very popular during Victorian times, and became even more sought-after thanks to a royal seal of approval – the breed was a favorite with Queen Victoria, and has remained one of the most popular purebred cats ever since.

APPEARANCE

The original Persians were considerably different to the ones we know today. They had longer faces, shorter coats, and smaller heads. Similar 'pet' cats can still be bought today.

Show Persians look distinctly different. They have large, broad heads, small, round ears, flat faces and rather squashed-in noses.

Persians are best described as 'cobby'. They have fairly short legs, a short brush-like tail, a short neck, a deep, broad chest and a ruff of hair as a mane. Their large, round eyes can melt most hearts.

The coat is the most distinctive feature. The topcoat is fine and long (growing to up to 6 inches/15.5 cms in length) and the undercoat is dense, fluffing out the top coat to such an extent that it is difficult to determine the cat's structure beneath it.

Persians come in a plethora of colors and patterns. Solid (whole/self) colors include white, cream, red, lilac, blue, chocolate, and black. All these also come with white (bi-color), in tortoiseshell, and tabby. A 'tipped' coat is referred to as 'cameo', and refers to the degree to which the hair is shaded. In a shell coat, there is only a little color on the tip of the hair; a shaded variety is where the coloring extends a little further up the hair; and a smoke variety has the most depth of tipping. Colorpoint (also known as Himalayan in the United States), where the cat's ears, face, legs and tail are colored, and van (color on the ears, face and tail) also occur in a variety of colors and patterns.

The cat's eye color will depend on the coat, and includes orange, copper, blue, green, and 'odd' eyes, where one is orange and one is blue.

CHARACTER

Laidback, placid and calm, the Persian makes a great house-cat. She loves snoozing and so is ideal for owners that are out at work all day. To prevent her getting too lonely, it is best for her to have another Persian for company – they can then play together if the mood takes them, or just cuddle up together for warm naps.

Physically, though, the Persian needs considerable care, requiring at least 20 minutes of grooming every day, together with attention to the eyes, which can be teary (see Chapter Sixteen). If you cannot commit the time to keeping this cat looking and feeling great, you must reconsider your choice of breed: an Exotic may be more suitable – it has many Persian features, but without the extensive coat.

 **SIAMESE**

HISTORY

The Siamese name belies the breed's place of origin. She is closely linked with Siam (now Thailand), though the Thai people referred to the breed as 'Chinese cats' which may indicate their actual place of birth.

The breed is one of the oldest of purebreds, dating back to around 1300 AD. The Siamese was something of a secret to Siam, where she was a treasure of royalty. Siamese cats roamed royal palaces, and it was forbidden for any of the cats to be taken outside the country, a transgression of the law punishable by death. Some cats did find their way to the West, however, initially as presents to honored dignitaries from the royal family.

The Siamese's link with royalty has bred many endearing myths about her. The kinked tail and squinty eyes, features of the early examples of the breed, have been explained in a number of ways. One story describes how a pair of Siamese were guarding a Buddhist temple when a golden goblet was stolen. They were sent to search for the treasure, and eventually found it. The male returned to the temple to tell of their find, and the female stayed with the goblet. Determined that it was not to be taken from her again, she tied her tail around the stem and stared at the treasure for several days and nights, until it was safely returned to the temple. Her vigilance caused the kink and the squint, which her subsequent kittens were born with.

APPEARANCE

The Siamese is one of the most elegant of cats. Her long, svelte body, powerful hindlegs (which are longer than the front legs) and piercing blue eyes make her one of the most easily recognized of all purebreds.

Again, there is a discrepancy between the breed's original appearance and its development for the show world. Over the years, the Siamese's features have been accentuated. Her head has become more triangular, her eyes more slanted and almond-shaped, her ears larger, and her body more athletic. Some breeders have continued to produce the traditional Siamese (known as 'appleheads' because of the rounder skull), though they are rarely, if ever, exhibited.

The Siamese coat is silky to the touch. Flat, it lies close to the body, thanks to a fairly sparse undercoat, which can make the breed susceptible to the cold. A Siamese requires little grooming, though the breed's personality makes her far from being a low-maintenance breed (see below).

All Siamese kittens are born white, and all develop a 'pointed' coat as they grow, though it can take up to a year for the coat to develop its color fully. There is a variety of different color points, including cream, red, lilac, blue, chocolate, and seal. Tortie and tabbie points in these colors mean there is a huge choice of color and pattern.

If you like the look of the Siamese, but would prefer a cat with a longer coat, consider the Balinese.

CHARACTER

The Siamese is the antithesis of the Persian – not only in looks but in temperament. This is not a cat that is happy to be left on her own – she'll show her displeasure by wreaking devastation on your home!

The Siamese loves people. If ignored, she will demand attention – not only vocally but physically. Many owners are familiar with the early-morning prod of a Siamese trying to open their eyelids in the morning! She is stubborn and strong-willed – she knows what she wants and she knows exactly how to get it. Combine this headstrong attitude with the cat's renowned intelligence, and you have a great force to be reckoned with. It is not unknown for these cats to work out how to open windows if they want to go out, or to raid the fridge if they fancy a bite to eat.

The relationship you get with a Siamese is a full and rewarding one, provided you give 100 per cent. They are great communicators, and are said to use 11 consonants and all five vowels in their language. Such a 'full-on' cat isn't everyone's cup of tea, though; if you want a quiet life, get a Persian – not a chatty, demanding Siamese.

 MAINE COON

HISTORY
America's only naturally-occurring native breed, the magnificent Maine Coon dates back to the mid-19th century.

Stories tell of how Marie Antoinette sent her cats to America to escape the French Revolution and that these cats were the ancestors of the Maine Coon, but the breed is more likely the result of the early settlers' cats breeding to longhaired seacats that turned up at Maine's port. The result is the glorious Maine Coon we know today.

The breed takes its name from the place of its origin (Maine, New England), and the fact that the early cats had a striped, ringed tail reminiscent of the racoon (coon).

APPEARANCE
The Maine Coon is a large, tough, handsome-looking breed. To survive the cold winters on the East Coast, this cat needed a heavy, weatherproof coat, and this is the breed's distinguishing feature.

She has an abundant coat of semi-long hair, with a soft, fine undercoat to insulate her. She has a ruff around her neck – a kind of furry scarf – which keeps her warm in cold weather, and which becomes less profuse in summer months. She also has 'ear muffs' – thick hair on her ears – and large paws to help her cope in snow. Her tail is magnificent: the hair is long and profuse, and looks distinctly brush-like.

The Maine Coon comes in a variety of colors and patterns. The breed is traditionally associated with tabby markings, but whole colors are popular too. Coats include: white, black, blue and white, black smoke and white, silver tabby, cream silver tabby, brown classic tabby, brown tabby and white, tortie tabby and white, silver tortie tabby and blue silver tortie tabby.

The Maine Coon has a muscular build, and is among the larger purebred cats. Males weigh in at around 8kg (18lbs) and females are only slightly less. This is no shapeless brute, however. Maine Coons are pretty-faced, elegant cats that are entirely well proportioned.

CHARACTER

With her athletic, powerful body, and great intelligence, she is a supreme hunter, and she loves the great outdoors. She is built to survive the elements and is not put off exploring outside in cold and wet weather, as many breeds are.

This breed is not best suited to life as a full-time house-cat, but she will enjoy living a dual life and spending time inside with her family. Playful, affectionate, and fairly vocal, the Maine Coon is quick to learn and is highly trainable.

One reported quirk of the breed is sleeping in uncomfortable nooks and crannies around the house. Maybe this habit dates back to the breed's history as a seacat?

 **EXOTIC**

HISTORY

This breed came about from American Shorthair breeders introducing longhair breeds to enhance their cats' coats. The result was a breed that they were quite taken with – the Exotic we know and love today.

First recognized in 1967, the Exotic has several breeds in her make-up, including the Burmese (page 39), the Persian (page 33), and the American Shorthair (page 40). Some breeders also used Russian Blues and British Shorthairs (page 41) in their breeding programs.

APPEARANCE

Appearance-wise, the Exotic is a shorthaired Persian. She has the big, round head, and cobby body of a Persian (e.g. the thick neck, short legs, and short, thick tail), but has a short coat. Facially, the similarities are very strong, with the Exotic's large round eyes and flat face bearing a strong similarity to the breed's longhaired cousin.

The Exotic's soft, plush coat has a luxurious feel to it, and comes in the same colours as are accepted for the Persian (see page 33).

CHARACTER

The Exotic shares a similar personality to the Persian, too. Placid and peaceful, the Exotic is loving and affectionate, and not too demanding of her owner.

ORIENTAL

HISTORY

The Oriental comes in two varieties – shorthair and semi-longhair. The shorthair version is best described as a colored Siamese, and the longer-haired type is a colored Balinese (which is, in itself, a fluffy Siamese). In structure and temperament, the Oriental is Siamese, but she lacks the pointed coat markings (page 35).

Early Siamese had colored coats (in fact, only a quarter were pointed), but breeders preferred the unusual color-pointed varieties and bred for this quality, eventually eradicating other coat patterns from the modern breed.

The colored cats were revived when a Siamese called Our Miss Smith produced brown-coated, green-eyed kittens in the 1950s. UK breeders carefully introduced Korat, Persian, and domestic shorthair genes to the Siamese to encourage different coat colors. The longhair type was created in the 1980s by an Oriental Shorthair mating with a Balinese.

The breed was originally called 'Foreign' by UK breeders, but the name was changed to 'Oriental'. However, white Orientals are still referred to as Foreign Whites in the UK.

APPEARANCE

The Oriental has all the athletic but slender grace of the Siamese, see pages 34-36.

Unlike the Siamese, only the white variety has blue eyes; the other colors have yellow or green eyes.

The coat comes in many colors and patterns – all are acceptable, apart from pointed (i.e. Siamese/Balinese), sepia and mink. The attractive tabby variety (classic, mackerel, spotted or ticked) was originally called the Egyptian Mau, as it bore a close resemblance to some of the first domestic cats.

CHARACTER

The Oriental character is very Siamese-like. These are bold, confident, chatty, and demanding cats that are devoted to their owners, and thrive in the company of humans – especially when they are being admired and adored.

 **BIRMAN**

HISTORY

The Birman is also known as The Sacred Cat of Burma, because she was said to descend from the country's temple cats. Various legends have developed surrounding the history, and most center on Sinh, a white temple cat dedicated to the golden, blue-eyed goddess Tsun Kyan Kse. When the temple was attacked, Sinh put her paws on the body of the dying head priest and adopted her goddess's colors – her paws remained white, her eyes turned blue, her points turned brown and the rest of the coat shone a golden color. The other temple cats were also transformed, and this inspired the monks to defend the goddess's temple.

Two temple cats were given to Frenchman August Pavie by a temple in Burma (now

Myanmar) as thanks for helping to defend it against attack. Sadly, only the female survived the journey to France, though fortunately she was pregnant. With careful outcrossing (breeding to other carefully chosen breeds), the modern Birman was born. It reached the UK and the US in the 1960s and has steadily grown in popularity ever since.

APPEARANCE

This is a luxurious-looking cat, with a thick, fairly long, silky coat, a brush-like tail, and piercing, round blue eyes. The coat is pointed, with the legs, tail, face (mask) and ears being a darker color than the body. The paws are not pointed, making it appear as if the cat is wearing mittens. Colors include: cream, seal, blue, red, lilac and chocolate, with tortie and tabby variations. Daily grooming is a must.

The body is long yet sturdy. Some claim the Siamese is in the Birman's history, and they certainly share the same elegance, though the Birman is stockier and has a broader, rounded head.

CHARACTER

The Birman is a well-rounded character – playful, friendly, intelligent, peaceful and laidback. They are loving and can be quite demanding of their owners – if they want attention, they will make sure they get it!

 **BURMESE**

HISTORY

In 1930, the founding queen of the breed was brought to America from the Burmese capital, Rangoon, by Joseph Thompson. The queen was a walnut-colored female called Wong Mau, who was a Tonkinese type in that she is thought to have been a Burmese-Siamese cross.

Wong Mau was bred to a Siamese, and was then bred to her subsequent kittens. The results of the matings produced Siamese-pointed cats, dark brown cats with minimal pointing (Burmese) and Tonkinese types. It was the second type that became the forefathers of the modern Burmese breed.

The breed arrived in the UK in 1949, and, over time, the European Burmese has become quite different to that in the US (see below).

APPEARANCE

The Burmese is a medium-sized cat with a sturdy body, rounded chest, round head, wide-set ears, and large, round eyes. In Europe, the breed is more Oriental-looking – with a more slender, muscular body, slightly longer legs (with the hindlegs longer than the fore), a more wedge-shaped, Siamese-type head, and eyes that are more slanted.

Both types of Burmese have a soft, silky, short coat that feels velvety to the touch and that positively shines with health and vitality. Colors include brown, chocolate, red, cream, blue, and lilac (frost/platinum) with tortie variations. The American breed has fewer colors than the European type.

CHARACTER

The Burmese is fairly vocal, intelligent, playful, outgoing, energetic and loving. The torties are said to be more extrovert than the other coat types. They love to be involved in everything you do, and are not happy to be ignored.

 AMERICAN SHORTHAIR

HISTORY

The American Shorthair derives from the early cats that the first American settlers brought over with them from Europe. The cats were probably working cats, used to keep the ship's rat population in check.

Setting up home with the settlers, these early cats continued to control rodents as well as to give companionship to their owners.

In the early 20th century, American breeders decided to preserve the breed, rather than leaving its development to nature and chance. The first litter was born in 1904, the result of a mating of a British Shorthair to an American one.

They were originally called Domestic Shorthairs, but the name was changed to the current one in 1965.

APPEARANCE

Together with the British Shorthair, this is one of the most natural-looking of breeds – the most 'moggie-like' of purebred cats. In fact, originally non-pedigree cats were allowed to be registered as American Shorthairs provided they fulfilled all the requirements of the Breed Standard. This practice is no longer allowed, but it has ensured a large, healthy gene pool.

The American Shorthair is robust, strong, and muscular – a healthy-looking cat through and through. Their faces, with their large, round eyes and full cheeks, are full of character, and they have short, thick, no-nonsense coats to protect them from the harsh elements.

The breed's diverse background has ensured a plethora of wonderful coat colors, including black, blue, cream, blue-cream, white, red, and tortie, with smoke, shaded, tipped, tabby, shaded tabby, vans (see pages 34, 46 and 253), bi-colors (color and white), and tabby and silver tabby bi-color variations.

CHARACTER

In keeping with everything about this breed, she has a very straightforward character. She is an easy-going, loving pet that enjoys exploring outside and often proves an accomplished hunter.

 ## BRITISH SHORTHAIR

HISTORY

Like the American Shorthair, this cat originates from ordinary domestic cats. Breeders began to fix the type in the 1800s to ensure that the breed's distinct qualities were preserved. By the Second World War, however, the breed was close to extinction, and it took some outcrossings to Persians and Orientals to revive the breed.

APPEARANCE

The British Shorthair is similar to her American cousin. She has a round face, large eyes, and a thick coat which is often described as 'crisp' because of the firm guard hairs in the topcoat. She is robust, cobby, strong and muscular, and feels much heavier than she looks. The males are considerably larger than the females.

The coat comes in a variety of colors and patterns including white, cream, blue, lilac, black, and chocolate, with bi-color, tortie, spotted, and tabby variations.

CHARACTER

An independent cat, she doesn't much enjoy being fussed over, but is friendly and loving. Her weatherproof coat equips her for all weathers and she enjoys being outdoors. Like the American Shorthair, she is a great hunter.

 ## ABYSSINIAN

HISTORY

The Abyssinian derives from the ordinary domestic cats of Abyssinia (now Ethiopia). The breed was brought to the UK by traders from Africa, as well as by soldiers returning from the Abyssinian war in 1868. Careful breeding to British Shorthairs ensured the breed's survival.

APPEARANCE

The most striking feature of this breed is the close-lying, sleek, ticked coat – where each individual hair has two or three bands of color. This would have proved invaluable camouflage for the cat in her native North African surroundings.

The ticked coat is similar to that of a hare and the breed was originally referred to as Hare Cats for this reason (in fact, the French still refer to the coat as lievre, meaning 'hare').

Coat colors include usual (ruddy), sorrel, fawn, chocolate, lilac and blue, with silver, tortie and tabby variations.

The Abyssinian is athletic, agile, lithe and muscular, and has a very elegant, refined appearance. In common with many breeds from hot countries, she has large, broad ears – providing a larger surface area from which to lose heat in scorching temperatures.

As with many breeds, the European Aby is much more Oriental in look than the American type. For example, in Europe, the head is wedge-shaped and long, whereas in America, it is more rounded.

CHARACTER

She can be aloof with strangers, but is utterly devoted to her family. Although she is a quiet breed, she can be demanding, is very smart, and will enjoy hours of play. Her athletic build makes her an excellent climber – indoors as well as outdoors!

 **RAGDOLL**

HISTORY

This beautiful breed was created by Californian breeder Ann Baker in the 1960s by crossing a white Persian female called Josephine with a Birman male called Daddy Warbucks. Josephine gave birth to a litter of kittens after being hit by a car, and this, combined with the fact that the kittens were all 'floppy', gave rise to the erroneous belief that the breed has a very high pain threshold. This is not true. What is true is that they have extremely placid temperaments – they relax so completely when handled that they become floppy, and this is how they got their Ragdoll name.

APPEARANCE

Ragdolls are gentle giants – they are large, heavy, and well built, though this is combined with a delicate appearance. The Birman influence is very apparent in the breed. They have full cheeks, a round muzzle, large, oval eyes, and a short, thick neck.

The semi-long coat is dense and silky and comes in three varieties: colorpointed, mitted (with longer Birman boots, page 39), and bi-colored, in seal, chocolate, lilac and blue.

CHARACTER

The Ragdoll temperament is second to none. Extremely placid, she is quiet and docile, and makes a great indoor house-cat. She is not that interested in hunting, and, because of this, has become popular in Australia, a country that views the cat as a great threat to its native wildlife.

Because the Ragdoll is so tolerant, children in the family must be taught how to handle her and to respect her, as she will put up with much more than she should.

SCOTTISH FOLD

HISTORY

Cats with folded ears have been reported for centuries, but it wasn't until the 1960s that a breed developed around this interesting natural phenomenon.

In 1961, William and Mary Ross discovered a neighbor's white farm cat in Tayside, Scotland, that had folded ears. They were fascinated with Susie, as she was known, and, when she had a litter of kittens with a local tom, they were given one of the kittens, called Snooks. She was then bred to a British Shorthair, to produce a white male called Snowball.

Several geneticists became involved in the breed, including Pat Turner, Peter Dyte, and Neil Todd, and subsequent breedings to British and American Shorthairs eventually produced the breed that is so popular in America today.

APPEARANCE

As the name would suggest, the breed's forward-folding ears are the key characteristic of the Scottish Fold. There are various degrees of ear folding in the breed, from those that have ordinary, erect ears, to single folds where the ear is bent forwards quite simply, through to show-quality triple folds where the ear lies very tight to the head. The erect-eared cats are used in breeding programs, to avoid genetic skeletal abnormalities that result from breeding a folded-ear cat to a folded-ear cat.

Scottish Folds are a very sturdy-looking breed, with a compact body, round head, a short, muscular neck, short nose, and large, round eyes.

The coat is thick, and all colors and patterns are acceptable (with the exception of colorpointed). A longhaired version of the breed is available. Susie is believed to have carried a long-hair gene, and the subsequent breeding to British and American Shorthairs (who themselves have some Persian blood) means longhaired kittens are not infrequent.

CHARACTER

The Scottish Fold is a sweet-natured puss that loves laps. In fact, she loves most things – dogs, other pets, children – and her face looks as if she is permanently smiling. She is placid and laidback, sometimes literally so – owners report that Folds often sleep on their backs!

BENGAL

HISTORY

The Bengal was created by Jean Mill, a geneticist interested in conserving the wild Asian Leopard Cat. Jean bred a male domestic cat to a female Asian Leopard Cat, to produce a female kitten called Kinkin, who was bred back to her father. Over time, further breeding programs were established, and, in 1983, the first Bengal was registered by Jean Mill – Millwood Finally Found. The breed has been growing in popularity ever since, though they are still relatively rare and expensive, compared to other breeds.

APPEARANCE

The appeal of these cats is how similar they look to small wildcat species. They are large, muscular, and powerful, and careful breeding has created a wonderfully patterned coat, available in black, and spotted and marbled tabby in brown or snow.

The Bengal's head is longer than it is wide, with high cheekbones, and large, oval eyes. The neck is thick, and the hindlegs are longer than the forelegs.

CHARACTER

Understandably, given the breed's close link with the wild, early cats were aggressive and nervous, but breeding to good-tempered domestic cats and using only the very best Bengals has diluted the fearful instinct towards people. Breeders are aware of how important temperament is in the breed, and, as a result, the vast majority have impeccable characters and are friendly, gentle cats.

CORNISH REX

HISTORY

Serena, a farm cat from Bodmin, Cornwall, had a naturally-occuring wavy (rex) coat. Her owner, Nina Ennismore, bred her to a domestic male, and the resulting litter included ordinary-coated kittens and only one rex kitten – a male called Kallibunker. He was bred back to his mother, and the descendants were mated to British Shorthairs and Burmese. The breed reached America in the 1950s, where Oriental and Siamese cats were introduced. This accounts for the transatlantic differences in the breed (below).

APPEARANCE

The Cornish Rex is one of the most easily recognizable of breeds. She has a short, wavy coat made entirely from undercoat – no guard hairs are present. As a result, the coat is very soft and velvety. All colors and patterns are acceptable.

This is quite a delicate-looking cat, though owners can attest to the breed's hardiness. In the US, the breed is more delicate, thanks to outcrossing to Oriental breeds. In the UK, the influence of the British Shorthair and Burmese can be seen in the breed's slightly more cobby, sturdy build.

The head is small in relation to the rest of the body, and is dwarfed by the breed's large ears (which are smaller in UK cats than in the Orientally-influenced US ones). In keeping with the cat's coat hair, the whiskers and eyebrows are wavy. The legs are long and lean, and the spine is slightly arched. The tail is long and tapering.

CHARACTER

The Cornish is a pixie-like creature, not only in looks but in temperament. She is lively, mischievous, extrovert, playful and very agile.

 **DEVON REX**

HISTORY

You would think that, given the similar coat type, and the close geographical proximity of Devon and Cornwall, that the Cornish Rex would have some influence on the Devon Rex's development. You would be wrong. A litter of cats bred by Beryl Cox from Devon produced an ordinary litter with one curly kitten, appropriately named Kirlee. This cat was bred to Cornish Rexes but no rex kittens were produced, suggesting that a different recessive gene is responsible for the mutation. When the kittens were bred back to Kirlee, half of them had the curly coat. From here, the breed developed, with some British Shorthairs and even Persians being introduced along the way.

APPEARANCE

It has to be said that the Devon looks like an alien from another planet! The early cats, with their patchy coats, were even more strange-looking. Thankfully, this has now been rectified and most have a good distribution of coat. Although the coat is wavy, like the Cornish Rex, the similarity ends there. Unlike the Cornish, that has no guard hairs, the Devon has a coat that consists of down and guard hairs.

The Devon is smaller than the Cornish, and her proportions are different too. She has a large, heart-shaped head, huge ears set low down and well apart, oval eyes also set well apart, and long, crinkled eyebrows and whiskers (that are brittle and prone to breaking). The Devon looks just as she is – mischievous and clownish.

CHARACTER

Life with a Devon Rex is never dull. They are fun-loving, amusing, mischievous and extremely loving – an asset to a cat-loving home.

🐾 TURKISH VAN

HISTORY

The Turkish Van is the famous swimming cat – she loves water. She was brought to Britain from the Lake Van region of Turkey in 1955, and has never lost her zeal for the wet stuff. Vans will swim in the bath, play with running water from a tank, or splash in a puddle – they are real water babies. The breed reached America in the early 1980s but has remained relatively unchanged since it was first discovered.

APPEARANCE

The Turkish Van coat is so distinctive that it has influenced cat terminology – now all coats that are patterned in a similar way in the other breeds are referred to as vans. The base color is a chalky-white, with colored markings on the top of the head (on the ears and in front of them), and the tail. Sometimes, thumbprint markings appear on the spine, typically by the base of the tail. The most popular color is the auburn (red) variety, but other colors are permitted (though they differ between cat-governing registries).

The Van has a semi-long, silky coat that lacks undercoat, and a glorious, brush-like tail. The body is long, sturdy and muscular, and the head is wedge-shaped. The eyes can be orange, blue or odd (a combination of the two).

CHARACTER

The Turkish Van looks really glamorous, but is quite tough and resourceful at heart. This cat had to struggle to survive in her native region, and she has retained this intelligence and independence to the present day. With people she is friendly, and she is particularly loving towards her human family.

Part 3

Tracking Down Your Cat

Chapter 5

Cat Outlets

You've decided which type of cat you want – whether purebred or mixed-breed, adult or kitten, male or female. Now it's time to find your perfect puss.

SHELTERS

Your first port of call should be your local animal shelters, including all-animal welfare charities as well as those devoted just to cats (see Useful Addresses). They are ideal for finding mixed-breed cats of all types and ages, and occasionally purebred ones. If you are looking for a kitten, the summer months are the best time of the year to make your search (nature has designed cats to produce young in warm weather, when there is abundant food), though kittens occasionally turn up in cooler months.

You might prefer to opt for an organization that has a 'no-kill' policy – where they promise never to destroy healthy animals. Some shelters, through lack of choice, will euthanase a cat if, after the statutory length of time outlined in the law, she has not been claimed or rehomed. Although, no organization would destroy healthy animals through choice, some people prefer to offer their help and money to organizations that offer long-term shelter to all their charges.

Most shelters either neuter the animals before they are adopted or make you sign a pledge that you will have the cat altered. They deal with stray and abandoned animals all the time and must make sure you won't contribute to their number. In the United States, you may also have to agree never to have the cat declawed.

Reputable shelters will be clean, with toys available to the cats. The staff will be friendly, caring, and knowledgeable, will assess each cat in their care, and will know the type of home best suited to her. If the cat is timid, for example, they will not recommend she goes to a busy household with children; however, she may be ideal for a sedate retired couple.

A good shelter will be choosy about the homes their cats go to. They will ask many questions about your lifestyle, why you want a cat, past experience etc., and may conduct a home visit to check whether your home and location is safe and suitable. They should also be pleased to answer all your questions about a proposed adoption, so don't be afraid to ask about anything you are unsure of.

Inevitably, some people will be turned down as prospective owners. Perhaps their lifestyle is too hectic (e.g. they are away on business, or regularly work very long hours) and they are therefore unable to devote themselves to caring for a cat. Do not feel upset if you are turned down – shelters only have their cats' best interests at heart. If you are rejected, you should consider a less demanding pet until such time as your lifestyle is better suited to cat ownership.

Shelters usually expect a donation for the cat or kitten, which will cover their expenses and enable them to continue with their invaluable work.

BREEDERS

If you are adamant that you want a purebred cat or kitten and you cannot find one at an animal shelter, or if you want to show your cat (and require a cat with a known history), then you should contact breeders. All recognized cat breeds have clubs, and they, in turn, will be able to pass you on to breeders with litters available.

The internet is a good starting point. Use a reliable search engine and locate official breed clubs; they will probably feature links to club-recognized breeders. Alternatively, you can contact your national cat governing body, such as the Governing Council of the Cat Fancy (GCCF) in Britain, or the Cat Fancy Association (CFA) or The International Cat Association (TICA) in the United States (see Useful Addresses).

Purebred litters can usually be found all year round. Queens kept indoors in artificial light are often fooled into thinking it is summer, because of the extended day length, and so can produce litters at any point in the year.

Finding a purebred litter can be difficult if you have your heart set on a numerically small breed. However, you should not lower your standards and plump for the first litter you find. Be as scrupulous as you can.

Once you've phoned around and found a breeder with a litter (or an anticipated litter), then do your homework. Contact members of the breed club and ask their honest opinion of the person in question.

• Are her cats healthy?
• Are they successful in the show world?
• Are there any known genetic problems in her lines?
• Is she known for producing many litters?

Once you are happy that she has a good reputation, you can ask to arrange to meet her and to see where the litter will be raised. This will give you a chance to check that the kittens will be reared in the home, that the environment is clean, and will also allow you to meet the queen. Do be wary of cat farms where queens are kept isolated and unsocialized and bred too regularly, as the kittens are prone to health and behavioral problems. (See Chapter Six, Assessing Cats.)

PET SHOPS

Pet shops are fantastic for buying pet food and accessories, but never buy a kitten from a pet shop. Most pet stores have stopped selling kittens and puppies, but some still do.

- The practice encourages impulse-buying, and there are no proper checks on whether you are suitable (no home-checks etc.).
- While in the pet shop, there is little socialization for the kittens (they may get used to people walking past, but won't be familiar with the sound of the washing machine, or other everyday household noises).
- You will not be able to assess the parents' temperaments or to have assessed the conditions in which the kittens spent the first few weeks of their life.
- Disease can be spread easily from kitten to kitten if they are kept together (as they invariably are).

- Sometimes pet-shop kittens are taken from their mother too early, and there is
  no way of being certain of the age of the kitten you are buying.
- There will be little after-sales care and advice following your purchase.
  However knowledgeable the staff, will anyone be able to answer a feeding query on a
  Sunday evening when the store is closed?

However sorry you feel for the kittens, do not buy them. It will perpetuate the trade, and will mean that more kittens suffer in the long run. Why buy a kitten from a pet store when there are thousands of homeless kitties in shelters? Wouldn't you prefer your money to go towards helping other down-and-out kitties, instead of boosting a shop's profit margin?

OTHER SOURCES

Responding to newspaper adverts for kittens or taking on a kitten from a friend or neighbor's accidental litter is not ideal. Yes, the kittens may be in desperate need of a home, but you can never be sure that you are getting a healthy kitten. The kittens could be harboring cat flu or leukemia and could well become seriously ill within days of your taking them on.

Of course, the same is true of shelter cats, but generally the kittens are checked by a vet, inoculated, and are observed closely for any signs of disease. If you do take on a friend's cat, or a kitten advertised locally, then ask to see evidence of the mother's vaccinations (see Chapter Twenty-six). Ask if the kittens have been wormed or inoculated (and ask for proof), and make sure you do all the pre-sales checks outlined in Chapter Six.

Chapter 6

Assessing Cats

Mixed-breed kittens are often homed around the age of eight weeks, but purebred kittens do not leave the breeder until 12 weeks in the UK, and between 14 to 16 weeks in the US. This extra time means the breeder can ensure all the kittens have received their primary vaccinations (Chapter Twenty-six), can be litter-trained, and be adequately socialized.

The importance of socialization cannot be underestimated. Simply put, socialization involves introducing the kitten to everyday life – its sights, smells and sounds, and therefore prepares her for the future. A kitten that is kept in a quiet, bare room for the first two to three months will be terrified when she finally is homed and has to encounter washing machines, children, dogs etc. If she has been raised in a busy but loving home, she will be confident in the world around her. It can take years to transform a nervous kitten into a well-rounded adult, and sometimes the negative effects of a poor upbringing can never be reversed.

It is therefore very important to find a breeder that has a lifestyle very similar to your own. If you have children, find a breeder that has kids of the same age group. If you have a dog, give yourself a head start and choose a breeder who has one too.

With shelter cats, the kittens' past is often not known. However, because these kittens are rehomed earlier than breeders' cats, you have the opportunity to be responsible for your kitten's early socialization and to introduce her to different things while she is still young and receptive to new experiences.

MOTHER LOVE

It is important to see the kittens with their mother. Often, shelters will have the mother of the kittens and you will be able to assess her temperament. A breeder will certainly have the mother (if not, steer clear of the breeder), and may also have the father. Interestingly, although toms have nothing to do with raising a litter, studies have shown that kittens inherit personality traits from both parents.

The parents should be confident and friendly. Nervous cats often produce neurotic kittens. Ask yourself if you would be happy for your kitten to turn out like the mum. If the answer is 'no', then look for another litter.

THE ENVIRONMENT

The kittens should be raised indoors in the breeder's home so they will be used to people and a normal household environment.

- Are the conditions clean?
- Is there lots of stimulation for the kittens (toys should be available to them)?
- How does the breeder treat the kittens?
- How do the kittens respond to her?

If you have any concerns whatsoever, make your excuses and leave. The kitten you choose will be an important part of your life for many years to come, so don't opt for second-best.

CHARACTER TEST

All kittens should be playful and exuberant. If they hide away from you for the duration of your visit, then you should be concerned. Most healthy, well-socialized kittens will be a little apprehensive at first, but curiosity will take hold and they will venture to check you out.

It is a good idea to take along a piece of string or similar that you can use to test the kittens' playfulness. Any self-respecting kitten will not be able to resist pouncing on a wiggling string or a long feather, and you should be wary of any that don't take the bait.

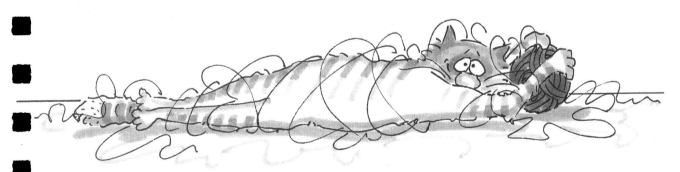

You should also assess how the kittens interact with each other. It is easy to spot different emerging personalities – in any one litter you can often find the bold bully, the tolerant tom who takes his siblings' batterings, the shy, clueless-looking one, and the manic lunatic that just races around at top speed.

Most kittens have a mixture of character traits. Ask the breeder or shelter worker for his or her advice as to which one would best suit you. They will have clear ideas about the different characters, and will be able to make a rough assessment as to the type of home that would suit each one.

If you do not have very much cat experience, or if you are too busy for some intensive work rehabilitating shy or overly bold kittens, then you are advised to choose a kitten that is playful, interacts well with her littermates and mother, and that is fairly outgoing, but not overly so. Your ideal kitten will not be too independent, and will enjoy being petted. This can be assessed by picking the kittens up gently (putting one hand under their chest and another under their bottom to support them), and cuddling them close to you. Stroke them gently and talk to them in a soft, soothing voice. Most kittens will struggle at first, but will soon be won round by the attention and will make the most of the cuddle.

Of course, if you want an independent cat that isn't too keen on human interaction, by all means choose the bold puss (if there is one). Or, if you really are smitten by the shy, doleful kitten that hides under the sofa, then choose her – but do so for all the right reasons. Be aware of the work that will be involved in bringing her out of her shell and instilling her with confidence, and don't just choose her out of impulse or pity.

If all the kittens are sleepy and sluggish, it could mean sickness or poor socialization, or it could be due to something perfectly innocent such as your visiting shortly after their feeding time, or the fact that they have just dropped fast asleep after hours of relentless playing. In such circumstances, it is best to arrange another viewing with the breeder, so you can assess the kittens at their most active. If they are still dopey on the second visit, and are not easily roused, then be concerned.

HEALTH CHECKS

Once you've narrowed down your choice to a kitten (or adult cat) that appeals to you, you should next assess her health. Make a squeaky noise and see if she responds. If she doesn't, it could indicate deafness (a problem that especially plagues white cats). Deaf cats can make great pets, but they will need to be kept indoors (because they cannot hear dangers such as traffic), and will require extra care and love to help them feel secure in a world that is silent for them.

- Assess the kitten's size. A larger kitten is likely to be healthier than a small, 'weedy' one.
- Make sure you see the kitten move. Is there any hint of a limp in any of the limbs?
- Assess the kitten's body shape. A pot-belly could indicate a heavy worm infestation.

- Run your hands over her coat. It should be soft and clean, with no bald patches.
- Part the fur in several places and make sure the skin is smooth and clean. Is there any evidence of scabs or flea dirt (black specks)?
- Hold her up close and listen to her breathing. There should be no hint of wheeziness and her breathing should not be labored.
- Look into the kitten's eyes – and try not to melt! Make sure the eyes are bright and clear, with no discharge. The presence of a third eyelid across the eye usually indicates illness.
- The kitten's ears should be clean. Any redness, dark wax or odor can indicate mites or an infection, as can head-shaking or scratching at the ears.
- The nose should be slightly moist with no discharge.
- Place one hand under her lower jaw and another over the top of her mouth and gently open the kitten's mouth. The gums should be a healthy pink, her teeth should be white and clean, and there should be no hint of bad breath.
- Finally, check under the kitten's tail to make sure that the anus is clean and dry.

All the above checks should also be made with adult cats. Some cats, particularly older rescued cats, can get very excited when they meet someone they'd like to spend the rest of their lives with, and may dribble. This is perfectly normal, if it is accompanied by noisy purring and the cat is making it quite clear that this is love at first sight. The cat is doing it because she sees you as a mother-figure and is expecting you to feed her, so she drools in anticipation of the milk. However, if the cat is showing little interest in you, and is still dribbling, you should check whether the drooling is the result of a dental problem or other health disorder.

Sickly cats and kittens can make full recoveries, and can blossom into wonderful companions. But you should know what you are letting yourself in for. If you are expecting a healthy cat, then make sure you get one. If you are experienced in looking after cats and are honestly prepared for the time, commitment, expense and possible heartbreak of raising a poorly puss, then go for it. If you are not, then do not feel obliged to take on the responsibility – leave it for a more experienced cat lover.

PAPERWORK

Once you are happy that you have found the perfect puss for you, and provided the breeder is happy that you can offer a loving, caring home (a home visit may be arranged in the meantime), you should agree on a date when you can collect the kitten. Delay the date if you have a holiday due or if you are planning any major home renovations that could upset your kitten. If you are working, arrange to collect the kitten on a Friday afternoon, so you have the whole weekend to settle her in.

The breeder may arrange for the paperwork to be completed before you collect the kitten, and will probably insist on a deposit, or the amount to be paid in full beforehand.

When you take charge of the kitten, the breeder should also give you a registration form, vaccination certificate, details of worming treatments, a receipt for the amount paid, and a diet sheet outlining what the kitten should be fed and when. You may also be given more information, such as on grooming (in semi-long and longhaired breeds). In the UK, you will probably also be given free insurance for the first six weeks or so.

If you have made any other arrangements with the breeder, such as the fact that the sale is conditional on a satisfactory health check by your vet, or that the breeder is willing to take the kitten back if you can no longer care for her, then you should make sure your agreements are put in writing. Most responsible breeders will be more than happy to give lifelong advice should you need it, and will be eager to take the cat back in extenuating circumstances.

FAMILY HISTORY

If you choose a purebred cat, the breeder should give you a pedigree, showing the cat's purebred status. What is contained in the pedigree varies between countries, so you should check with your national cat-fancy governing body as to what you should expect, but usually the pedigree shows the cat's full, official name, the parents' names (and sometimes further generations of ancestors), the cat's registration number with the governing cat-fancy organization, and the name and address of the breeder.

The breeder can usually dictate the terms on which you take the kitten, and may indicate on the paperwork that you cannot breed from the kitten. This may be because the kitten has a slight fault (such as coat markings) which renders her, and future generations, unsuitable for the show ring. If you fail to observe the breeder's wishes, you will be unable to register the resulting kittens, and will therefore have great difficulty finding homes for them.

Do be warned that there is no guarantee that a cat registered with a governing body is healthy, has show potential, or even that the cat really is purebred. There is no way each organization can visit each kitten, and the system is one built on trust – which a small minority of people abuse.

SHELTER PAPERS

There is a fair amount of form-filling to be done when you adopt a rescued cat too. Again, procedures vary, but you may have to provide references from your veterinarian (or details of any veterinarians you have used in the past), details of past cats you have owned, information on your lifestyle and family, and on your work. The shelter must be happy that you will provide a responsible, permanent home for the cat, and that she won't turn up on their doorstep again a few months down the line. If the shelter doesn't vet you, it isn't doing its job properly.

Part 4
Getting Ready

Chapter 7

Buying Equipment

You've found your cat, you've passed the breeder's or shelter's rigorous requirements, and you now just have to wait until the kitten or cat is ready to leave for her new home.

To help the time pass while you wait for your new pet, you should make sure you make all the preparations ready for her home-coming. The first step is to buy all the necessary equipment.

BEDS AND BEDDING

It will help the kitten to settle in her new home if she has a bed to call her own. Some cats don't take to cat beds, and far prefer human beds, or the sofa, but you should make sure kitty has a snug bed, in case she wants to sleep on her own or if you'd prefer not to share your bed with puss (it gets very crowded in a multi-cat household).

There is a phenomenal range of beds on the market, with price tags to match all budgets.

- **Beanbag beds**: most cats love milk-treading on these; some are nervous of the rustling noise at first, but soon get used to it. Make sure the material is strong – or the contents will spill out (much to your cat's delight). The major disadvantage is that they are often not washable.
- **Fleecy round beds**: warm and practical; they often come with a removable, washable pad on the base in case of accidents.
- **Hooded/covered beds**: these give great protection against draughts, and they prove popular with cats and kittens as they love small dark dens to snuggle up in.
- **Duvets**: usually washable, these are warm and versatile, and can be placed wherever you wish – for example, if the cat insists on sleeping on the sofa, the duvet placed on one corner will at least protect your furniture.
- **Sleeping bags**: feline sleeping bags are especially cozy in colder weather, and appeal to those cats that love warm, dark spaces.

- **Radiator cradle**: these are soft, furry hammock-type beds that fit over a radiator. Cats love them. Not only are they incredibly warm, but they also help to make a new cat feel secure, as they are off the ground. If they are also by a window, the cat will spend hours dozing in the sunshine and watching the world go by. Older cats will need a strategically-placed stool to help them reach the cradle.
- **Four-posters**: yes, there really are four-poster beds for cats. In fact, you can buy chaises longues, miniature sofas – the sky's the limit. Yes, these novelty items are good fun, but in all honesty cats tend to prefer to kip on a pile of newly-washed clothes waiting to be ironed!

- **Cardboard box**: a cardboard box, with the sides cut down to about four or five inches (10-12.5 cm) will help the kitten to feel cozy and protected, but will still enable her to get in and out easily. Line the box with a cat duvet, fleecy veterinary bedding, or an old jumper. Or you could even improvise a covered cat bed, which kitty will adore. Obviously, the cardboard cannot be cleaned, but it is easily replaced.

Whatever bed you buy, make sure it is easily cleaned, and that the bedding is machine-washable – important not only for accidents but also for flea control.

The size of the bed is important too. Cats and kittens love snug places – they will prefer a small bed that they can curl up in rather than a huge one (though the owner's double bed seems to be the exception that proves the rule!). When buying for a kitten, buy a bed that will snugly fit her when she is fully grown, and fill the excess space with a blanket so she is not overwhelmed by the size.

LOCATION, LOCATION, LOCATION

The location of the bed makes all the difference when it comes to settling your kitten or new adult cat into her new home. Finding herself in a new environment, your kitten's wild survival instincts may come to the fore. She will seek out small, dark hiding places where she will feel protected from any threats, and from where she can view everything around her. Consider her point of view when placing the bed. Putting it in the middle of the floor is not ideal. However, placing it in a quiet corner of the room, under a table and near to a warm radiator will prove far more popular.

Whenever kitty is ready for a catnap (after feeding or play), then pop her in her bed, and stroke her to encourage her to settle. She'll soon seek out her bed in future when she fancies a sleep. If she doesn't approve of where you've put the bed, she simply won't use it. In such cases, move the bed to one of the areas she prefers.

FEEDING BOWLS

Your kitten will need at least two bowls – one for food and one for water. There is a huge variety of bowls from which to choose.
- **Ceramic:** popular choice, easy to wash, but can break if dropped. Come in lots of different designs and can look great on your kitchen floor.
- **Stainless steel**: unbreakable, but can scratch, and some kittens freak out at their own reflections.
- **Plastic:** cheap and durable, but will scratch eventually and can be quite abrasive. Some cats get sore noses from regularly feeding from an old plastic bowl, so replace fairly regularly, or opt for a different material.

Whatever type of bowl you choose, remember that cats prefer to eat from shallow bowls rather than deep ones.

FOOD

Make sure you find out from the breeder the type of food that she recommends you feed. Often, the breeder will give you a few days' supply, but it is as well to be prepared beforehand. Changing to a diet that the kitten isn't used to is not recommended and can cause tummy upsets (see Chapter Fifteen).

LITTER-TRAY

You can choose a standard litter-tray or one that is covered. A covered litter-tray is advisable if you have 'ambush' cats in the house who will not respect your new cat's rights to relieve herself in peace. It also has the added advantage that smells are contained within it, but the tray should still be changed regularly – just because it doesn't pong, it doesn't absolve you of your cleaning duties! If the tray is dirty, your cat will probably refuse to use it.

Whatever type of tray you choose, the base should be at least three to four inches deep (7.5-10 cm) to give ample burying opportunities; and it should be large enough for your cat to comfortably maneuver around in it.

Make sure the litter-tray is not placed in the same vicinity as the cat's food bowls. Although it is convenient for the owner to have all the cat's accessories in one area, it is not hygienic and the cat may refuse to use her tray (would *you* eat your breakfast in the bathroom?).

LITTER

Make sure you have a good supply of cat-litter to see you through your kitten's first week or so. Initially, you should choose the same litter that the breeder uses, which will help the kitten to transfer her house-training knowledge to her new home.

If, once she is settled, you would like to change the litter (perhaps to a lightweight version that is easier to carry when shopping), then change the litter gradually. Mix in a small amount of the new litter into the other variety and kitty will hardly notice the difference. Over the course of a week, add more of the new variety until, eventually, the changeover will be complete.

Some cats aren't really fussed what they use, but others are quite choosy. If your cat refuses to use her tray, it could be that she finds the litter uncomfortable on her feet. Change to a less bulky litter, such as a variety that consists of small, fine grains. Ideally, you want something that is as close to sand as possible – which the wildcat would have used in the desert.

LITTER ACCESSORIES

You will also need a litterscoop, to remove the poop or clumps of wet litter, while keeping the clean litter in the tray. This cuts down on the number of times that a complete litter change is required.

You can also purchase litterbags, strong plastic liners that fit into the tray and upon which the litter is placed. When the tray needs changing, you just remove the bag and put in a new one. They aren't suitable for all cats, though. If you have a determined digger that loves to burrow to the bottom of the tray, the bag will split; if you have a fastidious feline that likes to cover her 'doings' thoroughly, she is likely to 'giftwrap' the tray, covering it all with the sides of the bag. If she needs to use the tray again, before you put everything back in order, she'll be left with no option than to relieve herself on top of the plastic – or elsewhere altogether. With these types of cat, dispense with the liner altogether.

Litter deodoriser can be added to the tray to help absorb nasty odors. They aren't ideal for kittens – to help with house-training you want the kitten to recognize the tray as a toilet; it doesn't help if it smells of roses! Some adult cats do not like strong-smelling deodorisers either, and can show their displeasure by going elsewhere.

The only way of preventing nasty odors is through a thorough scoop-and-clean program, see page 105.

COLLAR

A permanent form of identification (microchipping, pages 78, 216) is recommended, but it is also useful for your kitten to get used to a collar so she can be returned to you by anyone who may not have access to a microchip scanner.

There are some wonderful collars on the market, with or without bells (page 75), in every conceivable pattern, color and material, including reflective collars that improve the visibility of the cat in poor light.

The collar should be adjustable, so it can be altered as your kitten grows, and you must be able to fit two fingers under the collar once fitted.

However, you must make sure that the collar you choose is a safe one and will not strangle your puss if she gets it caught on something, such as a branch. Most collars now have a band of elastic fitted that will provide extra give if caught – hopefully enough to allow your cat to struggle free. However, among the best options are collars that have plastic clips that immediately release under pressure.

An identity tag should be fixed to the collar, giving your details so you can be contacted if your cat is found.

Some cats simply refuse to wear a collar. They will happily allow you to put it on, but will promptly remove it. You can try to experiment with different types of collar, but die-hard collar-haters usually work out ways of removing each one, and can get into danger trying to get out of them. For example, if puss is used to a clip-release collar and is then given an ordinary collar, she may think that if she applies pressure to it, it will come off. It won't. She may strangle in the attempt. In such cases, you'll have no option but to surrender to your cat's wishes (it won't be the last time), and you'll have to rely on a microchip as the only form of identification.

HARNESS

A harness is a useful piece of equipment when introducing a new cat to your garden (Chapter Nineteen), or if you have a house-cat that likes to have an occasional sniff outside. Never use an ordinary collar or lead – a cat will instantly back out of it. Buy a specially designed cat harness from your pet store, which fits all around the body to give you more control. Harnesses come in different sizes according to your cat's size, and look much more difficult to fit than they actually are. Just follow the instructions carefully. Make sure you buy one that has flat, fairly thick straps (the rope-type ones can dig in).

A tip: when taking your cat out in her harness, do not expect her to walk like a dog. You should follow her around, making sure the harness is slack; this way, she will hardly notice that she is even wearing a harness. If she feels pressure from the harness, or if she is scared by something, she will do a fantastic impression of a lunatic kangaroo, bouncing and twisting at speed to get free. Always have practice sessions indoors before taking her out – you do not want her to escape if she is not used to being outdoors.

Some cats find wearing a harness too stressful and will never accept it. In these cases, it is kinder to forget the idea.

SCRATCHING POST

Cats need to scratch to remove the outer husk of their nails to reveal a sharp new one underneath. They also scratch for territorial reasons – leaving scent from their paws for other cats to 'read'. If you do not provide your cat with a scratching post, she will make her own – out of the back of an armchair, a door, and anything else she can lay her paws on.

If you watch cats scratching against a tree outdoors, they always lean up and scratch, so your indoor post should be high enough for your cat to have a good stretch and scratch. Your kitten will soon outgrow a small post, so it is worth investing in a full-size adult one.

Sisal is the best material for a scratching post. Cats love the carpet varieties too, but if your puss gets used to the sensation of ripping carpet, she could extend the association to your own floorcovering!

House-cats should be provided with a cat-tree – a super-deluxe arrangement with at least two tall columns of scratching posts and various tunnels, nests, and perches. If you have several cats, you will spend hours watching them all leaping up and down, in and out, ambushing the cat below or above them. Single cats love perching on top of cat-trees too, and they are great fun for nutty kittens. Who knows? If kitty enjoys climbing her tree, she might stop scaling your curtains...

TOYS

The range of cat toys is incredible. From remote-controlled mice through to jangly balls and catnip-filled parcels, the sky's the limit.

Great favorites are fishing-rod type toys, with a toy or feather on the end of a very long piece of string, attached to a rod. There are also interactive toys, such as a motorized mouse on a racetrack, for house-cats to amuse themselves while you are at work. Kongs are also great for cats. They are tough rubber toys filled with catnip or a treat, that the cat can bounce around or chew quite safely.

If your puss doesn't show interest in her toys, perhaps they are too big for her. Some cats are intimidated by large toys – outdoors, they probably prefer hunting mice to rats. Other, bolder cats love bigger toys – these are likely to be the same cats that bring rabbits home to you!

CATNIP CRAZY

Catnip (Nepata cataria) is a herb that produces a slightly hallucinogenic effect in about fifty per cent of cats (including big cats, such as lions), causing them to roll or race around like crazy. They will become extra-playful, or lick the herb in a trance-like state. Others aren't affected by it at all. It is perfectly safe, non-addictive, and gives playtimes an extra edge.

Many garden centres sell varieties of catnip that you can grow yourself – even in a window box.

Many toys can be home-made. A couple of screwed up bits of newspaper thrown into a cardboard box with holes cut into it will amuse a cat for hours. Cotton reels (but never thread) are also popular.

Most toys should be played with under supervision in case of accidents, particularly toys on elastic, which can strangle a cat if she gets caught up in it. Toys with small, removable parts should be avoided in case they are swallowed in the frenzy of play. Remember always to use your commonsense – something most cats don't seem to have!

GROOMING EQUIPMENT

Your choice of grooming equipment will depend on your cat or kitten's coat type. Ask the breeder or shelter what brushes and combs you will need. For more information, see Chapter Seventeen: Coat care.

CRATE

A crate is a large metal cage, which is invaluable when raising kittens. It sounds much more austere than it actually is. If some comfortable bedding is placed inside, together with some safe toys, and a blanket is placed over the top to create a cozy den, puss will love her little home. The crate should be large enough for a small litter-tray (located away from the sleeping area), and a bowl of water.

The crate is a safe spot in which the kitten can be kept when you are unable to supervise her, and will aid introductions to other pets in the home. If you have room, it can be kept as the cat's den for the rest of her life, or you might want to dismantle it until you acquire your next cat. Either way, it is money well spent – especially considering the peace of mind it provides.

CAT-CARRIER

A cat-carrier should be sturdy, escape-proof, easily cleaned and covered on three sides to help the cat feel safe and protected. Cardboard carriers are not ideal – one defiant wee and they weaken considerably, and some cats do a perfect impression of Edward Scissorhands, shredding the cardboard in a matter of minutes.

Wicker looks great, but cannot be cleaned easily, and, if the strands break, they can be quite sharp. In some models, the carrier door does not fit as snugly to the basket as it could, giving escape artists a great opportunity.

Plastic carriers are strong, durable and washable, and come in many different sizes and designs.

Generally, cats like to feel quite snug, so a huge carrier is not always the best option. As a guide, the cat should be able to turn around in the carrier – anything larger and she could feel exposed to danger or be bounced around on the car journey.

If you have a long journey planned with an older cat, a larger carrier should be considered, however, so she can move around to prevent stiffness.

TOP TIP

If you have a cat that refuses to come out of her carrier when at the vet's, consider a top-loading one.

CAT-FLAP

Another must if your cat is to be allowed outdoors. A few days of getting up and down to the door to let the cat in and out, then in again, and you will regret not having fitted a flap for her. They are easily installed and will give your cat free access to the outdoors, or to a covered pen if she is a house-cat. Before fitting it, do make sure it will be at the right height for your cat, and not too high for her.

You must be able to lock the flap to control your cat's access to the outdoors. No cat should ever be let outside after dark (the majority of car accidents involving cats happen in poor light). Unneutered queens should be restricted to indoors, as should sick cats, and you might also want to keep puss indoors in bad weather or if there are fireworks nearby.

As well as being able to keep puss in, you should also consider how you are going to keep other cats,

racoons or even skunks outdoors! Cat-flaps that come with magnetic collars offer a solution. When the cat approaches the flap, her collar will act as a 'key', allowing her to enter and barring access to other would-be visitors. (Some cats, keen on entertaining, have been known to keep their heads close to the flap while their 'friends' enter the property, however!)

Chapter 8

Cat-Proofing Your Home

The home is full of dangers for inquisitive felines, so you must make sure all hazards are removed before you bring kitty home. Make sure curiosity doesn't kill your cat.

DOMESTIC DANGERS

Crawl around your home to get a kitten's perspective. Is there a gap on the bath panel that she can crawl through and get trapped behind? Is the chimney blocked to prevent her climbing up? Can she reach any electrical cables?

Before the kitten comes home, all family members should be briefed on the domestic dangers, and basic house rules should be agreed. Here are some guidelines to help you.

- Always put the lid down on the toilet (kittens can drown if they fall in, or become poisoned if they lick water which contains bleach or other chemicals).
- The doors to the oven, fridge, freezer, dishwasher, microwave, washing machine and tumble-dryer should never be shut without first checking that the kitten or cat hasn't crept inside. It's worth sticking reminder notes on the doors of appliances to help people remember, especially for the first few weeks, before it becomes second-nature to check them.
- If a cleaning substance has been left on the bath or in a sink, or a floor has been cleaned with chemicals, the cat should be denied access to the room.
- Unattended candles are out of bounds.
- Needles and thread should always be put away promptly (it seems incredible that a smart puss would contemplate swallowing a needle or pin, but hundreds are admitted to surgery every year – and some don't make it this far).
- Medicines should be locked out of reach, as should household cleaning products.
- Breakable ornaments should be kept in a glass display cabinet.
- For the first few weeks while the cat is confined indoors, all windows and doors to the outside should be kept closed. Upstairs windows should always be closed.

Screens can be purchased that fit securely to windows, allowing air to enter, while keeping the cat safely indoors.

- Bones should never be fed to a cat – chicken bones pose the biggest threat, and many cats have suffered severe injury when a bone has become lodged in the throat. Before throwing bones away, foil any would-be garbage raiders by wrapping up the bones in layers of newspaper sealed with sticky tape, tie them in a plastic bag, and then put them in your outside bin.
- The string that binds many meat joints is fantastically appealing to a cat – and immensely dangerous if ingested. It should be disposed of in the same way as bones, above.
- Aerosols should never be sprayed near the cat's bowls, as their contents could contaminate the water/food and be ingested by the cat.
- Plastic bags should always be put safely away (cats love exploring bags, but may suffocate in a plastic one), and razors, glue, firelighters, knives and scissors should be kept out of harm's reach.

• Many plants and cut flowers are toxic to cats (see Chapter Nine); check with your garden center before bringing them into your home, as most cats like to nibble or play with them. A house-cat should always have access to special indoor grass that she can chew to her heart's content. Safe house- and garden-plants are listed on page 74.

ELECTRICAL CABLES

These pose one of the biggest risks to teething kittens or adult, playful cats. Not only can they electrocute themselves by chewing through the wires, but they can also pull them, bringing down heavy, breakable or flammable objects on top of themselves.

Go around your home and gather up excess electrical wire and fasten with a cable tie. Remove all dangling cables, by taping to the floor or wall or thread them through cable clips which are then tacked down.

Where this is not possible, thread a thick, chew-proof cable protector over the wires your cat has access to (available from hardware stores) or apply a cat-repellent (such as bitter apple, eucalyptus, or nail-biting deterrent polish) to cables. Obviously, the appliance should be unplugged beforehand, and taken away from any electricity socket. The item should only be reconnected to the electricity supply once the cables are dry.

If ever your cat is spotted playing with cables, she should be stopped at once.

SETTING LIMITS

Before bringing puss home, you should decide on any no-go areas. Some, such as the kitchen work surfaces, are imperative. Not only is it unhygienic to have a cat trampling around where food is prepared, but, more importantly, it poses great danger to your puss. Jumping up head first into a steaming kettle, knocking a pan of boiling water, leaping on to a kitchen knife, or walking across a hot hob are accidents that can all be avoided by keeping kitty on the floor. If she is removed every time, she will soon realize it is a waste of energy to keep trying (though loose foil on the work surface will also dissuade her – cats hate the noise it makes). Alternatively, a well-aimed jet from a water pistol can act as a deterrent, especially if you accompany it with a loud "No!".

If there are any other areas, such as the bedrooms, these should be agreed beforehand so everyone knows – and can implement – the rules when kitty comes home.

CAT-SAFE ROOM

It is important to prepare a room that puss can call her own. A small boxroom is ideal – cats prefer small spaces if they feel nervous, and it will be an easier room to fully cat-proof and prepare for her.

This room will be the place you first take her when you bring her home (Chapter Twelve), and the place she will sleep and spend time when you are not able to supervise her. If you have other pets, they should not be allowed to enter kitty's room – it will be her own little place where she feels fully secure.

Thoroughly cat-proof the room, as described above. Place a bed and a litter-tray in the room (though not in close proximity to each other), make sure the windows are lockable (some cats can open unlocked windows!).

SAFEGUARDING FURNITURE

To a kitten, your home is a playground – sofas are there to scale and curtains make great swings. If it would destroy you to find scratch marks on a prized antique table, or snags in some designer curtains, then seriously reconsider having a cat. Or perhaps a sedate, older puss (in her mid-teens) would be more appropriate than a younger cat.

There are ways of protecting your furniture, but there are no guarantees.

- Flip your hanging curtains over the top rail.
- Cover your sofa and chairs with a protective throw (this will prevent cat hair clinging to your furnishings).
- Cover your carpet with rugs.
- Tape plastic on top of the carpet where it meets a door, areas where cats are wont to scratch, especially if the door is closed to them.
- Alternatively, pull up the carpet, sand down your floorboards and place some cheap rugs on top.

Do be warned: no amount of home protection will stop a cat from scratching – the natural urge to claw is just too strong. She must be provided with a good scratching post or she will improvise her own.

Chapter 9

The Outside World

If the home contains some potential dangers to cats, then the outside world is full of them. Traffic poses the biggest danger, and thousands of cats and litters are killed or injured every year by air rifles.

Once your cat is outside in the big, bad world, there is no way of protecting her. This is why many people choose to keep their cats indoors (Chapter Eighteen).

If you decide to take the risk of letting your cat outside, the least you can do is to make sure that you do not contribute to the hazards she faces.

First step: cat-proofing the garden/yard.

GARDEN/YARD HAZARDS

- Use only cat-safe chemicals (such as pesticides or fertilizers) in your garden. Read the label clearly. If it isn't clear whether the product is non-toxic to animals, do not use it – don't take any risks with your cat's safety.
- Don't use rodent poisons – if your cat is hopeless at pest control, use a humane trap that doesn't involve the use of toxic bait.
- Remember, a cat doesn't have to eat poison directly in order to be harmed. Munching a mouse that has been poisoned can have equally disastrous effects.
- All chemicals should be locked away safely – antifreeze is particularly dangerous, and yet cats seem attracted to its sweet smell/taste.
- Never shut the shed door without first checking that puss hasn't crept in unnoticed for a nap.
- Ponds should be covered if you have a reckless kitten. Older, wiser cats tend to avoid them, but a kitten could be tempted to do some fishing, and get into difficulty.
- Iced-over ponds should be covered securely so your cat isn't tempted to walk on the ice, which may then break.
- Don't forget to cat-proof your garage (oil and other chemicals must all be safely locked out of harm's way).

DEFINING TERRITORY

The size of a cat's territory is linked to sex (males tend to have a larger domain, and neutered cats roam less than entire ones), how much the animal is fed, the area available, and the surrounding cat population. For example, a male feral cat living in a rural environment can have a territory of up to 150 acres. But a neutered urban pet has only one-fiftieth of an acre; she doesn't need more — she is fed regularly, and, because she is neutered, she doesn't need to roam to find a mate.

At the centre of your cat's territory is her garden. Interestingly, cats usually respect the man-made boundaries we use, such as garden fences, so other cats in your area will soon learn that your garden is a territory that is not up for grabs — a few hisses and aggressive postures from your puss and they'll soon get the message.

G'DAY! I'M YOUR LOCAL GARDEN HAZARD!

POISONOUS HOUSE- AND GARDEN-PLANTS

Generally, cats are pretty wise about what they can and can't chew, but, if they are tempted by a moving leaf or stalk, most cats cannot resist leaping on a plant and having a nibble. For a more complete list, search the internet — there are lots of sites dedicated to the subject, such as www.cfainc.org/articles/plants.html, or ask your garden center for advice.

Amaryllis	Forsythia	Monkshood
Azalea	Foxglove	Narcissus
Belladonna	Hawthorn	Oleander
Boxwood	Holly	Peace lily
Broom	Hyacinth	Peony
Buttercup	Hydrangea	Philodendron
Caladium	Iris	Pine needles
Chrysanthemum	Jasmine	Poinsettia
Clematis	Jerusalem cherry	Poppy
Conifers	Laburnum	Privet
Crocus	Laurel	Rhododendron
Daffodil	Lilies	Snowdrop
Delphinium	Lords and ladies	Sweet pea
Dumb cane (Dieffenbachia)	Lupin	Tulip
English ivy	Mistletoe	Wisteria

CAT-SAFE PLANTS

African violet	Fuschia	Parlour plant
Air fern	Gardenia	Primula
Begonia	Honeysuckle	Pussywillow
Boston fern	Ivy peperomia	Red African violet
Chinese evergreen	Jade plant	Rubber plant
Dandelion	Lady palm	Spider plant
Draecaena palm	Lilac	Wandering Jew
Dragon tree	Monkey plant	Wax plant
Earth star	Moss	Yucca plant
Flowering maple	Parlour palm	

TO HUNT OR NOT TO HUNT?

Controlling a cat's hunting is not easy – it is a skill which has ensured their survival for thousands of years and which they would be foolish to give up (ferals would die if they couldn't fend for themselves and revert to the wild, and many cats are kept solely as ratters).

Some organizations have a fanatical anti-cat fervor, claiming cats are responsible for killing huge numbers of wild animals and birds. It seems unlikely, though, that cats are responsible for dwindling numbers of wildlife, particularly birds. Cats and birds have existed alongside each other for thousands of years. Why have the numbers of birds only suddenly declined? If anything, fewer birds are being killed by cats today, as most felines are fed regularly, and their numbers are now checked through neutering. It is more likely that humans are responsible – changing farming methods, pollution, changes in seasonal climates and temperatures are more likely causes than the humble cat.

Nevertheless, it's never nice if your cat brings home a dead bird, natural though it is. Here are some ways you can help to prevent this.

- Do away with your bird table; it will encourage birds to your garden and will prove too big a temptation to your cat.
- Attach a bell to her collar to warn birds of her approach. (However, most cats keep their head perfectly still when stalking prey, and the noise of a bell the rest of the time will drive her to distraction).
- There is some evidence to suggest that red collars are more easily spotted by birds than other colors.
- Buy a special anti-hunting collar (search on the internet for stockists), which makes a noise whenever the cat jumps up.
- Do not let her out at the key hunting times: dawn and dusk (see Chapter Nineteen).
- Consider keeping her indoors all the time as a house-cat (see Chapter Eighteen).

Chapter 10

The Professionals

In your cat's lifetime, you won't be the only person responsible for her wellbeing. There are a number of professionals, such as the veterinarian, cat-sitter, or cattery, upon whose services you will rely. Before you get your puss, you should do your research to find the very best people for the job.

FINDING A VETERINARIAN

Your relationship with your cat's veterinarian is as important as that with your own doctor. This will be someone to whom you entrust your cat's life, so don't just opt for the nearest veterinarian, or the first you come to in the telephone directory. Personal recommendations are a good starting point, or perhaps your kitten's breeder or shelter could recommend someone nearby. Once you have some contacts, do your homework to find the best one for you – and your kitty.

- Location is important – after all, you have to be able to get to the clinic quickly in the event of an emergency. But most towns and villages have several veterinary surgeries close by, so don't choose location over all other factors.
- Choose a practice that specialises in small-animal work. Some practices, especially those in more rural locations, may concentrate on large animals, such as horses or livestock. You may even be lucky enough to find a cat-only clinic (there are hundreds in America, but only a handful in the UK). Not only will the veterinarians have specialist feline knowledge, but your puss won't be intimidated by having to share a waiting room next to a Great Dane or an over-exuberant puppy.
- What are the practice's consulting hours? Do they do early-morning, evening, or weekend appointments so you won't have to take time off work for non-urgent, routine care of your pet?
- What emergency care is available? In the UK, a veterinary practice must offer 24-hour support, but this is not a legal obligation in the States.

- Is there a member of staff in the practice 24 hours a day? In some surgeries, animals are left on their own at night.
- Would you prefer a small clinic, where you are likely to see the same veterinarian every visit, or would you prefer a busier, larger affair, which may have a more snazzy practice with all the up-to-date equipment? (Though there are always exceptions in both cases.)
- Is there an on-site hospital, or, if the practice is a branch clinic, will you have to travel to one further away in the event of your animal requiring specialist surgery or care?
- Does the practice run any specialist clinics, such as weight-loss, or dental care?
- What is the practice's policy on home-visits (particularly important with older cats, or if you have difficulty traveling to the surgery).
- Is it important to you that the practice provides alternative therapies as well as conventional ones? Many treatments have proved useful in cat care, with cats of all ages and with many different conditions.
- Finally, cost. Although this is important, and prices can vary greatly between geographical areas, you should not base your final decision on veterinary fees. Other factors, such as the quality of care, are far more important. If you are concerned about affording veterinary care, look into pet insurance, but remember that it doesn't cover preventative care. Several charities run low-cost care schemes for people on low incomes, which may be worth investigating (see Useful Addresses).

QUESTIONS TO ASK

You've narrowed down your search by quizzing the practice over the telephone. Now it's time to visit your short-listed clinics.

- What is your overall impression upon entering the practice? Is it clean, friendly, and professional-looking, or run-down and chaotic?
- Assess the waiting area. Is it crowded? Is there an allocated cat corner, at least room enough to distance yourself from other animals (that may not only stress your cat, but could pass on disease).
- Don't forget the receptionist. You will probably see him or her as much as you do the veterinarian. Is she kind and friendly, or will she bark at you every time you make an appointment or ask for advice?
- Veterinary nurses are important too. They will have a great deal of contact with your cat, and may perform routine procedures on her. Are they professional and enthusiastic about their work?
- What equipment does the clinic have? What on-site results-testing facilities are there? Or do results have to be sent off to be analyzed? (The wait can be anxious and can delay treatment.)

VETTING THE VETERINARIAN

Trust is a key factor in your relationship with your cat's veterinarian. If you don't feel fully confident in the veterinarian's ability, you will encounter many problems in the years to come. Veterinary experience and competence aside, if the veterinarian is unable to explain things clearly to you, you may doubt that he or she is doing the very best for your pet because you do not understand all aspects of the care that is being provided.

- Is the veterinarian an animal lover? What pets do they have of their own?
- Have they taken any specialist courses or embarked on advanced study in the feline field, above and beyond their initial veterinary qualifications?
- Are they able to explain things clearly and simply?
- Is there a good chemistry between you? Is this someone with whom you are happy to work with for the next 15 years or so?
- When you take your cat along for her first visit, does the veterinarian handle her confidently and kindly?

THE FIRST APPOINTMENT

Once you are happy that you have found the best veterinarian for you, you should register with the practice, giving details of the cat you will be collecting, and arranging a date for the first consultation. Ideally, this should be the same day or the day after you first bring her home.

The veterinarian will discuss microchipping, vaccinations, worming and flea treatments, and neutering, and will arrange a program of preventative care with you. They will also check the cat over, and, hopefully, give her a clean bill of health. Take along with you any details the breeder or shelter has given you about any health treatments puss has received.

Start as you mean to go on. Take along some treats to the clinic, and ask the veterinarian to give your puss a few. If you can prevent your cat taking a dislike to veterinarians, life will be much easier in the future!

CAT-SITTERS

A reliable cat-sitter is the best option if you need cat-care while you are away, particularly if you have a multi-cat household or other pets that require care. Elderly cats in particular usually hate a change in routine, and much prefer to stay in the comfort of their own home. A sitter can also water your plants and deter burglars (some insurance companies give lower premiums if sitters are used).

If you don't have a trustworthy, cat-loving friend who can do the job (or if you have called in all your favors), you might want to consider a professional (advertised in the cat press or on the internet). Always check the references of anyone with whom you entrust your house and your cats.

- Check out the company. How long has it been in business? Can the staff put you in contact with some of their clients?
- Ask about insurance. What would happen if the sitter was responsible for a house-fire or for the accidental injury of your pets?
- Ask for full contact details of the sitter, and for references.
- What experience do they have?
- How would they react in an emergency? Do they have any cat-care qualifications? (Some sitters are veterinary nurses.)
- Establish exactly what is provided. Some offer a comprehensive service where not only is the cat groomed, fed, cuddled and played with, but your house is cleaned and your shopping is done for your return!
- What is required of you? In many instances, you pay a daily fee, and may also be expected to provide food for the duration of the sitter's stay.
- Make sure the sitter has your contact details so you can be called in the event of an emergency. Your veterinarian's details, together with information on any medication the cat needs, should also be given.

FINDING A CATTERY

If you cannot find a cat-sitter, or if you would prefer your kitten or young cat to get used to cattery care from the start, then you should start to research viable establishments.

Your vet, cat-owning friends, your local cat shelter, or your kitten's breeder may be able to recommend catteries, or at least relay any horror stories they've heard of those you should avoid. Your telephone directory should produce other leads, but personal recommendations are always preferred.

The Feline Advisory Bureau in the UK (see Useful Addresses) publishes a list of catteries that conform to their rigorous standards. If you are looking for a cattery outside the UK, or if you cannot find a FAB-registered cattery in your area, check out their website to get an idea of the minimal requirements you should look for in a cattery – www.fabcats/org/lbcs.html.

QUESTIONS TO ASK

- How long has the cattery been in business?
- How large is the organization? How many staff and units are there?
- Is there also a kennels on site? If so, how close is it situated to the cattery?
- What is the cattery's daily routine?
- How often are the cats checked by staff?
- The cattery must insist that all its occupants are fully vaccinated (and in good time to be protected) and must ask for veterinary evidence to prove it. Your veterinarian will provide you with a record of your cat's boosters.

INSPECTING THE PREMISES

- Are the premises clean?
- The food and water bowls must be scrupulously clean and the litter-trays should be emptied regularly.
- Is the accommodation comfortable?
- Is the spread of disease minimized by there being a good gap (around two feet) between each pen?
- If you have a scaredy-cat that is intimidated by other felines, is the shelter sufficiently secluded? Or are other cats visible and/or close by?
- A cattery where all the units rely on the same air-conditioning system can spread disease from one occupant to another.
- Is there a communal exercise area? If so, steer clear.
- Will your cat have access to an individual, safe outdoor area in her unit?
- Is the indoor apartment warm?
- Security must be tight. The units must be absolutely secure, with no direct access from the door to the outside. A double-door system or similar is imperative.
- The staff must be cat- and people-friendly, and should ask you lots of questions about your cat's likes and dislikes.

THE BREEDS

No two cats look alike – that is part of their great charm. However, there are a number of recognised breeds to choose from, each with their own unique characteristics.

Siamese: *Stunning to look at and supremely elegant, the Siamese has a larger-than-life personality.*

Oriental: *This breed is best described as a 'coloured' Siamese, available in solid colours (above), or different patterns, such as the tabby (right).*

◀ Persian: *The long-coated glamourpuss of the cat world.*

▼ Exotic Shorthair: *A similar temperament to the Persian, but with a much easier coat to manage.*

Maine Coon: *Hardy, powerful and intelligent, this cat loves exploring the great outdoors.*

84

▶ **British Shorthair**: *A popular, friendly, and adventurous breed.*

▼ **Burmese**: *Vocal and energetic, the Burmese makes a loving companion.*

Birman: *Known as the Sacred Cat of Burma, this is a peaceful, affectionate cat, descended from temple cats.*

Ragdoll: *Created by crossing a Birman with a Persian, the popular Ragdoll is so called because of her laidback, placid character.*

Bengal: *A stunning miniature version of the Asian Leopard Cat, this breed is still relatively rare.*

▶ **Abyssinian**: *The characteristic ticked coat, where each hair has two or three bands of colour, provided excellent camouflage in her native North African habitat.*

Devon Rex: *Fun-loving and mischievous, there is never a dull moment with a Devon Rex in your home!*

Cornish Rex: *Pixie-like in looks and in temperament, this is a playful, lovable extrovert.*

TIPS FOR A STRESS-FREE STAY

- Book well in advance, particularly during Christmas, summer holidays and other peak times. Good catteries get booked up very quickly.
- Make sure your cat's vaccinations are kept up to date (remember that it can take seven to ten days after vaccination for your cat to be protected), and make sure the veterinarian gives you a certificate of proof.
- If you have an old or sick cat, it is best not to leave her unless you have no other choice. If your absence cannot be avoided, make sure you discuss with the cattery what should be done in the event of your cat dying or becoming seriously ill.
- If your cat is on medication, written instructions should be left as to dosage.
- Emergency contact numbers and details of your own veterinarian should also be left (the veterinarian used by the cattery may need further medical background).
- Always leave a worn piece of clothing with your cat, also ideally her bed, and some favorite toys, so she is comforted by familiar items around her, and the scent of home.

Part 5

Home Sweet Home

Chapter 11

Collecting Your Cat

After a long wait and all the pre-puss preparations, it's finally time to collect your new kitten or cat. Arrange with the breeder (or shelter) to collect your cat in the morning, so it gives you both plenty of time to get home and settled in before night-time. The breeder will probably ensure that the kitten has not been fed prior to being collected, in order to minimize the risk of car-sickness.

Ask a friend or family member to drive you, so you will be able to dedicate yourself to the kitten on the return journey. Don't forget to take along:

- Cat-carrier, lined with absorbent newspaper overlaid with warm, comfortable bedding (see Chapter Seven).
- Water. Many carriers come with a small water container that fixes to the front. It's unlikely that puss will need a drink, but if she does (particularly in warm weather or if it is a long journey), take along a bowl and bottled water.
- If it is a very long journey, you should take along a litter-tray and perhaps consider installing a crate in the back of the car in which you can place bedding, a tray, toys etc.
- Payment, if it has not already been arranged.
- Paper towels and plastic bags in case of accidents.

LOOSE ENDS

After the breeder or shelter has sorted out the paperwork with you (see Chapter Six), you should make sure you are clear about:

- Feeding regimes (what and how often) – the breeder will probably supply you with some food to see you through the first few meals.
- Any feeding preferences (particularly in adult cats).
- Any grooming instructions.

- Many breeders offer to board the cat (if you are local) for holidays etc. throughout the cat's lifetime. Is your breeder agreeable to this?
- The type of cat-litter the kittens are used to.
- Details of worming, vaccinations, and other health treatments received.
- Ask if you can take a piece of bedding home with you, so the kitten will feel secure with a familiar scent around her. (Taking a blanket or soft towel to the breeder when you first view the litter is a good idea.)

THE JOURNEY HOME

Place the cat-carrier in the footwell of the car, or sit on the back seat with the carrier next to you. Fix the rear seatbelt around the carrier so that it will remain secure in the event of an emergency stop or car accident. Never be tempted to hold the kitten on the journey home. An escaped kitten loose in the car is very dangerous when driving.

Talk to the kitten or cat in a soft, reassuring voice on the journey home. Be prepared for some serious yowling, though. Some cats love car journeys, but the majority associate it with going to the vet's and like to make their protestations known! Your kitten may be a little nervous because this will be the first time she is away from the breeder, and the new sights and smells may intimidate her – particularly if she isn't used to car journeys either.

Make sure the temperature in the car is not too hot. Open the tops of the windows so fresh air can enter, and never leave the cat unattended in a stationary car – it can quickly heat up and cause heatstroke, which can be fatal.

Chapter 12

Arriving Home

The journey is over, and you've both safely arrived home. In your excitement, don't take kitty out of the carrier and introduce her to the family and other pets all in one go. First, she needs to get her bearings and familiarize herself with the scent, sounds and sights of her new home. Give her plenty of time and space to build up her confidence. Act in haste, repent at leisure!

FIRST IMPRESSIONS

After arriving home, take the cat (still in her carrier) to her safe room (page 71), and close the door behind you. Keep any other pets well away – they will be busting themselves with curiosity – so puss doesn't feel intimidated.

Keep her in the carrier for a few minutes so she can observe her surroundings and get used to the smell. Sit down next to the carrier and talk to her reassuringly. Then open the carrier door and let her come out tentatively to investigate. Always let her come out in her own time as this will help her confidence. Keep the door open so she can dive back in if she feels spooked.

Don't make any sudden movements – remain calm and let her explore in her own time.

After the journey, she may need to use her litter-tray, so put her into it. Provided you use the same litter as the breeder, she should realize that this is her new toilet.

Kitty may also be due a feed. It may be worth offering her some food, but do not be surprised if she doesn't take it. Cats do not eat if they are stressed. If she refuses the food, take it away and offer her some more an hour later when she may feel a little more settled.

Once she's sniffed every inch of the room, and has then sniffed it all again, she may settle down in her bed for a sleep. Put a blanket in the bed that has the breeder's scent (page 92) – or, if she is a rescued cat, something from her former home or shelter, if possible. Place kitty in her bed, pet her gently, and talk to her lovingly. She will settle when she is ready.

MEETING THE FAMILY

After the new cat or kitten has settled into her new room for a couple of hours, then you can slowly introduce the rest of her human family. It is best to bring in one person, then, after five minutes, to add another, and then another. This is preferable to bringing in a partner and two kids all in one go, which may be too overwhelming for the kitten.

Everyone should sit on the floor and wait for the kitten to approach them – there should be no chasing, grabbing or even picking up. The kitten or new cat must feel completely in control of the situation. If she hides, tempt her out with a toy or a treat. She can be stroked gently on the back if she approaches someone. The moment she withdraws, she should be left alone.

All voices should be calm and reassuring – yelling will not endear your sensitive newcomer to her human family. Occasional treats can be given so she learns to associate your company with an enjoyable experience. After 10 minutes, evacuate the room, and reintroduce everyone again an hour or two later.

Provided you have chosen a rescued cat with a known history of being confident around children, or if you have bought a kitten from a breeder with similarly-aged children, your newcomer should not be too nervous of your family.

TOP TIP

Right from the start, children should be taught to behave sensibly around cats and to treat them with respect.
- *Gently does it! Teach youngsters how to stroke the cat – most think patting is in order!*
- *Stroke only her back and around the side of her face and under her chin. Tummies are out of bounds.*
- *Tails are never for tugging.*
- *If kitty is uncertain about being touched, she will shrink away from your hand. If she does this, leave her alone.*
- *Never chase.*
- *Never run around when the kitten is in the same room – she can easily get trampled or scared.*
- *The litter-tray is not a sandpit!*
- *The cat's food is not for human consumption!*
- *The cat should always be left in peace when she is eating and sleeping.*
- *The cat's room is out of bounds unless supervised by an adult.*
- *Hands should always be washed after stroking the cat.*

CHILD-PROOFING PUSS

If you don't have children, but plan to have them in your cat's lifetime, enlist the help of friends and family to make sure your kitten grows up not to see little people as terrifying aliens that should be avoided at all costs! Having a bomb-proof cat will also make life much easier when you entertain visitors with children.

RESIDENT PETS

Once puss is settled (the time this takes will depend on the cat's character), you can introduce her to any other pets in the household. Do make sure kitty has had the all-clear from the vet first, though. You won't want her to pass on any disease to other felines in the house, or fleas to your dog or hamster.

Don't expect your pets immediately to embrace each other as lifelong buddies – just as human relationships take time to develop, so too do animal ones. If you rush the process, they may never learn to trust each other, so go slow!

TOP TIP

Swap your cats' bedding every other night, so that they become familiar with each other's scent and learn to associate it with being comfortable and relaxed.

FELINE FRIENDS: FIRST INTRODUCTION

- Put kitty in her crate, and bring the resident cat into the safe room.
- The crate should be placed on the floor, so both cats are on the same level. This will allow them to assess each other easily and will prevent physical aggression.
- Close the door and let the adult cat investigate in her own time.
- Reassure her, stroking and talking to her.
- If it looks as if there will be some 'swearing' and aggressive postures, try to distract your adult cat. Call her to you, and give her a treat.
- If, despite your best efforts, there is hissing, arched backs, fluffing up and all the rest of the cat repertoire, don't worry. Both cats are safe, because of the crate. The more they get used to each other, the less posturing will occur.
- After 10 minutes, let the adult cat leave (if she wishes).

SUBSEQUENT MEETINGS

- The next time you attempt to introduce them, put your adult cat in the cage, and let the kitten loose in her safe room.
- Praise both cats if they remain civil to each other (but don't expect miracles).
- For a third meeting, move the crate with the kitten in it to another room in the house, and let the adult loose. Then alternate again, with the adult in the crate.
- By moving the pen to different areas in the house, eventually the newcomer's scent will gradually be disseminated throughout the home, and your adult cat will accept it as being normal.
- All the time, make more of a fuss of your adult cat to reassure her and to stop any jealousy. Although it is tempting to pity the small, defenseless-looking kitten, this will only fuel the adult's fear that the newcomer is a threat to her position. The kitten will not want attention drawn to her anyway in the presence of the older cat, preferring to fade into the background.
- Over the course of half a dozen or so controlled introductions, the cats will stop making such a fuss and will realize the perceived threat is not real – after all, no one can come to any harm while the cage is being used.
- Next, prolong their mealtime by an hour, so they are fairly hungry, then feed both of them in the same room. Initially, keep the bowls quite a distance away from each

other, but, over the course of several more mealtimes, move the adult's bowl closer to the crate.

- If the adult refuses to eat, you will have moved the bowl too close to the crate too quickly, so move it back to a distance at which she is comfortable.

OPEN INTRODUCTION

When you feel that both cats are comfortable in each other's presence (i.e. little attention is paid to the other and there is no aggression), then you can dispense with the crate.

The length of time this takes will depend entirely on the two cats concerned – with a friendly, laidback cat this may take only a day, but more timid cats may need as long as a week or more before an 'open' introduction is attempted.

Of course, in the meantime, the kitten will not be confined to her crate, but will be kept in her cat-safe room, venturing to other rooms in the house under supervision, while the adult cat is elsewhere in the house.

- Introduce the cats in a small, clutter-free room – somewhere with no hiding places into which one of them could dive and refuse to come out. The kitten's safe room is an option, provided your adult cat feels comfortable in there and doesn't view it as 'foreign territory'.
- Make sure the door is closed so they can't escape.
- Ideally, there should be an upward safety escape route (such as on top of an armchair or a high windowsill) which the adult cat can take if she feels overwhelmed.
- Make a fuss of the adult cat whenever she comes to you. Don't restrain either cat or they may feel trapped.
- If hissing takes place, try to distract them, by making a clicking noise with your tongue or calling one of them to you.
- When they are calm and well behaved, hand-feed them an extra-special treat, such as fresh chicken.
- Keep the initial 'open' introductions short and sweet, and ideally ending on a good note with no aggression.

TOP TIP

If you don't have other pets, the kitten's safe room can be separated from the rest of the house by a child-gate across the door. This will prevent any young children bugging your puss in her little haven, while she will be able to see and hear what is going on around her. If you have other pets that can scale such a gate, the door to the kitten's room should be shut.

• Gradually increase the number of introductions until, eventually, no supervision is required.

House-cats or older cats may take a little more persuading to accept a newcomer, but most will learn to tolerate a house-mate – and they may even become good buddies and playmates.

CANINE COMPANIONS

Obviously, your dog is friendly to cats (or at least not a die-hard cat chaser) – otherwise, why have you brought a kitten home? Before you introduce him to the new addition to the family, you should revise some basic obedience exercises with him so you will be able to control him. Down, Stay, and Leave are the key commands that you will find useful (see *Puppy Owner's Survival Manual*, in this series, which also features information on dog/cat introductions).

Do remember: if you can't fully trust your dog, you should keep him on a loose lead when the kitten is around, until you are completely satisfied that he can be trusted around her.

• Start the introductions with the kitten in the crate, as you would when introducing her to an adult cat (page 96).

- Introduce the dog to the room and let him investigate. If he gets too overexuberant, and tries jumping on the crate or similar, call him to you and tell him to lie down.
- If he gets a half-hearted swipe through the bars of the crate, he will soon learn to be a little more respectful of the new addition.
- As with introducing an adult cat, the meetings should be short and sweet, and, gradually, they will both become familiar with each other and they can be fed in the same room.
- With the 'open', uncrated introductions, keep your dog on a lead. Let him sniff the cat or let the cat sniff him, and act in a calm, reassuring way.
- Intermittently call the dog's name, and, once you have his attention, praise him and give him a treat. This should stop him obsessing about the kitten.
- Gradually extend the length and frequency of the introductions until they take little notice of each other.

With time, your dog and cat will probably grow to be good friends. Most dogs love having cats around – especially if they can steal some of their food – and cats enjoy having a living hot-water bottle on which to sleep.

SMALL PETS

If you have birds, rodents or other small animals as pets, you should be extra-cautious. Some cats learn to live amicably with the pet budgerigar or family rat, but most will view such pets as 'meat on feet'. For thousands and thousands of years, such animals have been a cat's prey and these powerful feline instincts are not tamed overnight.

Never leave the pets unsupervised, and make sure they are protected from sharp claws and jaws. If you have hamsters, for example, it may be best to house them in a plastic, fully-enclosed home, rather than a cage. Use your common sense, and don't ever underestimate how cunning a cat can be!

NAME GAME

Naming your cat should happen as soon as you get her. If she is called Kitten or Cat for the first couple of weeks while you all decide on a suitable name, she will begin to think this is her name, and will get quite confused when you start to call her Tiddles, or whatever you eventually decide.

If you adopt a cat from a shelter, you may be told the cat's name. If you decide to change the name, choose something that is quite similar to the original one. This will help the cat settle in a little more easily, as the name will be familiar to her. For example, if the cat is called Lady, you could change it to Sadie. If you do not know the cat's name, then choose whatever name you think best suits her.

Don't be surprised if your cat's name changes over time. I've had a Domino that changed to Dodo, then to Dodie – and sometimes ended up as Diddle Dumps or Miss Didds! Most owners have variations of a name according to what the cat is doing. A cat that is stealing the Sunday roast could be a stern-sounding Patrick, where otherwise he is known as Paddy!

- Say your cat's name to her as often as you can.
- Use a gentle, friendly tone of voice.
- Say her name while she is eating, playing, or being cuddled and she'll learn to associate it with enjoyable experiences. This will make things much easier when you call her. If she only hears her name when she is being told off, she is less likely to respond to it.
- Practice calling her to you from another room and always play a game, have a cuddle or give her a treat as a reward when she comes. This will make her more likely to respond to you when she is allowed outdoors (Chapter Nineteen) and will save lots of sore throats in the future!
- In a multi-cat household, most cats learn their own individual names, but some respond to any name you call – they seem to respond to your 'cat tone of voice' rather than to what you actually say!

FIRST NIGHT

Most kittens will settle for their first night in their new home, provided they are warm and comfortable, and feel safe. The kitten-safe room you have prepared is the best place for the kitten's first night, as she should feel secure in there.

If you do not have a 100 per cent safe room, she should be kept in a crate, containing a litter-tray and bedding.

- Do not play with the kitten within an hour of her going to bed, as it will excite her, and make it more difficult to get her settled.
- A small feed shortly before bedtime will help her to doze off.
- Put her in her litter-tray immediately before putting her to bed.

Once kitty is settled in her bed, leave the room and do not return to her until the morning. If you give in to her plaintive cries, however heartbreaking they are, your smart puss will soon work out that if she makes a fuss, you come running. If you are strict with yourself, she will soon learn the rules and will settle throughout the night.

WORDS OF WISDOM
"A home without a cat – and a well-fed, well-petted, and properly revered cat – may be a perfect home, perhaps, but how can it prove its title?"
Mark Twain

You may have to wake up a little earlier than usual for the first few weeks, as your kitten may be restless because she is hungry and wants her breakfast. Gradually prolonging the time you go into her room by five to ten minutes will help her to adjust to your routine.

In the wild, cats are quite active at night, but domestic cats soon adapt to their humans' routines and many sleep through the night until morning (some multi-cat homes are a little more chaotic, though, as you generally get one mischievous moggie that is determined to wake up everyone in the house).

TOP TIP

If you fully intend to share your bed with your kitten for the rest of her life, then by all means let her snuggle into bed with you. However, it isn't fair to let her on or in the bed if, in a few months' time, you will change your mind and she will have to sleep elsewhere.

A cat will happily sleep in a cat-bed or any other spot around the house, provided that is what she is used to. Once she's decided that she likes a human bed, she will resent sleeping anywhere else! It is only fair to puss that you are consistent from the very start.

Chapter 13

House-Training

Ⓗouse-training is the one area of raising a kitten or new cat that most owners dread, but it needn't be a chore. The majority of kittens will be fully house-trained by the time they reach their new homes, and most adult shelter cats will be completely trained too. All you need to do is to transfer what your cat has already learnt and apply it to her new home.

Even if your cat has received no toilet-training, do not despair – teaching a cat to be clean in the house is very straightforward, provided you follow some basic rules.

CAT CLEANLINESS

Cats are well known for their meticulous cleanliness, so you will be working with a willing pupil, who is more than eager to be shown where she can relieve herself without soiling her home.

The cat's evolution is responsible for her fastidiousness (see Chapter One: From Ancient Times, page 10.) In the wild, a cat would toilet well away from where she lived and be sure to bury the results, so as not to attract predators and to minimize the risk of disease.

Kittens would be encouraged very early on to do the same – today, domestic kittens still have this in-built instinct, and will leave the nest to relieve themselves as soon as they are able to do so.

GETTING STARTED

The location of the litter-tray is very important (see page 62). Once you've found a quiet spot in the house that the cat will feel safe in, well away from her sleeping and feeding areas, you're halfway there.

The litter should be comfortable for her to use. Initially, use the breeder's litter, but, if puss is reluctant to use it, opt for the finest-grain type you can find. Some cats find the larger pellets uncomfortable to stand on, or to dig.

ADOPTING A REGIME

Routine is the key to success. Put the kitten in her tray at the following times:

- On waking
- Before a nap
- After feeding
- After play
- After periods of excitement (such as meeting new people)
- Every two hours.

Such a rigorous regime may seem excessive, but it will pre-empt any accidents and reinforce what she is meant to do.

When you first put kitty in her tray, encourage her to dig, by digging the litter yourself (ensure the litter is clean first and wash your hands afterwards), or by taking her paw gently and encouraging her to dig. Provided she is happy in the litter you have chosen (page 102), her natural instincts should take over.

TOP TIP

If your cat doesn't make an association between the litter and what she is expected to do, take some urine from a puddle she has left, and put it into the litter-tray. The scent of her urine will encourage her to use the tray next time. Don't overdo it, though, piling heaps of feces into the tray, as cats do not like to use dirty trays. Put yourself in your cat's position – would you use a soiled toilet?

If you stick to the routine, kitty will start to go to her tray of her own accord, after meals etc., and will also seek it out if she needs to go to the toilet in the meantime.

Don't quit the routine too early though or you may encourage puddles. Kittens lead very busy lives, and, in all the excitement of exploring their new homes and living life to the full, they can simply forget to 'go'. Then, they are suddenly caught short and don't have time to get to the tray. Regular gentle reminders will prevent this.

If your cat doesn't 'go' at any of these times, don't force her to stay in the tray (she may become insecure being in it and then avoid it at all costs); instead, let her wander off, and try again in another ten minutes. In the meantime, watch her closely for any warning signs that she is about to have an accident (see below).

As your kitten gets older, so she will develop better bladder control and will need to be toileted less. Very gradually decrease the number of times you take her to her tray – perhaps every three hours instead of every two.

If accidents start appearing, then you have proceeded too quickly, and you should immediately increase the number of times you put her in the tray.

SPOTTING THE SIGNS

Be aware of the signs that your cat or kitten needs to relieve herself.

- She will look furtive, sniffing the ground and seeking out dark places and quiet corners.
- Just before she relieves herself, she will move around in a circle.
- Then she'll squat.

If you spot any of these signs, don't shout at her, just calmly distract her to stop her in mid-flow (make a clicking noise with your tongue, or make a high-pitched squeak), and then take her to her litter-tray. Give her lots of praise and affection when she uses the tray, and she will soon get the hint.

Shouting at the kitten will make her nervous of you, and she will think that you are mad because she is relieving herself, not because she is using the wrong place. Once she comes to this conclusion, she will then try to avoid going to the toilet when you are around, and the situation will get worse. She'll seek out hiding places more and more so she can 'go' without you noticing. Be kind and patient with your kitten and such Catch-22 scenarios can be avoided.

CLEANING ROUTINE

Pong management is best achieved by scrupulous hygiene.

- Choose a good, absorbent cat-litter.
- Scoop out as soon as you notice it has been used.
- Change the entire cat-litter regularly (according to the number of cats you have and how often they use their tray – twice a week is a good guide for two average house-cats).
- Disinfect the tray with a cat-safe disinfectant (from your pet store), rinsed with hot water, at least once a week. Do not use any other type of cleaner on the tray.

For the first couple of weeks, it is useful to leave a little urine in the tray to leave puss a 'scent message'. All other lumps and clumps should be scooped out of the tray straightaway.

What you do with the scooped bits depends on the litter and your plumbing. Some litters can be flushed down the toilet, others have to be disposed of in a sealed bag, placed in your outdoor rubbish bin.

When you perform a complete litter change, it must all be disposed of in a plastic bag (your plumbing would never cope with more than the odd scoop!).

ACCIDENTS HAPPEN

The occasional accident is bound to happen when you have a new kitten or cat. You should just clean it up thoroughly (see page 106 and as described above), and make sure you take puss to her tray more frequently to prevent it happening again.

Anyone that can even contemplate 'rubbing her nose in it' should not be allowed to have a cat: such punishment is sickeningly cruel and counterproductive. Punishment never works.

Even yelling at the cat after you've trodden in a 'present' won't help – she won't be able to associate the effect (your screams) with the cause (her accident). She'll just think you are a nasty, irrational owner, and this won't get your new relationship off to the best of starts. For persistent 'soilers', see page 107.

OUTSIDE TOILET

Once your cat is fully house-trained, and vaccinated, you might want to encourage her to do her business outside. She must always have access to an indoor tray, however, so she can relieve herself at night (when she should be kept indoors).

TOP TIP

After cleaning up an accident, wash the area in a solution of biological washing powder or a pet product specifically designed to remove all odours.

Cats have a very sensitive sense of smell and can still sniff the urine through ordinary disinfectants. They are more likely to urinate where they can detect the scent of urine, so all trace must be removed.

Some products can actually encourage a cat to urinate – to a finely-tuned feline nose an ammonia-based cleaner smells very similar to urine!

- Every day, move the litter-tray a couple of inches towards the back door.
- Introduce a small amount of soil to the litter, and add more every day, until the tray contains only soil.
- Once the tray has been at the back door for a couple of days, move the tray to just outside the back door. Only do this in fine weather, or the cat may be reluctant to go outdoors. Keep the door open so she knows where it is.
- Once she has used it a couple of times, introduce another tray which then can be kept inside the house.
- Over the course of a few days, gradually move the outdoor tray to the spot in the garden/yard that you ultimately want the cat to use.
- Once the tray is in the best spot for you, leave it there for a few days, so puss gets into the habit of visiting this area. Then you can dispense with the tray altogether. Provided the earth is freshly dug, she should start using that instead.
- Do make sure that children's sand pits are covered securely when not in use, so your cat can't use them.
- If your cat insists on using your prized flowerbeds as a lavatory, put some netting just under the surface of the soil. This should discourage her from digging. You can also purchase cat-safe crystals that act as deterrents.

Although you will save money by not having to change the cat-litter so regularly, there are notable disadvantages to letting your cat toilet outdoors.

- Cats are not always respectful of boundaries. Unless you make the necessary adjustments to your garden/yard (Chapter Eighteen), your cat could use your neighbors' yards as public toilets – which will not endear her (or you) to them. Cats trained exclusively to a litter-tray will often come indoors to use the tray before returning outside.
- You may not want your cat to toilet in your own yard (perhaps you are a keen gardener and do not want your plants dug up etc.).

- It will be more difficult to monitor your cat's toilet habits. The owner of a cat that only uses the tray will be able to notice if anything is wrong (e.g. increased or decreased frequency of urination, diarrhea, constipation etc.).

SOLVING PROBLEMS

REPEAT OFFENDERS

Where a cat is persistently having accidents, you should get her checked over by a veterinarian. Perhaps she has a urinary infection or other physical cause.

If she has been given the all-clear and still has accidents, try the following.

- Check the location of the litter-tray. Is it in a secure position? If it is by a cat-flap or door, perhaps the cat is nervous about being able to see other cats while she is in a vulnerable position. Make sure it is in a quiet, private spot in the house.
- Is the litter too coarse? Change to a finer texture, or to an unfragranced variety (see page 102).
- Is the tray dirty?
- Is the cat reluctant to use a tray that other cats in the house are using? Multi-cat households should be multi-litter-tray households, with several trays upstairs and downstairs. The number of trays you need will depend on how many cats you have, as well as their personalities. Some don't mind sharing with another cat or two; others refuse to have anything other than their own private bathroom!
- If your cat persistently soils the same spot, then she is doing so for a reason. Clean the area thoroughly (page 106) and cover with tinfoil. Cats hate the sound and texture of aliminum foil and will not walk on it.
- Alternatively, move the litter-tray to the soiling spot, and then gradually move it, inch by inch over the course of a week or so, to your preferred location.

MAKING A STATEMENT

Sometimes urination (and, in a few cases, defecation – known as middening) is a deliberate message left by the cat, used to mark her territory with her scent. It is not always a dominant gesture – it can be born out of intense insecurity.

For example, a cat that sprays near doors or windows is quite likely to be scared of other cats. She may be urinating, not only to tell other cats that this is her territory, but also to surround herself in her own scent – a kind of smell comfort blanket.

In such cases, the root cause – the cat's insecurity – should be removed. Make sure you have a lockable cat-flap so no other cats can enter your property, and do not allow her access to rooms where she is likely to see other cats outside.

When you are not able to supervise her, perhaps keep her in a small, cat-proof room (Chapter Eight) so her confidence can be built up slowly.

It is also worth consulting your veterinarian, who may prescribe a course of feline Prozac (yes, Prozac) or similar, or refer you to a professional pet behavior counselor.

If you have a multi-cat household, and one of your cats is urinating or defecating through insecurity, you should monitor them all closely to determine who is responsible. Once established, confine her to a cat-proof room so she feels safe, and, once her confidence is built up, gradually reintroduce her to the rest of the house.

SUMMARY

If your cat is experiencing house-training problems, don't despair. Cats are very clean creatures by nature, and there will generally be a good reason for their actions. 'Think cat' to discover the source of the problem, and be patient with puss while you re-train her to use a litter-tray.

With a little thought, a good house-training regime, and patience, accidents in the house will soon be a thing of the past.

Chapter 14

House Rules

It is important that kitty knows the house rules from day one. Just because she's a newcomer doesn't mean you should let her get away with things that, a few weeks down the line, you will yell at her for. That isn't fair on her. She will be utterly confused and won't know what she is and isn't allowed to do.

SETTING BOUNDARIES

Even before bringing puss home, everyone in the family should have discussed what rules you will impose. Some will be to do with safety, such as always putting the toilet seat down and not allowing puss on the kitchen work surfaces (see Chapter Eight), but others will be your own personal preferences. Here are some ideas.

- What hours will she be allowed outside (if at all)? If you let her out all day (once she's protected by her vaccinations) for the first six months, and then change her routine to an hour a day later on, puss will be climbing the walls out of frustration. If she's used to an hour a day from the start, she won't expect more. Remember: no cat should be let out after dusk (see Chapter Nineteen).
- Who will be responsible for grooming? Will it be on a roster system or will one person take care of it all?
- How often should puss be groomed? Kitty should know the routine from the start.
- Will begging be forbidden? If you feed puss from your plate just once, you will encourage her to leap on to the dining table or to paw at you for scraps every mealtime. If everyone sticks together, you should have a well-mannered moggie. If she is too persistent, shut her out of the room.
- Do you want to allow puss on the beds?
- Will she have complete freedom in the house, or will certain rooms be out of bounds? (It is always useful, for example, to have one bedroom which is a cat-free zone, for asthmatic visitors or those who have the great misfortune to be allergic to cats.)

Every home is different. You might positively encourage puss on to the bed, if that's what you want from your cat, or you might not allow her upstairs at all. Go with whatever rules work best for your family and lifestyle.

Whatever rules you decide, stick to them. Everyone in the house must be consistent if your cat is to be taught what is right and wrong. If someone allows her on the bed, whereas everyone else removes her, all your hard work will be undone. Do be warned – most cats will sleep where they like when your back is turned. The only way you can be sure your bed is a hair-free zone is to shut the bedroom door (and even then some cats are expert door-openers!).

Part 6
Cat Care

Chapter 15

Diet And Nutrition

If you have never owned a cat before, or are returning to cat ownership after a break of a few years, you are likely to be utterly confused by the different types of food on the market. The pet food industry is huge, with new brands appearing all the time. With so much choice, where do you start?

CHOOSING A DIET

The best starting point is with the breeder or shelter from whom you got your cat. They are likely to have experimented with different types of food and will have formed their own conclusions as to which is superior.

Initially, you should feed your cat whatever she has been fed previously. The breeder or shelter will have provided you with details of her diet, and this must be followed to the letter. A change of food could cause an upset stomach, particularly during the stressful period of moving homes.

If the breeder/shelter's recommended diet works for your cat, then why change it? If, however, you have difficulty getting hold of the food locally to you, or if after a period of a couple of weeks the food does not seem to agree with your kitty, then you could consider changing it.

DRY FOOD

These foods are usually 'complete' foods (though not always – check the label), meaning they are nutritionally complete. They provide all the nutrients needed for a cat's good health, and no supplementary foods are required.

They offer peace of mind to the owner, are simple and clean to feed, they help to prevent plaque build-up on the teeth, and they come in many different flavors and varieties for all life stages. The main advantage is that dry food can be put down in the morning for the cat to snack on throughout the day, without it going off. Some premium varieties are also designed to minimize wastage – meaning more food is digested and there is less to scoop out of the litter-tray.

This type of food isn't suitable for all cats. Very old toothless kitties can't manage to eat it, so it may be worth considering feeding your younger cat some wet food a couple of times a week, so that, in the event of her becoming unable to munch on crunchy food in years to come, she won't turn up her nose at the sloppier stuff.

Another important consideration when choosing a dry food is Feline Lower Urinary Tract Disorder (FLUTD), a condition which affects about one per cent of cats. It is caused by stones or crystals developing (through alkaline urine content) in the cat's lower urinary tract, making urination difficult and painful (see page 229). Stress, gender, and the environment are all contributory factors, as is diet. A diet high in magnesium can trigger the condition, so check that the type of food you are considering is low in this mineral (there are several brands that have been developed to minimize the incidence of FLUTD, by producing a more acid urine).

Fresh water should always be available to the cat, and this is particularly important when feeding dry food as it contains very little water.

TOP TIP

Unlike the dog which can live quite healthily on a vegetarian diet, the cat is an obligate carnivore – meaning she cannot survive without meat. Her nutritional needs derive from the days when she had to hunt to survive – and she hunted animals, not vegetables! One example of the cat's dependence on meat is taurine, a substance that is essential for a cat's eyesight, and which can only be found in meat sources; it cannot be manufactured synthetically.

SEMI-MOIST FOOD

These are biscuits which are moister than dry foods, but drier than wet foods. Some are 'complete' (page 112). They are palatable and can be left out for the cat to graze on throughout the day.

WET FOOD

Wet food comes in cans or pouches, and is the type favored by most cats. Many brands are 'complete', but you should always check the label.

It is useful to buy tins that will feed your cat one meal per sitting. If you have one cat, the smaller cans are a little more expensive, but are cost-effective, as most cats will refuse to eat anything but meat from a freshly opened can. Plastic lids can be bought to put over an opened can to keep the contents fresh, but the meaty smell of the food soon diminishes (in a matter of an hour), and a fussy cat is likely to turn her nose up at it. Pouches contain just enough for one meal per cat, so she gets fresh food every time and there is no wastage. (They are also lighter to carry, less bulky in your shopping bag, and easier to dispose of.)

To add a bit of crunch to the meal, you can add a few dry cat biscuits on the top. This will help to prevent the formation of tartar, and will ensure your kitty has a little variety (if only fed wet food, some cats will refuse to touch dry).

You might want to feed one 'wet' meal, additionally feeding a dry or semi-moist food throughout the day, leaving some biscuits in her bowl for her to snack on whenever the urge takes her. Do not leave wet food down for your cat – it will go off very quickly and will attract flies in warm weather. Remove anything your cat doesn't eat after five minutes.

If your cat is prone to FLUTD (page 113), you might consider feeding a complete wet-food diet. Its higher moisture content helps to dilute the urine and the incidence of the condition is lower with this type of diet.

TOP TIP

Because it generally smells more enticing than other types of food, wet food is a good option if you are trying to tempt a cat's appetite.

LIFE STAGES

Whether wet or dry, many brands come in different 'life stages', catering for the cat from kittenhood through to old age and accommodating her fluctuating nutritional needs through these stages. Many brands produce a kitten, adult, light/lite (for weight control) and senior variety.

- **Kitten:** this type will contain a fairly high calorie content (12-week-old kittens need around 260 KCals a day, and six-month-olds require about 280 KCals).
- **Adult:** how much an adult cat needs depends on her size. A small cat will need between 125-225 KCals depending on how active she is; a large cat will need between 325-585 KCals. (A pregnant female will need more – see Chapter Twenty-four.)
- **Senior:** from the age of seven, cats can switch to a senior variety of food, which is more easily digested and has lower protein levels. Dietary management for conditions such as kidney disease is important in oldies (see Chapter Twenty).
- **Light/lite:** these are low-calorie foods that can help a cat's weight reduction program, or help to maintain a good weight in cats that are prone to putting on the pounds (see pages 117-118).

TOP TIP

Cats prefer food that is served at room temperature, or heated up slightly. This probably relates to her role as a hunter – fresh prey is warm – and also means the food releases more aroma. If you have stored food in the refrigerator, always bring it to room temperature before giving it to your puss – otherwise, she is likely to sulk and refuse to eat it.

HOME-MADE DIETS

It is very tempting to think that a natural diet of fresh ingredients is healthy for humans and so must be the best for our feline friends too. This is not necessarily the case. The cat's nutritional requirements are complex, requiring 60 essential nutrients. Feeding a diet of tuna or chicken and thinking a multi-vitamin will make up any shortfall is not a solution – in fact, it can be dangerous. Overdosage of vitamins and minerals can be as dangerous as underdosage, so exact measurements should be given.

Pet food manufacturers have years of experience of providing the right food for cats, and spend millions ensuring their products provide the best results in a fiercely competitive industry. The best advice is to leave it to the experts.

However, if you have the time to prepare fresh meals every day, and the money to afford the ingredients, and you are determined to feed a home-made diet to your cat, you must seek advice from your veterinarian. He or she may be able to recommend a pet nutritionist that can help you devise a healthy diet for your puss.

WATER, WATER EVERYWHERE

Fresh drinking water should always be available to your cat. From her origins in a desert-type environment, the cat has evolved to survive on very little water compared to some other pets, but it is still vital to feline health. An average cat requires about a quarter of a pint a day. A wet diet will provide most of this requirement, but a dry or semi-moist food will contain little, and the cat will need to drink more to make up the difference.

Some cats are fussy about the water they drink, preferring puddle water to the water in their bowl. This may be because they are sensitive to the chlorine levels in your local supply of mains water. Consider filtering the water from your faucet if this is the case.

It is a fallacy that you should provide a saucer of milk for your cat to drink. Most cats love milk, but sadly milk does not always love them. Shortly after weaning, a cat loses the ability to digest lactose (milk sugar), and drinking milk will result in tummy upsets. Water is all she needs to quench her thirst.

As a treat, there are proprietary brands of cat milk available on the market, or, if you insist on giving your cat cow's milk, make sure it is first diluted well with water.

TOP TIP

All cats differ in their personal tastes, but here are some favorites that may work with your cat. They can be used occasionally during training, to tempt your cat's appetite, or to coat a tablet (where the medication can be given with food).

- *Cream cheese*
- *Pâté*
- *Commercial cat treats*
- *A little fresh cream*
- *Fresh, cooked chicken meat*
- *Fish (tinned or fresh – always ensure bones are removed). Tuna, pilchards, salmon and prawns are favorites.*

MEALTIMES

Evolution has designed the cat to survive on small amounts of prey throughout the day. Unlike a big cat that may eat a gazelle once a week, the smaller wildcat is used to catching birds, lizards and rodents, so her digestive system is used to small but frequent snacks (the average diet is about five mice a day).

These same feeding patterns should be replicated in the home – meals should be small and frequent. Nutritional studies have shown that a cat with food left out for her all day returns to her bowl 36 times! This isn't to say you should prepare this number of meals for her, but it does mean that you should aim for two or three small meals a day, with dry food left out in the meantime.

Kittens should have more meals than adult cats, as their stomachs are relatively small and they cannot digest large amounts of food. When you first bring your kitten home,

TOP TIP

Cats enjoy nibbling on grass, and it is thought that it provides essential roughage to prevent constipation and to allow furballs to be brought up. If your puss is an indoor cat, you must provide her with some indoor grass (sold at pet stores), which is grown very easily in small containers. Watered regularly and kept in a sunny spot, it will provide your cat with something to graze on – and should prevent her munching on your plants (see Chapters Eight and Nine).

the breeder or shelter is likely to recommend four or five meals a day. If, because of work commitments, you are unable to accommodate this, feed three meals a day, with dry or semi-moist food left out for her to snack on.

The number of meals can gradually be reduced to two or three meals a day by the time she is six months old.

QUANTITIES

All cat food labels give recommended amounts that should be fed, depending on the weight of the cat and how active she is. As a general guide, an average-sized cat that weighs between 6 and 10 lbs (2.72-4.53kg) will need 2-3oz (57-85g) of dry food, 2-4oz (57-113g) of semi-moist food and 5-8oz (141-225g) of wet food. This can be split into however many meals she eats each day.

The majority of cats do not overeat, so you can generally feed on demand, leaving dry or semi-moist food for your cat throughout the day for her to snack on.

PROBLEMS OF OBESITY

Some cats do not have a 'stop' message from their tummy to their brain. This sometimes happens in shelter cats who may have lived a life where they never knew where the next meal was coming from. Such cats are insecure around food and will often eat and eat and eat whenever a meal is offered, in anticipation of a 'famine' period in the future. In a caring home, where regular meals are provided, this means endless eating for the cat, who is still unsure whether her good luck will continue.

Obesity can also occur in middle-aged cats who are less active than they used to be (particularly neutered animals who will roam less), but continue to eat the same amount.

When you live with a cat, it is very difficult to notice any gradual weight increases, so take a step back and assess your cat. Look at her from above. Is her body like a brick or balloon, or does it have a well-defined shape and a visible 'waist'? If you are concerned that your cat is overweight, you must see your vet. The issue isn't just about how your cat looks – her health could well suffer. Obesity can contribute to diabetes, thyroid conditions, and heart and kidney problems. It will also affect her movement and quality of life.

CAT TALES
Himmy the tabby cat holds the record as the world's heaviest puss. He died in 1986 in Queensland, Australia, weighing 47lbs (21kgs).

Many veterinary surgeries run weight-loss clinics, with regular weigh-ins and feeding advice. Often, weighing out a precise amount of low-calorie food and giving no extra treats or tidbits is all that is required. Obviously, overeaters should not be given limitless amounts of dry food to snack on through the day, as you can do in the case of more controlled cats.

If you have a multi-cat household, monitor your cats closely when they eat, just in case Miss Greedy Guts is wolfing down her food and then stealing everyone else's.

THE FADDY FEEDER

Some cats develop unhealthy food obsessions that can be infuriating if you are the owner. Although this can occur in all cats, old ones seem particularly prone to it, often refusing to eat anything other than one particular food or flavor of food.

The lack of a varied diet throughout adulthood can cause food faddiness in later life. Get your cat used to eating dry food, wet food (gravy and jelly varieties), and all in different flavors. If you feed only one type, you will experience difficulties if that food is discontinued, or if, because of health reasons, puss has to have a different diet.

However, you must make sure that you do not cause your cat to develop a food fetish. If you put food down for your cat and she turns her nose up at it, do not remove it and replace it with something tastier to encourage her to eat. Worse still, don't produce increasingly mouthwatering food the longer she refuses to eat. This will immediately teach your cunning little cat that, the longer she holds out, the higher the stakes.

The problem is, cats are infinitely more obstinate than humans. The advice "She'll eat if she's hungry" will be given to you by friends and family, but it simply isn't true! Incredible though it is, cats will starve themselves to death rather than eat something they've decided they don't like.

In these circumstances, you'll have no choice than to surrender. However, you can start to introduce her to new foods by gradually introducing a little at a time to her existing food. Done very slowly, the changeover is likely to be almost imperceptible to puss.

Clearly, preventing faddy feeding from the start, by giving your cat a variety of foods from the start of her life, is by far the better option.

LOSS OF APPETITE

- Is the bowl in a cat-friendly location? Does she feel certain that she won't be ambushed by other cats, or pushed out of the way by the family dog?
- Is the bowl too near the litter-tray? Cats will refuse to eat in the same area as where they eliminate.
- Is the bowl too close to other cats in the house? Some cats are very good at gobbling down their food and then growling under their breath at any other cats that are still eating. With nervous cats, the intimidation works and they walk away, leaving the other cat to finish up the meal. If this is the case, feed the cats separately, in different rooms.
- Put her food in a different bowl. Some cats aren't keen on plastic bowls, especially when they start to scratch through overuse (see page 61).
- What is the weather like? Cats generally eat less in warm weather, and may miss the odd meal simply because they are not hungry.
- Is your cat being fed elsewhere? Many cats lead double lives and have a couple of homes on the go!

If your cat doesn't eat for more than 24 hours, or if her refusal to eat is accompanied by any unusual behavior or symptoms, seek veterinary advice.

If your cat is refusing food because she is sick, then you should ditch all the rules and stop at nothing in your search for tasty food that will tempt her appetite. Talk to your veterinarian about what you should feed. Generally, fresh, cooked chicken meat is a favorite (not too rich for sick cats), and flaked white fish (with all bones removed) is another good option. The smellier the food, the better (pilchards often do the trick). Try heating up the food a little to make it more appealing and to release the food's aroma.

SICK AS A CAT

Cats are very good at being sick! It is usually wonderfully dramatic, with their head stretched forward, their stomach convulsing, pumping in and out, and often accompanied by an unearthly noise. Faced with such a sight, it is easy to overreact and believe puss is in her death throes. Nine times out of ten, she is bringing up a furball, or regurgitating her food.

Food regurgitation is not the most pleasant of things to deal with – particularly if you have other cats who are mad-keen to eat what has been brought up. Ugh! Often, it is caused by the cat gobbling her food too quickly – particularly if dry food is given (as it expands quickly inside her). Feed gobblers little and often, or switch to a wet diet. If your cat is sick more than occasionally, you must seek veterinary advice.

Chapter 16

Regular Checks

Cats do not require a great deal of care, and are quite low-maintenance, compared to more labor-intensive pets. However, they do require some regular checks and care to keep them in tip-top condition and to spot any problems before they get out of hand.

DAILY EXAMINATION

Once a day, when your cat is curled up on your lap, being petted, perform the following checks. Done gently, puss will think it's all part of her cuddle.

- Run your finger against the growth of the fur to check for any evidence of parasites or flea dirt (black specks).
- Does her coat look healthy, or is it dull and scurfy?
- Run your hands over her entire body to check for any lumps, cuts or scabs.
- Check that her nose is clean and is not dry or cracked.
- Check under her tail to see if her bottom is clean. Any change in coloration, cracking, or wetness may indicate a problem.
- Inspect her nipples. Any lumps, changes in coloration or weeping should be investigated.
- Run your fingers along her spine. You should be able to feel the bones, but they should not be too prominent.
- Gently stroke her tail. Are there any unusual kinks or lumps that have appeared?
- You should also check the contents of the litter-tray. Instead of blindly scooping any clumps, check the urine is not more smelly than usual and is not blood-tinged. Is there any change in the consistency of her feces?
- If your cat is a little on the heavy side, you should check her weight once a week. Weigh her cat-carrier and then put her inside it and weigh it again. Subtract the first weight from the second to find out how much she weighs. (For information on dealing with obesity, see Chapter Fifteen.)

If you have any concerns, or note any changes, you should consult your cat's vet.

EYES

A cat's eyes should be bright and clear, with no evidence of a third eyelid (often the sign of illness). The eyes should be clean and dry.

Longhaired, flatter-faced breeds can be prone to weepy eyes because fluid cannot drain through the tear ducts properly. These cats will need their eyes cleaned and dried regularly (from once a day to twice a week depending on the severity of the problem).

- Moisten a piece of cotton pad with tepid water and wipe around the eye very gently.
- Remove any build-up in the corners of the eye and wipe any tear stains underneath the eye.
- Moisten a fresh pad to clean the other eye (to prevent cross-infection).
- Dry each eye (with separate pads) thoroughly.
- If tearing becomes excessive or the fluid changes in color and consistency, consult your veterinarian, as an eye infection could be responsible.
- A veterinarian should also be consulted if the cat sustains a scratch or other wound to the eye (from briars or a cat fight).

EARS

A cat's ears should be checked at least once a week. Being pricked (erect), the ears are prone to picking up ear mites (page 204), which irritate the ear intensely and spread like wildfire between cats (and to other pets too). Excessive scratching at the ear and head-shaking are all signs of mite infestation, together with red, sore ears and a build-up of wax/dirt.

Generally, it is best to leave the ears alone. However, if there is a little wax, and there are no signs of irritation to the ear, they can be wiped gently with ear-cleaning cloths (available from pet stores). Do not push anything into the ears, or you could damage them. If you notice any odor, redness, excessive dirt, or irritation, seek veterinary advice.

Some cats develop polyps in the ear. These are black/blue growths that are more commonly seen in older cats. They are often accompanied by infection and irritation and so a vet should be consulted if your cat develops them. They can be surgically removed in most cases, but a risk assessment should be made about putting the elderly animal under anaesthetic.

The tips of the ears should also be checked, particularly with white-eared cats who are prone to sunburn. They can turn cancerous if repeatedly exposed to the sun, so keep a close eye on pale pusses. Sunblock should be applied in sunny weather, but this is often licked off, so you should try to keep your cat indoors during the hottest part of the day (from 11am-4pm), and discourage her from sleeping on windowsills where she is heavily exposed to sunlight.

TEETH

A cat's teeth are designed to hunt – to kill and to rip up the prey with her sharp fangs. In the wild, they would be kept clean by crunching on bones or such-like, but, in the domestic home, they are not put through the same rigors. Dry cat food helps to prevent some plaque build-up and some treats are specifically designed to clean the teeth, but, in addition, it is best to give your cat's teeth a brush once or twice a week. This should reduce the number of times your cat will need to undergo a full veterinary dental procedure (for which anesthetic is required).

• Use a small toothbrush. You can buy cat toothbrushes in pet stores, but a child's-size brush also works well. Alternatively, you can buy a rubber fingerbrush which has a textured surface and which fits over the tip of your finger. If your cat is not used to having her teeth brushed, it is best to use a fingerbrush.
• A small pea-sized amount of cat toothpaste should be applied to the brush. Do not use toothpaste intended for human use. Cat toothpaste will not foam (and so does not require rinsing) and is often meat-flavored, so your cat enjoys the taste.
• When your cat is relaxed on your lap, gently stroke the side of her mouth. Most cats enjoy being petted here and will rub against you to deposit scent.
• You can then progress to lifting one side of her mouth and gently using the fingerbrush to rub her teeth.
• Work around all the teeth and finish with a special treat as a reward.

A cat is more likely to accept having her teeth cleaned if she has been accustomed to the procedure from kittenhood. Time spent with a youngster, getting her used to having her paws and claws touched and her teeth brushed, will save you lots of scratches in the years to come!

If your cat won't let you brush her teeth, take things really slowly. Just stroke the side of her mouth at first. After a couple of weeks of doing this, progress to putting the fingerbrush in the side of the mouth and brushing just one tooth. End the session with a treat. If you take it one step at a time, she should eventually accept the routine. If not, you'll have to resort to a helper restraining her gently in a towel while you perform the mini-dental. A dental paste is also on the market which is meant to prevent plaque build-up. Squeeze the sachet on to your finger and let your cat lick it off. Simple! Regular brushing is recommended, however, for your cat's long-term dental health.

When you brush your cat's teeth, you should also check that her breath is clean-smelling, that her gums are healthy, and that all her teeth are in good order. Consult a veterinarian if you notice bad breath, red, swollen gums, missing or broken teeth, and anything else that is out of the ordinary. However, don't be alarmed if you notice that your kitten is losing her teeth – her milk teeth will naturally fall out from 20 weeks onwards, and her permanent, adult teeth will grow through.

WHISKERS

Occasionally, a cat loses a whisker or two. Don't panic if you find one on the carpet, or if one drops off during grooming – it will soon grow back! If several whiskers fall out at once, however, consult a veterinarian to ensure that there is no underlying problem.

NAILS

Cat claws are layered like onions. When a cat scratches at a tree or her post, the outer husk will be pulled off to reveal a sharp new tip underneath. Most cats rarely need their nails attended to, as they manicure themselves regularly, but house-cats or older cats, who may not climb or exercise as much as outdoor/younger cats, may benefit from having their claws trimmed occasionally (particularly those on the hind feet).

- Only cut those claws which appear long when the cat is at rest (when ordinarily the claw would be completely retracted).
- Take your cat's paw and gently press down on each toe to reveal the full claw.
- Using guillotine-type nail clippers, snip just the very end of the claw (the 'hook').
- Never clip anywhere near the dark line that runs along the claw. This is the 'quick', the

nerves and blood vessels. If cut, it will be immensely painful to your puss, could cause an infection, and will bleed profusely. A potassium permanganate pen can be used to stop the bleeding, but if you take good care, you should never have to use one.

Again, a kitten that has grown up having her feet touched will be much more amenable to this procedure. If your cat has ticklish feet or is petrified that, in fact, you are trying to amputate her foot, you will have to resort to stealth. With clippers at the ready, you may have to wait for your cat to fall asleep with a paw stretched out in front of her. Clipping the odd nail whenever the opportunity arises is a favorite pastime of house-cat and veteran owners! (Experienced cats learn to sleep with all their paws tucked safely under their body whenever clippers are around.)

Only clip the claws if they are overly long. Cutting them in an attempt to stop her scratching will be counterproductive. Snipping the tips leaves a bluntish end, and the cat will probably scratch even more vigorously to remove this husk and get to the sharp claw underneath.

If you are in any doubt about the procedure, or have never done it before, you should ask your veterinarian to show you how it should be done. If your cat is professionally groomed, nail care is usually included in the price.

You should also regularly check your cat's feet and between her toes for any cut or for dry, cracked pads, nail-bed infections, or foreign objects (such as thorns).

TOP TIP

Declawing, where the cat's claws are removed, is illegal in the UK, but is still practiced in the US. It is incredibly cruel to the cat, and puts her at great risk. The surgery does not simply remove the claw, but also a toe bone and the surrounding ligaments and tendons. There are often health and behavioral complications following surgery, and the procedure causes the cat great pain and stress.

Scratching is a natural behaviour in the cat. She uses it to stretch and tone her muscles, and to mark her territory. Without claws she cannot perform these instinctive activities and will also be defenseless against other animals and unable to climb properly.

It is completely indefensible to mutilate a cat because she does not fit in with the owner's lifestyle, and fortunately most veterinarians, cat registry bodies and all animal welfare charities agree. If you value your sofa more than your cat's wellbeing, you shouldn't have a pet.

There are kind, effective alternatives to declawing – including providing your cat with ample scratching opportunities (posts), or even using nail covers which fit over the claws.

Chapter 17

Coat Care

Cats come in many different coat types – from the glamorous, longcoated Persian to the bald-looking Sphynx, there is a cat to suit all tastes. Making sure your puss remains wonderfully cuddlesome can mean anything from a quick brush once a week to intensive daily grooming, but the results are well worth it – a cat that looks great, smells wonderful, and feels fantastic.

COAT TYPES

A cat's coat type is directly influenced by its origins. For example, cats from warm countries, such as the Siamese, have short, sleek, thin coats. Cats from colder climates, such as the Norwegian Forest Cat, have thicker, fuller coats.

The cat is pretty well designed to look after her own coat. Her rough tongue does a superb job of brushing through the coat, distributing natural coat oils through it, and removing dead hair. Regular grooming isn't simply to keep the cat clean, it also ensures her coat is well-insulated, keeping her warm in cool weather and cool in warm weather.

So, if the cat can do such a good job, why do we need to interfere? Today's cats are often quite different to how they were originally bred. Where humans have interfered with a cat's coat, breeding for thicker or longer coats, the cat often needs a helping hand to keep on top of her hair care. The prime example, of course, is the Persian, who, without regular grooming from the owner, will become a bundle of painful mats in a very short time indeed.

Grooming also helps to form a close bond between owner and cat, is enjoyable for the cat, and will help to cut down on furballs and excess hair in the home.

- **Longcoated**: this coat, as seen in the Persian, is incredibly long and thick, and is also high maintenance.
- **Semi-longcoated:** this coat, seen in cats like the Ragdoll or Maine Coon, is long but not as thick as the longcoat. Medium maintenance is required.

- **Shortcoated:** this category covers a wide range of coats, from the thin Siamese coat, to the thicker, more plush coat of the Exotic or Russian Blue. All types are fairly low maintenance.
- **Rex:** the Devon and Cornish Rex have a curly, quite sparse coat.
- **Sphynx:** the Sphynx appears hairless but actually has a fine down of fur, particularly on the face, feet and tail.

Do remember that temperature will affect a cat's coat. For example, in cold weather, a cat's coat is likely to become thicker, and will look quite different to the same coat in hot, summer months once shedding has taken place.

TOP TIP

If you live with a cat, then you live with hair on your clothes, on your furniture, in your bed, and, invariably, in your cornflakes. It's a fact of life. Grooming will help to eliminate some of the excess hair from your home, but not all.

Lint rollers or sellotape are very good at removing hair from your clothes and furniture, but often stubborn hairs work their way into the carpet and are more difficult to budge. This is a particular problem in house-cat or multi-cat households.

Tip: put on a pair of rubber gloves, dip them into some water, shake off the excess, and then stroke the carpet. Yes, stroke the carpet. This removes hair brilliantly. It takes a while to do an entire carpet (and you are likely to wear through a pair or two of gloves), but the results are spectacular – your carpet will be back to the colour it is supposed to be! Alternatively, dispense with the carpet altogether and polish up your floorboards!

START THEM EARLY

It is very important that a kitten is groomed from a young age, so that she grows up to accept the procedure. She will be easier to handle, and will accept it as being an ordinary routine of life.

Start off by petting your cat. When she is in raptures, purring her head off, rubbing against you and rolling around on the floor in front of you, use the brush as an extension of your hand, continuing to stroke her. This will get her introduced to the sensation of being groomed, and she will love it! Gradually increase the length of the sessions, starting off with just a few minutes a day, so she doesn't become bored by them, and always finish with a tasty treat as a reward.

WHY DO CATS GROOM?

Cats do not groom only to keep themselves clean.

- *Grooming can help the cat to cool down (the moisture from licking evaporates and lowers their temperature).*
- *It can be form of diversionary behavior. For example, a cat that has been quarreling with another may start to groom to defuse the situation, turning her attention away from the situation and hoping the other cat will do the same.*
- *A cat usually grooms when she is content and feels secure, but she may also groom if slightly stressed. The act of grooming is reminiscent of her mother's love and care, and helps to distribute the cat's scent through the coat, thus reassuring her.*
- *Some cats, particularly attention-seeking Siamese, can take grooming to extremes. If bored or insecure, they may groom excessively, to the point of causing skin and coat problems. This behavior should be treated by a professional pet behavior counselor.*
- *Grooming between cats is a form of bonding and acceptance – a way of exchanging their scent, helping with hard-to-reach spots, and a symbol of trust and affection. If a cat licks you, it is a great compliment.*

If you adopt an adult cat that is not used to being groomed, take things slowly. Keep a soft brush next to your chair so you can take advantage of any opportunities that come your way. For example, if a sleepy puss is lying contentedly on your lap, you can gently start to brush her as part of your petting – this will help her to associate being groomed with a pleasurable experience. Stop after a couple of minutes and resume stroking her with your hand.

If she ever becomes stressed, never restrain her. You will aggravate her and she will become more panicked. Just stop grooming and try again when she is relaxed.

If you inherit a cat with mats, then don't attempt to groom them out. It is likely to take an awful long time, and will probably be painful to puss. Not a good way to kick off a new relationship, especially when it is all about building trust and confidence. Instead, take her to a professional groomer and get her clipped off. She won't look great, but she will be more comfortable and you can then start her grooming from scratch, keeping on top of it to ensure mats do not recur. (Provided you cover all the mirrors in the house, your puss should get over the indignity of looking like a shorn sheep.)

GROOMING REGIME

This will entirely depend on your cat's coat type. Hopefully, the breeder or shelter from where you got your cat will have given you specific grooming instructions. Here is a guide to what is needed; if you have any further queries, you are advised to contact the breeder/shelter, or a professional groomer.

SPHYNX

These cats only need an occasional groom with a soft baby brush. However, they do need to be bathed regularly, as their skin becomes very oily (the skin secretes oils for a coat that isn't there!).

REX

These coats are quite straightforward to care for. Generally, a good stroke is all that is needed for day-to-day care. If showing or if the cat needs a more thorough groom, a rubber brush can be used. However, it is possible to overgroom, resulting in an excessively sparse coat, so only brush when absolutely necessary.

SHORTCOATED

- Take a slicker brush which has plastic coated ends to the 'pins'. This will get down to the undercoat, but won't scratch the skin.
- Brush along the cat's back gently but confidently and gradually work around the entire body. (The back is the least sensitive part, used to being stroked, and will get her accustomed to the sensation of being groomed before you move on to the more sensitive parts of her body.)
- Don't forget the cat's tummy, the tail (which should be groomed very gently), the chest, and the 'armpits'.
- If your cat looks as if she's getting fed up, just groom the sides of her face, which she should love (most cats will rub their cheeks against the brush of their own accord).
- Give her an occasional treat as a reward.
- Then take a medium-toothed comb and work through the coat, removing any unnoticed knots. Make sure you get to the bottom of the coat, but be gentle so as not to scrape the skin.
- If you suspect your cat has fleas, you might want to use a narrow-toothed flea comb at the end of the session, once all knots have been removed. This should catch the odd critter, but there will always be those that manage to hop out of the way, so your cat should be treated with an appropriate parasiticide and the house should also be treated (see Chapter Twenty-six).

TOP TIP

As an occasional alternative to bathing a shorthaired cat, try a grooming wipe. These are cleaning cloths which can be stroked over your cat's body to give her a quick freshen-up. They aren't as effective as bathing your cat, but are useful as a stopgap.

- Finish by smoothing the coat with a piece of chamois leather or velvet for a smooth, polished finish.
- Once a week should be fine for most shortcoated breeds.

SEMI-LONGCOATED

- A semi-longhair will need grooming around two or three times a week.
- Spray a fine mist of room-temperature water on to the cat's body, so it is very slightly damp, and brush along the back with the slicker brush (above).
- Work along the body systematically, being sure not to miss any areas.
- Semi-longhairs often have bushy tails and ruffs (manes), so be sure to pay particular attention to these areas.
- Check under the tail, in case any fecal matter is present. If so, wash and rinse away using a damp flannel (designated for cat use only!), and brush through thoroughly.
- If you come to any knots that won't brush out easily, take hold of the affected hair in one hand and use a brush or comb to ease out the knot. Holding the hair will prevent any tugging and pain to the cat.
- Any persistent knots should be cut out with blunt-ended scissors, rather than cause pain to the cat by trying to remove them with a brush.
- Then work through the coat with a medium-toothed comb to pick up any last dead hairs and to detect any unnoticed knots.
- Finish with a treat.

LONGCOATED

For a long coat, you will need a slicker or pinbrush, a wide-toothed comb and a narrow-toothed comb.

The cat should be groomed every day to avoid tangles and knots. Make sure you do a thorough job – a quick surface brush may make the cat look good, but serious mats can develop underneath the topcoat.

CLEAN MACHINES
A cat will spend a good proportion of her life grooming. It has been estimated that a 12-year-old puss will have spent three years cleaning herself!

- Spray a fine mist of water on to the coat.
- Brush along the cat's back and then work all around the body, making sure you reach all parts.
- Brush down into the coat so that you are not just brushing out the surface. Do be careful not to scratch the skin.
- Once the coat has been brushed, work your wide-toothed comb through it. Comb slowly – if you rush, you are likely to pull out knotted hair which will be painful to your puss. Working slowly, you can stop when you come across a tangle.
- Always hold the knot with one hand, while working it out with the comb, as described for the semi-longhair coat, so as not to pull on the coat.

- Once the coat is tangle-free, comb through with the narrow-toothed comb. This is a particularly useful tool for grooming facial hair as well as removing any last dead hairs in the coat.
- Finally, brush against the lie of the coat so your cat looks like one luxurious soft ball of fur.

SHOW WORLD

If you would like to enter your cat for shows, you should talk to a professional groomer or your cat's breeder about what is and isn't allowed in the show ring. For example, a small amount of talcum powder is sometimes applied to a Persian's coat to remove any greasiness, but this is not permitted for shows.

TOP TIP

A shorthaired cat will generally need brushing once a week. For a quick in-between groom, make your hands slightly damp (not wet) and then stroke your cat. This will help to remove any dead hairs until you can groom her more thoroughly.

BATHING

I won't pretend that this is going to be easy. Cats and water can make an explosive combination (though Turkish Vans are renowned for their love of the water). However, it needn't result in an armful of scratches and a sulking cat that won't talk to you for a week.

Starting young is the key. If your cat realizes from a young age that bathing is something that is over quickly and painlessly, she will put up with it – especially if you reserve an extra-special treat and heaps of love as a reward at the end.

A confident attitude will also help. Cats always rebel when they spot a chink of weakness. For example, a veterinarian can give a cat a tablet first time, every time. A nervous owner can spend hours trying exactly the same procedure, but the cat won't have any of it. Why? Because they know they can get away with it. With a veterinarian, they immediately suss that this guy means business, so they might as well surrender and get it over and done with now. The same goes for bathing. If you handle the cat in a calm, confident way, the cat will realize that you mean business and that rebellion is pointless. At least that's the theory.

Shortcoated breeds only need bathing occasionally, and most average mixed-breeds never need bathing at all. Show cats are bathed more regularly to keep the coat looking its best. Long- and semi-longcoated breeds will need more regular bathing, according to the cat's needs. Unneutered toms benefit from a dip in the tub to control odor and a

greasy coat (particularly 'stud tail' where the base of the tail becomes quite dirty-looking), and bathing can also reduce allergic reactions to cats.

- Groom the cat, as described above. Never attempt to bath a knotted coat – it will simply make them worse.
- Put a rubber mat at the bottom of a sink (which is a much better size and height than attempting to use the bath).
- Fill the sink with about three inches (7.5cms) of warm (but not hot) water.
- Attach a nozzle spray to the taps, and get all your equipment to hand – a gentle cat shampoo, a cat conditioner (useful for semi-longs and longs), and a towel.
- It is best to have a helper on hand until you are confident that you can manage single-handed.

- Put cotton wool (cotton) in the cat's ears to prevent water from dripping into them.
- Hold the cat firmly and place her in the sink. You may need to hold her scruff to keep control and to calm her (kittens are held by the scruff when moved from danger by their mother so they have an instinctive reaction to freeze when held this way).
- Using the shower attachment, gently wet the coat all over, making sure you get down to the skin. Cat coats are designed to repel water from the surface and to remain dry underneath, so make sure you get the entire coat thoroughly wet – particularly in long coats. Try to keep water away from the cat's eyes.
- Work the shampoo into the coat, having read the instructions carefully beforehand. Should the shampoo be applied directly to the coat, or should it be diluted in a saucer of water first?
- Lather all over the body, and don't forget to do underneath the tail. Keep any suds well away from the cat's eyes.
- Pull the plug in the sink, then rinse the cat really thoroughly and make sure there are no pockets of suds in the undercoat that have gone unnoticed. Any trace of unrinsed shampoo can leave the coat looking streaky or scurfy when dried and can make it incredibly itchy for the cat.
- Watch out for any parasites that can be seen in the water. If you spot any, your home will need treating (see Chapter Twenty-six).
- Apply conditioner if necessary. It can be useful for longer-coated breeds and will aid brushing after the bath. Again, rinse well.
- Then heap lots of praise on your bedraggled cat, wrap her in a towel and rub her gently with it to remove the excess moisture.

DRYING OFF

Most cats can then be taken to a warm room to sulk and dry off. Always give a treat so she doesn't hate you too much. Longcoated and semi-longcoated breeds can be blow-dried, which will help to voluminize the coat. Keep the dryer on a low setting and ensure it stays a good distance from the cat so as not to burn her or cause her to overheat. Brush as you dry her. If you don't have a helper to hold the cat, buy a hairdryer stand.

Part 7
Feline Lifestyles

Chapter 18

The House-Cat

Faced with increasing dangers to their cats, such as traffic and air gun attacks, many owners are choosing to protect their precious wards by keeping them inside. It may seem cruel to keep a creature that is so wild at heart away from the great outdoors, but, provided she receives alternative stimulation to keep her mind and body active, most cats adapt remarkably well to life within four walls – and her safety will be assured.

ADVANTAGES OF INDOOR LIFE

- Safe from all the major dangers that cause premature deaths in cats, house-cats generally live much longer than those with access to the outdoors.
- They are safe from cars, air guns, and theft.
- You will be able to protect your cat from accidental poisoning. If you have an outdoor cat, you might avoid using rodent poisons and toxic chemicals in your garden, but you cannot guarantee that your cat won't encounter them elsewhere.
- Barred access to other cats, house-cats are much less likely to pick up diseases, infections and parasites.
- They won't encounter dogs, foxes or other animals that could potentially harm them.
- A house-cat won't run off if scared by thunder or fireworks (many cats disappear forever this way), either running into the road in fright or eventually finding a new home miles and miles from their original one.
- Your relationship with your neighbors won't be jeopardized by your cat digging up the plants of gardening enthusiasts.
- As an owner, the main benefit is security. Not for you the hours of panic when the cat is late coming home. Every moment of the day and night, you will know your cat is safe and well.

Peace of mind does come at a price, though. Looking after a house-cat involves a lot of hard work. Your puss won't be happy with a quick cuddle when you come home from work. She will need varied play and lots of love and attention to keep her content. If she is deprived of adequate stimulation, she will become bored and unhappy, and serious behavioral problems (such as obsessive licking and destructive tendencies) can develop.

IDEAL CANDIDATES

It is not fair to adopt an adult cat that is used to spending time outdoors and to expect her to be happy as a house-cat. Her years of hunting, playing and exploring the outside world will have stirred many instincts, and she will miss the excitement of the outdoors terribly.

A kitten, on the other hand, will adapt very well. She won't know what she's missing because she would never have experienced anything other than an indoor life. Very old cats can make good house-cats too. As they hit their late-teens, most oldies spend less and less time outdoors, preferring home comforts such as snoozing on comfortable chairs and watching the world go by from the safety of a sunny windowsill.

Some breeds or personalities adapt to a house-cat lifestyle better than others. A placid, laidback Persian makes an ideal candidate, but a 'manic' Siamese needs heaps of physical and mental stimulation. This is not to say that more demanding cats cannot make good house-cats; rather, you will need to be more creative in catering for their specific needs (see below).

If your cat has feline leukemia, FIV, or any other disease transmissible to other cats (see Chapter Twenty-six), you have a responsibility to the local feline population to keep your puss indoors. Deaf cats should also be kept indoors for their own safety.

CREATING A CAT-FRIENDLY HOME

Your home will be your cat's entire world, so it must be safe and stimulating for her. The usual safety checks should be made (see Chapter Eight), but it is very important that everyone in the family – and visitors too – understand the importance of keeping windows and outside doors shut at all times. They should only be opened if the cat is secure in another room.

If your cat gets out, she won't be at all equipped to deal with the dangers of the outside world. Ordinary cats grow up to be a little streetwise, but your house-cat will have lived in a protected world and will be entirely unprepared when faced with aggressive neighborhood cats, stray dogs, traffic etc. If she gets scared, she could run and run, and not be able to find her way back, so be extra-careful to prevent any escapes.

The cat harness can be used to introduce your cat to the area around her home, so that, in the event of an escape, she will be familiar with her surroundings and will hopefully be able to find her way home.

MENTAL STIMULATION

Outdoors, the cat's mind is stretched in every way. She is alert to every noise or movement, she will investigate new scents, and pounce on every leaf blowing in the wind. Indoors, things are pretty humdrum. Everything is safe and familiar, and it is easy for cats to stagnate. It is your job to inject some zest to indoor life.

• A kitty kong is a great interactive toy to keep your puss busy. Made of tough rubber, it has an opening at one end in which paper impregnated with catnip can be stored. The cat can chew to her heart's content, trying to get to the catnip, or can fling the toy around. It bounces unpredictably, which will keep her amused for hours. Alternatively, the catnip can be removed, and some cream cheese or pâté can be put in. This should only be an occasional treat, however, or your puss will become too podgy to play.

• A buster cube is another good buy. This is a tough plastic cube in which there is a hole, linked to an inner maze of passages. Place some dry treats inside, or a small portion of her daily dry food, and your puss has to move the cube around for the treats to fall out randomly. Make sure you buy the puppy version – the adult one will be too big and unwieldy for your puss.

• A house-cat generally enjoys the company of other cats, with whom she can play. Toys that encourage them to play together are very good at alleviating boredom while you are not at home. A mouse on a racetrack or in a piece of Swiss cheese are just two types on the market. One cat can shoot the mouse around the track and another cat will invariably join in, returning the mouse around the track to the first cat – a kind of 'mouse tennis' game.

• Buy toys that are designed to hook over your doors. Dangling down on elastic, they will entice your puss to play whenever she walks past. When they are touched, they squeak or squawk, and will encourage further play. Just as your cat is about to get bored with the toy, she will let go of it, and it will shoot off at an angle (because of the elastic), and so will spark more interest.

• Windows are your cat's only link with the outside world. Being the nosey creatures that they are, cats enjoy sitting on the windowsill and seeing what's going on outside. Clear away any plants or ornaments cluttering your windowsill, so your cat has plenty of room to sit. If your windowsills are not wide enough, move a chair to the window, so your cat can sit on the back of it to get a good view.

• Before you go to work, at lunchtime (if you can), and throughout the evening, you should play, play, play with your cat. It has been estimated that a cat needs more than 30 short spurts of play per day. This is based on the average cat needing five mice a day to survive, and the fact that only one in six hunting attempts is successful.

• Leave a small number of safe toys around the house for her to play with when you are unable to be with her (Chapter Seven), and keep a selection put aside for times when you will play with her. This will prevent her getting bored with all her toys quickly.

• Try to replicate hunting situations – your cat will much prefer trying to get a toy mouse out from under a small gap at the bottom of a cabinet than pouncing on one in the middle of the room. It will seem more realistic. A cardboard box with holes in for the cat to poke her front leg through is another favorite – throw a ball or some screwed-up paper inside, and let her loose!

• Another popular game is to use the rod/stick of a dangle toy and move it under a rug. The cat will go bananas, pouncing on the rug and trying to get underneath it. Of course, only use an old rug that you don't mind your cat 'killing'. Designate this mat as your cat's playmat, and she should leave all other rugs and mats well alone.

• Jazz up toys she has grown tired of by sprinkling some catnip on to them.

• Get a video in for your cat to watch! Believe it or not, there are videos made specifically for cats. One, made by a leading pet food manufacturer, features moving lights, squeaky noises, toys, and food etc., and most cats are enthralled by it.

• Train your cat. House-cats are often easier to train as they are more in tune with their owners and enjoy the mental stimulation. See Chapters Twenty-one and Twenty-two.

TOP TIP

Don't forget – you must grow grass for your house-cat to nibble on (see page 116).

PHYSICAL STIMULATION

A cat's body will be exercised through periods of play (see pages 136-137). You can encourage her to release any more pent-up energy by using a fishing-rod type toy. The joy of this toy is that you can exercise your cat while sitting in the armchair or standing in the middle of the room. It also ensures you won't be attacked by accident, as your hand is a long way from the end of the toy!

Get her interested in the toy and then move it around the room quickly. Flick the end of the toy up the stairs so she races after it, then bring it downstairs again. Throw the end over the top of her cat tree or scratching post (she'll have a good scratch while she's there). Flick the toy into a cardboard box, on to the windowsill, anywhere to get her moving, which will tone up different muscles.

Remember, cats prefer short, frequent bursts of activity to one hour-long slog, so keep your play sessions short and sweet.

To provide your cat with exercise while you are at work, why not adapt a spare bedroom into a cat-activity room? It may seem excessive, but will save your cats wrecking your home. Some people have actually carpeted the walls and ceiling of a cat room, and built networks of planks for the cats to walk and chase each other on. The cats will have a wonderful time literally climbing the walls – particularly athletic, energetic climbers such as the Siamese.

To increase your cat's stimulation, you can build or have built a lean-to or similar at the back of the house. Linked to the main house by a cat door, your cat can come and go as she pleases. The lean-to can be nothing more than a sturdy pen made of chicken-wire panels. It will allow your cat to enjoy the sights, smells and sounds of the garden, the sun and the wind, but will keep her safely enclosed. Do make sure the foundations are deep and that the pen is absolutely secure before letting your cat loose in it.

If you have the time and money, you can be more creative, turning a larger strip of your garden into a cat area. Fill it with cat-safe plants (see Chapter Nine), grasses for her to nibble and pounce on, etc. A clever use of climbing plants along the panels and over the roof can minimize the caged, chicken-pen appearance.

Alternatively, you can give your cat free access to the garden by tightening up security and making it utterly escape-proof. Firstly, you must have a completely enclosed garden. A high wall or fence all the way around, fitted with an inward overhang, will prevent

TOP TIP

Suddenly, for no obvious reason whatsoever, your cat will act like a creature possessed, leaping on anything that moves, climbing the curtains, racing up and down the stairs and making little chirrupy noises. After five minutes, she'll stop, then groom herself or go back to sleep.

These crazed sessions are your cat's way of getting rid of excess energy, and are much more common in house-cats than in outdoor ones. They are also more likely to happen at dawn or dusk (the dawn raid where you wake up to a cat running over your face or hunting your toes through the bedclothes is one of those special joys of cat ownership...).

If your cat's 'mad five minutes' start happening every five minutes, urgently review your play regime – she needs more stimulation!

your cat being able to escape. Do check local regulations regarding high fences before beginning work, and talk to your neighbors, who may have objections to your plans. Make sure your cat can't dig underneath and ensure there are no trees that she can use to leap over the top.

Skilled do-it-yourselfers should check out the Feline Advisory Bureau's fantastic fact sheet and webpage devoted to the subject, (see Useful Addresses).

Chapter 19

The Indoor/ Outdoor Cat

T he vast majority of cats live a dual life, switching between indoor and outdoor life with great ease. Although it is easy to adopt a laissez-faire attitude, letting your cat come and go as she wishes, it is best to regulate her outdoor access for her own safety.

ESTABLISHING A ROUTINE

Cats are crepuscular, meaning they are most active at dawn and dusk. This is when they get most of their hunting done, and means that they are often focused on prey rather than being alert to their surroundings – such as traffic. Because the light is not very good at dawn and dusk, the cat is less visible to car drivers, and many accidents occur at these times.

Keeping your cat in from before dusk and not letting her out again until after dawn will reduce the chances of her being involved in an accident and will cut down on rodent/bird corpses in your house! In Switzerland and Australia, all cats must be kept indoors after dark to protect wildlife (and the feline population).

In the winter months, when it is dark very early, you should invest in a reflective collar to make your cat easily visible to road users (and to you!). You might also prefer to adapt your cat's schedule, letting her out for longer in the morning when it is lighter and not letting her outside in the evening at all.

Cats tend to do most of their fighting at these times too – particularly males. If neutered later in life, they still go through certain macho posturing out of habit, and can get into all sorts of scrapes with other cats. Although these can happen at any time through the day, cats seem particularly territorial at night, dawn and dusk. Keeping your cat in will prevent nightly yowling and other horrific noises, and will cut down on fighting injuries.

Cats are generally nocturnal, but, if they are not let out at night, they will usually settle and most sleep through until morning, only getting up when the owner's alarm clock sounds. The key is to figure out what works best for your lifestyle and then stick to a routine. The ever-adaptable cat will reorganize her hunting, playing, sleeping schedules around you.

You might want to unlock the cat-flap all day, or you might want to let your cat out for only an hour or two a day. Whatever you decide, make sure it is not dark outside, and pick times when the traffic in the area is quiet.

FIRST-TIMERS

Do not let your new kitten or cat outside until she is protected by her full course of vaccinations. Even if she is fully inoculated by the time she comes to you, she should be kept indoors for at least three to four weeks so she can settle in and bond with you before venturing outside. (If you move to a new house, the same procedure should be used.)

Kittens are much easier to introduce to your garden or yard than adult cats. They cannot run as fast, and so you can head them off if you see they are about to climb a fence or squeeze through a gap in the fence.

An adult cat is quicker on her toes! Because of this, you might want to introduce her to the garden or yard in a harness (see Chapter Seven). This will allow her to sniff around and get her bearings while still being safely attached to you. After a few sessions, you might let her out of the harness.

MIAOW!

- Choose a warm, quiet day – if she hears thunder or fireworks, she may bolt.
- Make sure your garden is safe (see Chapter Nine).
- Delay one of the cat's meals before letting her outside. If she is hungry, she is more likely to come back.
- Open the back door and let your cat take her first tentative steps outside. It is better that the cat walks outside (rather than being carried), as she will be able to follow the scent of her footprints back to the house.

- She will slowly sniff around at first, but will become bolder with time.
- After five minutes or so, show her some fresh chicken (or something equally mouthwatering) and encourage her to follow you. Call her name in a friendly, happy tone of voice.
- Slowly walk back to the house, with the cat in tow, and close the door behind you. Give her a little of the chicken and the long-awaited meal.
- Short sessions like this are an ideal way of introducing your cat to the outside world. Over the course of a couple of weeks, you can prolong the length of time she has in the garden or yard.
- Initially, leave the back door open so she has a fast, easy way back to the house in case she gets spooked.
- Once you are confident that she knows her way back, you can close the door and she can rely on her cat-flap.

USING A CAT-FLAP

Most cats are clever enough to work out how to use a cat-flap with no prompting, but some just don't get it and need a helping hand.

- Make sure the flap is at the right height for your cat (see Chapter Seven).
- Set it to the open, unlocked position.
- Ask a member of the family, or a friend, to sit outside and to kneel on the floor, so he or she is visible through the cat-flap.
- Your helper should be armed with a treat, such as a piece of fresh chicken, something your cat would jump through hoops – or flaps – for.
- You should sit together with your cat on the other side of the flap.
- Ask the helper to call your cat's name and to show her the treat.
- Puss will probably tentatively edge forwards and may nudge the flap with the nose or paw. Most will summon the courage to continue through the flap for the treat.
- If your cat is a little nervous of it, and won't make the final step through, then open the flap outwards an inch or so for her, so she can smell the treat through the gap.
- If she still doesn't push through, open the flap fully for her to walk through.
- Entice her through the flap a few times, so she is confident walking through it, and then lower it. She will soon work out that she has to push it to get through.
- Give a treat and lots of praise and cuddles when she does so.
- If your cat isn't tempted to use the flap when baited with chicken, try using her favorite toy. Pull it through the flap to encourage her to chase it.
- Don't forget to lock the flap at night, or at other times when you want to restrict your cat's access to the outdoors.
- If you get into a routine, your puss will stop even trying to get out at night, and will only attempt to use it when she knows it will be open.

INDOOR CAT-FLAPS

A cat-flap can also be used within the house. For example, if you have a dog, it is useful to have a cat-flap fitted to your cat's safe room (see Chapter Eight), so the cat can enter her den but the dog cannot. She can then retire to her own space for a sleep, or a bite to eat, safe in the knowledge she won't be harassed and that the dog won't steal her food.

If you have a house-cat, a cat-flap can be used to give your puss access to a safe outdoor room, such as a lean-to (see Chapter Eighteen). They are also useful for an indoor/outdoor cat, and prove particularly invaluable in a multi-cat household. If you lock the pen's cat-flap (or door) to the outside, your cats can use their outdoor pen area after dark, protected from night dangers but still able to feel part of the action.

LOST AND FOUND

All cat owners have experienced the trauma of a missing cat. Sometimes, the cat is absent for a couple of hours, sometimes for a night, sometimes for days, weeks, and months, and, sadly, some never return.

In most cases, the cat comes back – she has just been having a whale of a time somewhere, and has simply lost track of the time. Some get locked in people's sheds, some get spooked by something and run, and then have to try to find their way back. Some are victims of road-traffic accidents, and some simply get a better offer and decide to live with someone else!

If your puss goes missing, try not to panic. Most return. Keep the cat-flap open all the time and keep fresh dry food in her bowl, together with some water, in case she returns when you are not in. Search your neighborhood, calling her name, or shaking a box of cat biscuits. Ask everyone nearby to have a look in their sheds or outbuildings in case she crept in unnoticed and then has accidentally been shut in.

GOODBYE FOREVER! Ginger

Contact all the animal rescue charities and shelters in a twenty-mile or so radius of your house, and also call veterinary surgeries. Put an advert in your local paper, giving a full description and offering a reward, and distribute posters and leaflets in your area. Some pet insurance companies offer money for advertising a lost pet, which may help towards your costs. Ring around the shelters and veterinary surgeries every day to see if she has been brought in.

Don't give up. Most cats come back – they may have used up a few of their nine lives in their adventure, but the majority return with a voracious appetite and a few tales to tell.

TOP TIP

It is a good idea to take a clear color photo of your cat or kitten at different stages of her life, so you can use one in a poster if she goes missing.

OUTDOOR WORKING CATS

Some cats, perhaps rescued from a feral colony, can never be happy as a pet cat. If they are not caught at a sufficiently young age, some – but not all – ferals can never be domesticated (see Chapter Two).

However, they can be usefully employed as working cats. They usually make ideal mousers, and will happily live in a barn or weatherproof outbuildings, provided they are given regular meals and water. You will be able to keep an eye on their health and wellbeing, providing veterinary care where needed, and, of course, you should ensure that the ferals are neutered.

UNINVITED GUESTS

The ease with which cats can learn how to use a cat-flap is best illustrated by the fact that they are more than happy to use everyone else's! Don't be surprised if you find a few neighborhood cats roaming around your house, or munching on your cat's food. Cats are so nosey, they find it difficult to resist checking out other people's homes.

Cute though it can be to meet other cats this way, it isn't ideal. They could be bringing in fleas, you don't know if they have any diseases, they could start spraying their new-found territory, and your own cat is likely to take great offence at the uninvited guests.

In nervous cats, such visits could cause great stress – their one safe haven in the world (their home) will have been tarnished with the scent of other cats and this could cause your own puss to urinate indoors as a way of surrounding herself with her own smell (see Chapter Thirteen).

Other cats and small animals (such as racoons and skunk, in the US), can be kept outside by a cat-flap which can only be opened by a special magnetic collar fitted to the cat (see page 67).

IN A FLAP: PROBLEM USERS

AVOIDING AMBUSH

In a multi-cat household, cat-flaps can be used to ambush others as they enter or leave the house. If there is one mischievous moggie in your cat clan, the other cats generally learn to race through the flap at high speed or to give as good as they get. However, if you have a cat that is particularly nervous of using the flap because of the risk of attacks, you should lock all the cats indoors and only let them out when you can supervise them. You should also sit by the back door with a water pistol to squirt the naughty puss every time she lies in wait for the others. She'll soon get fed up and avoid her ambush positions if she associates them with getting squirted.

OPEN SESAME

There are many owners who have permanent draughts in their home because, when they first got their cat, they tied up the cat-flap to teach the puss to use it, and it has remained open ever since!

In these cases, the cat has trained the owner very well. By showing reluctance to use the flap when it is shut, the puss has learnt that the owner will keep the door open for her. Why should she waste her own energy, when the owner is willing to do all the 'hard work' for her?

Do the exercises on page 142, to retrain your cat how to use the flap, then let her get on with it. If a cat really wants to go out, and she has understood that the flap is her gateway to the outdoors, she'll soon learn to push it open, and you can return to living in a warm, draught-free home.

Chapter 20

The Older Cat

Cats are hardy, healthy creatures that are generally long-lived. It is not unheard of for a cat to reach her twenties, and the vast majority make their mid- to late-teens. Because most of us will have older cats, and for longer, it is important to address the subject of caring for an older cat.

From a veterinary viewpoint, a cat is 'senior' from around the age of seven years – halfway through the average cat's lifespan! Nutritionally, a seven-year-old cat's needs are quite different to those of a younger cat, and she will need to switch to a lower-protein diet around this time (see Chapter Fifteen).

Of course, a seven-year-old might officially be termed a 'senior' but most are as sprightly at that age as they were at two years. When they reach their mid- to late-teens, however, most exhibit at least some signs of aging.

These signs are not always easy for the owner to spot. Cats grow old gracefully and, when you live with a cat, it can be difficult to notice any gradual changes that occur. Here are some pointers to consider.

SIGNS OF OLD AGE

- An older cat will be less mobile than a younger puss. She may not be able to jump up on to furniture quite so easily. Place little steps around the house for her. For example, if she likes sleeping on the windowsill but she struggles reaching it, place a stool near the window so she can reach it in stages.

- You may need to groom your cat more. As they age, cats can become stiff and be less able to twist their neck to groom those hard-to-reach places.

- Your cat's coat may become thinner, and she will feel the cold a little more. Very old cats will benefit from a hot-water bottle wrapped in a towel placed under their bed. Or you can purchase a microwaveable heat pad that keeps warm for hours and hours.

- She may go out less. An older puss is likely to sleep more, and will enjoy her creature comforts more. She is likely to become less effective as a hunter, and many very old cats are perfectly happy dozing in a warm spot in the garden or even becoming house-cats (see Chapter Eighteen).

- An older cat will love sleeping-bag type beds to sleep in, as they are extra-warm. Or you can roll a small duvet into a tunnel for her to sleep in – she will love you for it. If you don't provide her with a snug bed, she'll find her own – usually by tunneling under the covers in your bed!

- She may play less, but will still need mental and physical activity to keep her mind and body ticking over. Adapt her play sessions to her physical abilities, but don't do away with them altogether. Even twenty-somethings enjoy behaving like kittens sometimes!

- Very old cats like their routines and will not take kindly to any big changes. If you go away on holiday, for example, your oldie will much prefer a cat-sitter to come and look after her in the familiar surroundings of her own home to a spell in a cattery.

- The nightly 'where are you?' cries are another feature of life with an oldie. Often older cats wake up in the middle of the night and seem to panic if they can't find their owners. Or they just demand a cuddle in the early hours of the morning.

- Older cats are less able to digest their food, and many lose weight. Any weight loss should be checked out by a veterinarian as it can be a symptom of several diseases associated with old age. Feeding several small meals of a senior variety of cat food often helps the cat to maintain her weight if she is otherwise healthy.

- If your cat loses her appetite, warm her food up a little or add something really smelly to it (such as pilchards) to encourage her to eat.

- She may have the odd accident. Any loss of continence should be checked by a veterinarian, but, if there are no health reasons, it could be that she just couldn't get to her litter-tray quickly enough. Place several in the house (upstairs and downstairs) so she is never far from one.

- Check the contents of her litter-tray. Any change in the frequency of defecation and urination, or in the consistency, color, or smell, should be reported to the veterinarian.

- Monitor your cat's breath – if you turn green when your cat yawns, take her to the veterinarian. Bad teeth can lead to gum infections, loss of appetite or difficulty eating.

- Older cats generally become much more affectionate, craving attention and warm laps.

- Keep a close eye on her drinking habits, and report any changes to your veterinarian. Increased thirst can be attributable to diabetes, kidney problems, or hyperthyroidism which can all affect older cats.

- There have been huge leaps in veterinary advances recently, and many illnesses can be managed quite effectively if they are caught early enough. A regular check-up with your veterinarian is a very good idea.

- Make sure your oldie isn't harassed by younger cats, other pets, or children. She will need to sleep more, and will enjoy her peace and quiet. It isn't usually a good idea to introduce a kitten to a very old cat. Far from giving her a new lease of life, she is likely to resent the change – especially as young kittens are usually far from respectful of their elders!

GOLDEN OLDIE
The oldest recorded cat was Puss, a tabby from Devon, England, who died one day after his 36th birthday in 1939.

TOP TIP

It isn't quite true that one cat year equals seven human ones. Cats mature more quickly than humans towards the beginning of their lives, and, once adulthood is reached, development is more steady, with every cat year equaling four human years.

Cat years	Human years	Cat years	Human years
1	15	11	60
2	24	12	64
3	28	13	68
4	32	14	72
5	36	15	76
6	40	16	80
7	44	17	84
8	48	18	88
9	52	19	92
10	56	20	96

With every subsequent cat year, add four human ones – so a 21-year-old is actually 100 years old!

This is a very basic guide. Some breeds or individuals mature more quickly or slowly. For example, the Maine Coon is a slow developer, only reaching adulthood by the age of three or four years. For kitten development, see Chapter Twenty-four.

- Finally, enjoy your cat. The relationship with an oldie is an extra-special one. You both know each other inside out, through years of living with each other, and the trust and love creates a wonderful bond. Make the most of your time together.

WHEN TO LET GO

It is one of life's sad facts that cats just don't live long enough, and eventually you will have to make the decision to put your cat to sleep. This is the hardest part of owning a cat, but it is also the most important.

When you adopt a cat, you take on full responsibility for her care and wellbeing. This includes making sure she does not suffer. If your cat becomes ill and the veterinarian has told you there is no hope of recovery, you should assess your puss's quality of life. Is she in pain or distress (for example, through loss of continence)? If so, you should seriously consider euthanasia.

Euthanasia is the technical term for putting an animal to sleep. It is done by injecting barbiturates into the cat's vein so she loses consciousness and dies. It is entirely painless to the cat, and is just like falling into a deep sleep.

Although it is difficult to cope with, you should stay with your cat while she is given the injection. You will be able to stroke and reassure her while she gently slips away. Yes, it is incredibly difficult for you, but, after years of love, the least you can do for your pet is to ensure she does not die alone, surrounded only by strangers.

Most veterinarians will do a home visit, if you would prefer euthanasia to be done in your own home. This option is more costly, but may be much less stressful for your cat.

MAKING ARRANGEMENTS

What to do with the body is something that is best decided well in advance – while your cat is still young and healthy. You will be able to think clearly about your options rather than making a spur-of-the-moment decision under pressure.

You might like to bury your cat under her favorite tree in the garden, or to buy a plaque to commemorate her. You might want to have her cremated and to keep or scatter her ashes. There are some lovely caskets on the market, including some very tasteful wooden sleeping cats that look like ordinary ornaments.

Your veterinarian can dispose of the body for you, or organize a cremation. Not all veterinary surgeries offer private cremations, however. Often, they are mass cremations and you cannot be sure of getting back your own pet's ashes. Ask if the company your veterinarian uses offers a private, individual service. If they don't, search on the internet for your nearest pet crematorium that does.

COPING WITH GRIEF

Losing a cat is a terrible experience and understandably so. After being an integral member of your family for so many years, the loss is acute and the grief very real.

Many people are taken aback by the overwhelming sense of loss, but the feelings are perfectly natural. Cry when you want to cry, and talk about your special cat if you feel the need. If you do not have friends or family that understand what you are going through, check out the internet. There are lots of pet-loss sites that offer great support from people all over the world who have experienced exactly the same feelings of sadness, anger and despair. One particularly good site can be found at www.petloss.com.

Various pet-loss befriender schemes are in operation in different countries, through which you can talk to trained bereavement counselors. Your veterinarian should have details of national schemes.

Talking about your cat – what made her special and the happy memories you have of her – will become much easier with time, and smiles will eventually replace the tears.

Part 8

Cat Tricks

CARING FOR KITTENS

All kittens are irresistible, but they require considerable time to train and socialise if they are to grow into well-behaved, confident and loving companions.

If handled with love and respect, your kitten will grow up to be content in the company of children.

THE FAMILY CIRCLE

A kitten will generally accept resident pets, provided she is exposed to them early, and initial introductions are carefully supervised.

▲ Young kittens take well to training – but keep sessions short and fun.

◄ A regular grooming routine from a young age will ensure that your cat accepts – even enjoys – the procedure.

156

▲ Check that your garden is completely cat-safe before letting your kitten outside.

▶ A kitten must be fully vaccinated before she is allowed to venture outdoors.

157

▲ Kittens will play with any items they can lay their paws on.

A cat-tree with sisal posts, toys and tunnels, is a must-have – and will help you divert attention away from your best furniture.

It is important that a ▶
cat has her own bed – a
place where she can find
peace and quiet when she
wants to retire for a snooze.

◀ *A cardboard box, lined with*
cosy bedding, makes a
comfortable, temporary bed
for a growing cat.

Most cats will rest wherever ▶
they can find a warm, soft
spot – and a house-mate
usually makes an ideal
makeshift bed!

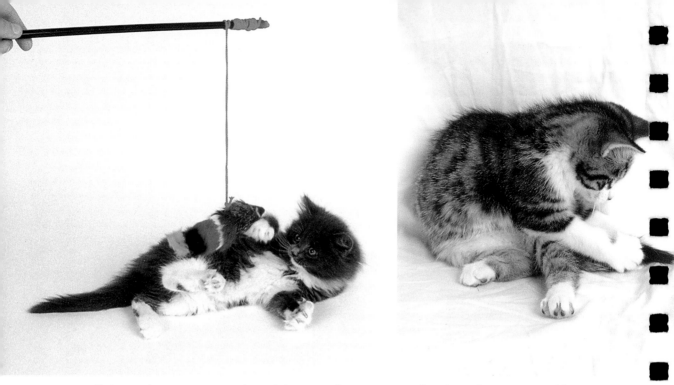

Fishing-rod toys are very popular with kittens and cats...   ... though a tail proves irresistible to most.

A playful, kittenish streak stays with a cat well into adulthood and even into old age.

160

Chapter 21

The Cat's Mind

Cats are smart creatures, no one can deny it. They work out how to pull their owners' strings to get what they want, when they want it, and also plot cunning schemes to steal food and to sleep in the warmest spot in the house. This raw intelligence can be harnessed to train your cat – yes, train your cat!

METHODS OF TRAINING

You might think your cat cannot be trained, but consider all the things she has already learnt from living with you. She knows her name, how to be litter-trained, she probably knows that the alarm clock invariably means breakfast will soon be served, and she will come running the moment she hears the food cupboard being opened. Many cats learn how to knock on the door or ring the bell to get the owner to let them in, or they realize that, if they are being ignored, scratching the carpet or the sofa soon gets them the attention they want. Now, it's just a case of adding more tricks and exercises to your cat's impressive repertoire.

The dog's background predisposes him to training – he likes to please his pack leader and will work hard for praise and approval. Although training comes more easily to dogs, cats can make wonderful pupils – provided the right approach is adopted.

MOTIVATION

The cat will only train if she thinks there's a point to it. Why bother expending energy for the sake of it? Unlike the dog, she is less likely to leap through hoops simply

CLEVER CATS
The Wesleyan University, Texas, has conducted studies into animals' problem-solving skills, which showed that cats are better at finding their way out of difficult situations than dogs. In fact, cats exhibited the same intelligence as primates, though they took slightly longer to work out problems.

to impress you – she'll only do it if *she* wants to.

Always reward behavior you want to encourage, and ignore behavior you want to discourage. Your cat will soon learn that she can influence what *you* do – if she raises a paw, or whatever you ask her to do, you'll give her good things. If she doesn't, nothing happens.

The key to training is to make it worth her while by using rewards that she really values (be it chicken, or cream cheese). If she enjoys learning a new trick or obedience exercise, she'll work with you. If she is bored by the whole thing, she'll go to sleep.

Some cats are too fixated on food and lose the plot entirely at the first whiff of a treat. They will jump up to get the treat and lose all concentration on anything else. In such cases, use praise and petting instead. A cat will do most things for a stroke around her cheeks and a chin-rub.

Alternatively, you can use a favorite toy to lure your cat. For example, if you want her to sit on her back legs and beg, a toy can be dangled above her head. The reward in each instance would be to let your cat have a quick play with the toy before continuing with the training.

TOP TIP

If your cat is prone to piling on the pounds, make sure you subtract the treats used for training from her daily food allocation.

TRAINING TIPS

Training should be short and enjoyable. A five-minute exercise done four or five times throughout the day is much better than one, long half-hour session. Short, frequent sessions will ensure your cat remains fresh and willing to learn, will break up the monotony of the day, and will help her to consolidate what she has learnt.

The right location is also essential. Choose a room that is free of distractions to help your cat concentrate on the task in hand. If you train in a room where people will be coming and going, progress will be slow – or non-existent! Distractions should only be added once your cat has conquered a particular exercise.

Never train immediately after a cat's meal (she will want to groom and snooze and will not be easily motivated), or if you are tired. You both should be on your best form if you are to enjoy your session together and if you are to achieve results.

Finally, be patient – don't expect too much from your cat too soon – and do not have unrealistic expectations. It takes an awful lot of work to create a cat that can walk to heel as close as a Collie, but why would you want to? Cats are cats and training is just a way of spending some fun, quality time together.

CLICKER TRAINING

Clicker training for dogs has taken the Obedience world by storm, and some people are now using the same methods on cats. It involves a plastic box, which is held in the palm of your hand. The box has a metal 'tongue', which, when pressed with your thumb, makes a distinctive 'click'. This sound is always followed by a treat so she learns to associate the click with an enjoyable experience. Eventually, the clicks and the treats are phased out, as your cat makes progress and the rewards become less critical.

As a method of reward-based training, the clicker is particularly effective as it is so precise. If a treat is used solely as a reward, it can never be given at exactly the right moment that your cat performs an appropriate behavior. You have to fumble in your pocket for the treat and hand it down to her. By the time your cat receives the treat, the good behavior will have been and gone, and instead you will be rewarding something completely different.

For example, if you ask your cat to raise her paw, by the time you give her the treat, she is likely to have put her foot back down to the floor. She may then think she is

TOP TIP

Special training treats can be bought for use as rewards. They are generally freeze-dried chicken or liver pieces which are clean to use, easily stored in a fanny-bag or pocket, or held in your hand without getting your fingers mucky. They are just the right size too – if you give too big a treat, your cat will spend too long chomping and will disrupt the flow of training. Specially-made training treats are just enough to reward your cat and leave her wanting to earn more.

rewarded for sitting. The clicker can be used to tell your cat what she has done right at exactly the right time, and the treat can then follow afterwards.

The key to clicker training is to break down the exercise into simple stages, to teach them step-by-step and then to put all the stages together. All the exercises in Chapter Twenty-two are taught this way.

When teaching a new exercise, give a click the moment the cat makes a move towards doing the right thing. For example, when teaching her to give you her paw, give a click even if she makes the slightest movement. This way, she can be encouraged to make more confident movements, and, eventually, she will be 'giving you five' with no hesitation at all (see page 169).

SOFTLY, SOFTLY

Some cats are quite alarmed by the sound of the clicker. To stop your puss freaking out, hold the clicker in the middle of your hand, and wrap your fingers around it. You can even put your second hand around the clicker hand. Then, when you click, the sound will be quite muffled. Followed by a really tasty treat, she will soon become less wary of the sound, and you can gradually reduce the muffled effect. Eventually, she'll enjoy the 'click', associating it with a reward.

Chapter 22

Training Program

Here are some exercises and tricks to get your training off to a good start. Once you've mastered the basic principles of training (see Chapter Twenty-one), there's no end to what you can teach your cat.

As well as being a way of having fun with your cat and of exercising her mind, training can be used for practical purposes. For example, teaching a cat to give a paw (page 169), will make clipping her nails much simpler, and, if you have a houseful of cats, teaching them to sit patiently at their bowls (page 170) will save you tripping over them every time you serve their meals.

SIMPLE EXERCISES

COME

It's been said that a dog owner will go to the back door, call her dog inside from the garden, and the dog will come. A cat owner will go to the back door, call her cat, make a cup of tea, sit down and read the newspaper, and, eventually the cat will come. Cats like to do things in their own good time.

It can be infuriating for an owner – especially if you are calling the cat indoors because you have a vet appointment lined up, or need to get her inside before you go out. Working on the recall exercise (coming when called) should help to speed things up.

- Get your cat all loved up – stroke her, rub the sides of her cheek and talk to her in your special 'cat' tone of voice.
- Move a couple of steps away from her, and call her to you – "Kitty, come!"
- Usually, she'll come straight away to get some more strokes. If she doesn't come, use any trick in the book. Shake her biscuit box, show her a toy or a treat. If she refuses to come, it's because you are not making it worth her while. The stakes should be high. Offer her some ham, chicken, or fish – whatever her favorite delicacy is.

TOP TIP

It's always best to start your training when the cat is a kitten. Youngsters learn quickly and you can get them into good habits before they learn some bad ones! But training can be just as successful with adult cats. In fact, some people prefer working with older pupils.

George Techow, a circus owner of the late-19th century, worked purely with adult cats. He taught cats to walk tightropes, jump through hoops of fire, somersault, balance on bottles, and walk only on their front legs. George claimed he could not work with kittens, and instead trained young adult cats, aged between one and three years. The best pupils, he said, were strays, because they were used to living by their wits to get by.

- As soon as she comes to you, give a click (page 163), and give her a treat.
- Repeat the exercise, moving a few steps away from her once more. Each time, give her lots of praise when she does as you ask.
- Once she understands that treats are on offer, together with great praise and adoration, she should respond more quickly.
- After five repeats of the exercise, play a game with her, using her favorite toy, and resume your training session later in the day.
- Over several training sessions, gradually increase the distance between you and your cat, so she has to come further to you. Always click and treat when she obliges, and give lots of praise and a quick pet. (Some cats work better for a cuddle than for food – use whatever best suits your puss.)
- Now she has really got the hang of what "Kitty, come" means, it's time to refine the performance. Try to speed up her response. If she dawdles, don't reward her. Just move a few steps further away and call her again – make her really want to come to you. Call her in a soft, but excited, tone of voice, and show her a really wonderful treat. When she comes quickly, click and treat her, and lavish heaps of praise upon her.
- Then move into a different room, and call your puss. Once she's mastered this, go upstairs and call her. When she will come quickly to wherever you are in the house, try the exercise outside in your garden.
- The great outdoors has heaps of distractions against which you will be competing for your cat's attention. Let her have a sniff of the garden before attempting to train. Once she's settled, practice the recall exercise, but only call her to you three or four times so she doesn't get bored. Then let her play in the garden. If you call your cat and then immediately take her inside afterwards, she will be less likely to come to you next time.

SIT

Cats are great sitters, and particularly love sitting by a window for hours and hours on end. However, teaching a cat to sit on command is more of a challenge.

- Cuddle your cat to make her more responsive to you (page 165).
- Call her to you (above), and if she sits in front of you, click and treat.
- If she comes, but continues to stand, then hold a treat just above her head, so she has to look up, and sit back to reach it. With some cats, you can just use your index finger – they will follow your finger, wanting to rub their heads against it.
- The moment her bum hits the floor, click and treat. Give lots of praise.
- If she takes a while to understand, be patient. She is likely to try to get the treat out of your hand, but just keep hold of it, and alter the position of your hand to lure your cat into the right position.
- After a few sessions, she'll soon understand what she is meant to do when your hand is above her head, and you can withdraw the treat as the lure, and use it only as a reward after she has been clicked. Eventually, even this reward can be withdrawn, and it will only be given occasionally – for the very best of responses.
- Only when she understands what you want her to do should you introduce the word "Sit". If you say it at the beginning, she won't have a clue what it means and will associate the word with jumping up, miaowing, or whatever she is doing instead.

DOWN

This is a more difficult exercise. When they are training, cats are really alert and energetic, and don't like lying down – it's just too passive and inactive for them. Your chances of success will be better if you try this exercise towards the end of your training session, once your puss has expended any excess energy.

- Pet your cat, so she is putty in your hands.
- Then lie down on the ground and put your hand on the floor.
- Rub your fingers together or wiggle them to encourage your cat to rub her head against them.
- When she does so, keep your fingers on the floor and gently rub around her head. Hopefully, this should be enough to get her to flop down on to the floor in pleasure.
- As soon as she does lie down, click and treat, and give her a good cuddle.
- Practice little and often, and, eventually, you will be able to get her to lie down simply by lowering your hand and saying "Down".
- Gradually phase out the reward, until it is only an occasional treat. The rest of the time, her reward will be the sound of the clicker.
- If your cat is a little more reserved and the petting approach does not work, hold a treat in your hand to lure her down.

FUN HEEL

Most cats love following their owners around and will enjoy this exercise enormously.

- Pet your cat so she is more receptive to you, and so you can lure her with your hand – she'll follow your hand to get more strokes from you. (Treats can also be used.)
- Stand up, ask your cat to "Come", and to "Sit" in front of you, facing towards you.
- Show her your right hand (held at the cat's head height), and wiggle your fingers to encourage her to follow it.
- When she does, move your hand around the side and back of your right leg, and then use your left hand to continue to lure her round until she is sitting fairly close and directly level with your left leg.
- Give her a click and a treat, lots of praise and affection.
- Practice this first section before moving on to the next part.
- With time, you will need to lure her less, until eventually a discreet backwards gesture with your right finger will be all that is required to get her into position.
- Now it's time for the second part. Again, give your cat a good cuddle to get her in the right co-operative frame of mind.
- Put her in the heel position, hold your left hand down the side of your leg, so it is near your cat's head, and take a couple of slow steps forward.
- All the time lure her to follow you by using your finger or a treat.
- When she is walking next to you, click.
- Stop, get her to sit next to you, give her another click and treat, and then give lots of praise and strokes.
- With practice, you will be able to walk further with her beside you, and you can also introduce turns.
- When she understands what's expected of her, you can introduce the word "Heel", so she associates the word with the action.
- Phase out the clicks and rewards so they are only given occasionally.

 TOP TIP

If a cat doesn't understand what you want, she is likely to flump down on the floor. This is a submissive gesture, where she is trying to please you – she can't work out what is required of her but knows she has to do something, so she'll try to appease you through body language.

If she does this, give her a cuddle to reassure her, and reassess your training exercise. She obviously doesn't understand what she is meant to do, so break down the exercise into smaller sections. If you have been training for more than 10 minutes, finish with an exercise she knows, reward her, stop the session, and start afresh tomorrow.

NOW FOR THE GOOD MEWS

Some cats are real chatterboxes. Siamese-types are renowned for enjoying the sound of their own voices, but many mixed-breed cats are talkers too. Even quiet cats miaow occasionally – particularly when you are preparing a meal for them.

Think about what makes your cat mew, and use it in her training. For example, if she mews when you are about to put her food down for her, give her a click as soon as she does so, say "Speak" and keep hold of the bowl to encourage her to mew. Again, click and then give her the meal.

If she mews to greet you when you come into the house, say "Speak", click and give her a treat. It won't take her long to figure out that if she mews when you say "Speak", she gets a treat. Once she associates the word with the action, you will be able to encourage her to mew on command.

TRICKS TO TEACH

PAW

- Don't start this exercise by petting your cat or she may become too excited and attempt to cuddle you when you kneel down beside her.
- Put your cat in the Sit position (page 167). With your hand, gently lift one of her paws, say "Paw", and immediately give a click and a treat.
- Repeat this several times.
- Some cats are a bit skittish about having their feet touched, but they are reassured by the fact that it is immediately followed by a treat.
- After a few practices, say "Paw" but don't touch your cat. Hopefully, she will have worked out what you want and may tentatively move her paw.
- Even if there is only the slightest of movements, give a click and a treat, and make a big fuss of her.
- Repeat, and she should get bolder, lifting the paw higher.
- Once she really has the hang of what's going on, you can refine her performance by withholding the click and treat for only the best behavior.

GIVE ME FIVE!

This is a variation of the paw-giving exercise.
- Put your cat in the Sit position (page 167). With your hand, gently lift one of her paws, say "Shake hands" or "Give me five", and immediately give a click and a treat.
- Repeat this several times.
- After a few practices, say "Give me five" but don't touch your cat. Instead, hold your hand just in front of her foot.
- From the previous practices, she will realize that if her paw makes contact with your hand, she gets a click and a treat. She will therefore tentatively touch your hand.

- The moment she does so, click and treat, and give her heaps of praise and affection.
- Over several practice sessions, bring your hand further away from her until she will always touch your hand, wherever it is.

WAVE

Once your puss has learnt to 'give you five' , teach her to wave her paw up and down.

- Put out your hand as if you want your cat to touch it with her paw. Your hand should be quite high (though still within your cat's reach).
- As she goes to touch your hand, move your hand downwards so she has to bring her paw down too. Click and treat.
- Repeat a few times and give lots of praise.
- Then bring your hand down and then up again. Click and treat once more.
- Keep practicing until she will move her paw up and down a couple of times.
- Once she has mastered this, say "Wave" as she does it.
- With time, you can use only a finger to encourage her to move her paw, and, eventually, the command "Wave" should be all that is needed.

HOOP

This looks a really impressive trick, but is really quick and simple to teach.

- Hold a hoop upright on the floor, between you and your cat.
- Show your cat a treat and when she shows interest in it, move the treat slowly so she has to step through the hoop to get to it. Give her a click and a treat as a reward.
- If you find it difficult to hold the hoop, a treat and a clicker, then ask a helper to hold the hoop, or, alternatively, get your cat all loved up and use your hand as a lure.
- Keep practicing, and, with time, say "Through" as she walks through the hoop.
- You will be able to gradually withdraw the treat/hand lure and get her to jump through by using your command word.
- Over time, raise the hoop further off the floor. Do so gradually, so you are not expecting too much too soon. Progress is best made slowly.
- Eventually, you will be able to sit your cat on a chair, and get her to jump through the hoop mid-air to a chair located the other side.

DINNER IS SERVED!

If you have more than one cat, mealtimes can be chaotic. As you are in the kitchen, putting the food into their bowls, you will probably be mugged by moggies, trying to jump up on the kitchen worktop, or rubbing against your legs. Trying to carry the bowls to their eating places without treading on the cats is a feat in itself. However, mealtimes can be an orderly affair if you teach your ravenous rabble to sit quietly at their places.

- Whenever you feed your cats, try to get into a regular routine as to who sits where to eat (you probably do this already).
- The cats will soon work out where they should run to in order to be fed.
- Say "Bowls!" just as you are about to put the bowls down.
- There's no need to use a clicker in this exercise – being fed is reward enough.
- Over time, they will learn to associate the word "Bowls!" with their feeding positions, and the fact that they are about to be fed.
- Next, start to say "Bowls!" just before you get to the feeding location, and the cats should race on ahead of you, into their relevant positions, as they have been used to doing over the past couple of weeks.
- With time, you will be able to say "Bowls!" earlier and earlier, until, eventually, your cats will run and sit patiently while you are still serving up. Heaven!

ROLL OVER

This can be taught in a number of ways, depending on your cat's personality. If she's a toy freak, use a dangle toy to lure her; if she's obsessed with food, use a treat; and if she loves being stroked, get her purring and then use your finger to influence her.

- Practice the Down exercise, page 167.
- Once she's down, use your lure to encourage her to roll on to her other side.
- Give a click and a treat. Use your lure as the reward – either the food treat, a play with her toy, or a chin-rub.
- Keep practicing, getting her to roll one way and then the other, and once she's got the hang of it, say "Roll over" as she does so.
- With time, click less. For example, start off by clicking after she rolls one way. Then click after two rolls, then three, and so on.
- With practice, you can lure her less, until, eventually, she will roll over whenever you say the command word.

UP

- Use your cat's favorite lure – be it a treat, a toy, or your hand (see above). A hand-lure is particularly popular – most cats will go up on their back legs to get a stroke.
- Show the lure to her, and then lift it up a little way above her, so she has to sit back on her haunches to reach up to it.
- As soon as she does this, click and treat, giving her the lure.
- Practice a few times, and say "Up" once she will do so reliably.
- With time, she will need less luring, going up whenever your hand is above her.
- Eventually, the command "Up" will be all that is required.
- To get your cat to stay up for longer periods, delay the click. For example, when she is first learning this exercise, click her even if she goes up for just a second. With further

practice, make her wait a couple of seconds for the click, and gradually extend the length of time further, the more you train.

GAMES TO PLAY

FETCH

Dogs aren't the only animals that can play fetch – spice up your cat's play sessions by teaching her to retrieve.

- Before starting this trick, revise the recall/come exercise (page 165).
- Once she will reliably come to you when called, throw a small toy for your puss. Don't throw it too far – a couple of steps is fine to start off with.
- She will chase after it, and will invariably put it in her mouth.
- As soon as she does so, call her to you, and she should bring the toy with her.
- Click and treat, and then throw the toy for her to fetch again. Being allowed to continue to play with the toy is a great reward for her.
- When she will reliably bring the toy to you, say "Fetch", so she associates the word with the action.
- Gradually, over the course of several training sessions, throw the toy further and further away.

TOP TIP

Some cats can learn as many tricks as you can throw at them, but others seem to have a limit as to how much information they can retain, and shut down after five or so tricks.

'Five-trick cats' will look at you quite blankly if you try to teach a sixth trick, and will invariably respond by going through their repertoire of five tricks, hoping this is what you want from them. Other cats can learn a sixth trick, provided they then forget one of the other tricks you've taught them: it seems they have a finite amount of brain power dedicated to training – once you've reached the limit, they have to forget other things to make room for new ones!

However, once she's learnt a trick, it's just a case of revising the early stages of the exercise to refresh her memory. Take one trick at a time. You might never get to the stage of getting her to sit, lie down, give a paw, wave, jump through a hoop, or retrieve a toy just by using command words (some lures may still be needed), but that's not important. As long as you have fun together, who cares?

Part 9
Breeding Cats

Chapter 23

Coming Of Age

A cat can reach sexual maturity between five months and eight months of age, according to the individual and the breed. Oriental breeds can mature as early as four months, whereas Persians are generally late developers. Sexual maturity in mixed-breed cats is linked to the animal's weight. A queen will generally come into season when she weighs around 5lbs (2.3kgs), and a male will hit maturity around 7lbs (2.5kgs). This is only a guide; do not think your cat cannot reproduce because he or she is lighter than these weights – always be safe, not sorry and get your cat neutered.

It is remarkable that a cat who has just finished teething (sometimes *still* teething) is physically equipped to produce kittens when she is still very much one herself. Do not overlook your cat's sexual development, or you could end up with a house full of kittens. Neutering before your cat reaches adulthood is *always* the best option (page 176).

PHYSICAL CHANGES
- An adolescent kitten will be around three-quarters the size of an adult cat.
- A male (tom) will start to grow a thicker coat around his 'mane'/neck area.
- His skin will also thicken to protect him in territorial disputes with other toms. When vaccinating or microchipping unneutered males, or those that have been 'fixed' after sexual maturity, a vet may find it a little more difficult to pierce the skin.
- The tom will develop penile barbs (page 183), large jowls, and his scent gland at the base of his tail will become more active (so-called stud tail – pages 130-131). All these can be prevented through neutering.

BEHAVIORAL CHANGES
- A tom that is on the cusp of sexual maturity may start to grab any entire female cats in the household by the scruff of the neck. This means he is about to mate her (or is practicing how to do so), and you should immediately separate him from any females and make an urgent appointment to have him neutered!

- Sexually active cats will spray in the house – and the smell is appalling. Being mixed with hormonal messages to other cats, it is very strong and is difficult to remove.
- Spraying isn't limited to males. Queens will spray just before and during a season – it is a kind of feline advertisement of her availability to any toms in the vicinity.
- Toms will hump blankets and anything else they can lay their paws on. Fleecy veterinary bedding is a particular favorite!
- Entire (unaltered/unneutered) cats are more independent. They are utterly focused on sex, and so are less in tune with, or affectionate towards, people.
- Toms will be more aggressive with other unneutered males.
- Toms and queens roam in search of mates. This can result in them being lost for days, or even being involved in car accidents (when they follow a scent, they do not concentrate on what is going on around them).

PREVENTION IS BETTER THAN CURE

Many health problems can be prevented by neutering (altering) your cat. Entire toms are prone to abscesses, caused through fighting with other males, they are more susceptible to diseases such as feline leukemia and FIV (feline immuno-deficiency virus – feline AIDS) through sustaining bites and scratches, as well as other diseases (as can females). Neutered cats generally live longer than their entire counterparts because they are less likely to contract life-threatening diseases, and have reduced chances of being involved in a car accident through roaming.

"Cats mean kittens, plentiful and frequent."

Doris Lessing

Sexually-motivated behavioral problems are much more difficult to cure once they are established and are also best prevented through neutering. For example, an adult cat that is used to spraying in the house may continue to do so even after he has been neutered because the behavior has become habitual. The same applies to humping – the cat may routinely simulate sex even though he won't exactly know why he's doing it anymore!

Toms neutered after sexual maturity can continue to show aggression to other males. Again, the hormonal cause will have been removed, but their aggressive behavior, reinforced over months or years, becomes fixed in their brains and they cannot break their routine.

Do the smart thing and get your puss neutered before these problems take hold.

NEUTERING

Professional breeders and exhibitors excepted, breeding is the last thought in our minds when we acquire a cat. Nonetheless, we have to think about the subject. Cats, depending upon their breed or type, can become sexually mature from as early as 14 weeks and then are capable of breeding and producing kittens themselves.

Cat sanctuaries and rescue homes worldwide continually struggle with the problem created by the sheer number of unwanted cats and kittens. Indiscriminate breeding is the main reason, so it is part of our responsibility as cat owners to avoid it. Cats are not small dogs and no matter how vigilant, if your cat goes outside at all, and is unneutered, mating is likely to take place.

THE FEMALE

Female cats (queens), like dogs, will only allow mating when they are in estrus (heat) which is when they are said to be 'calling.' Ovulation occurs in the cat under the stimulus of mating. Once sexual maturity is reached, the average cat will call typically about every three weeks. However, this is variable. With some of the Oriental breeds, calling can be an almost continuous affair until the cat is mated. Even indoor cats can be a problem when calling, since, as the name suggests, it can be a noisy affair! They are frequently more interested in sex than eating and so will commonly lose condition.

There are other disadvantages. A cat in continuous call, as it is known, sometimes suffers serious hormonal imbalance which, in turn, can result in more chronic problems. These situations do not occur in nature since, once sexual maturity is reached, the female cat rapidly becomes pregnant and will have repeated litters throughout her life. In the case of the pet cat, this shortens the mother's life and increases the already difficult problem of securing suitable homes for a seemingly endless supply of kittens.

If you are lucky, you may not have such a highly-sexed female but cats are seasonally polyestrous – most will call from spring until autumn/fall on an approximate three-week cycle.

THE MALE

Remember: it takes two to make a bargain! The male cat has a part to play in the equation. Cats, males in particular, are territorial and will mark their territory by urine-spraying. Unaltered – entire – male cats try to exert much larger territorial rights than their altered brethren. They are therefore much more likely to be challenged, particularly in urban and suburban environments, by other males. Fighting becomes synonymous with entirety in the uncastrated male cat!

ENTIRE MALES AND FIGHTING TOMS

We are all aware of these terms. In the male cat, however well house-trained, once his sexual urge has been awakened, urine-spraying will not only be confined to the cat's perceived territory outdoors, urine-spraying on furnishings is considered fair game and all that is needed is the scent of a calling queen to trigger the reaction.

The establishment of territorial rights and concomitant challenge puts the uncastrated male at a very much higher risk of contracting serious feline infectious diseases. Feline immuno-deficiency virus (feline AIDS) and feline leukemia virus are but two examples which are transmitted through cat bites.

These diseases apart, simple cat bites and scratches can be dangerous. Cats' claws and teeth are potent weapons, sharp and penetrating. Cats' skin is pliable and quick-healing. During a fight in which the skin is punctured, be it by claw or tooth, it heals over leaving infection within. The result is sepsis and abscess production. A sudden large swelling appears which may or may not burst of its own accord to reveal an unpleasant septic wound. The result: a sick cat, and concomitant veterinary fees.

BENEFITS

As shown, both male and female cats clearly benefit from being neutered (altered). It has been shown that altering (de-sexing) leads to a well-balanced, less temperamental animal. With some behavioral abnormalities it is advocated in order to prevent problems, e.g. feline aggression.

DISADVANTAGES

As a veterinarian, I understand the objections made by certain people with the undoubted welfare of the cats at heart. They feel that altering (neutering) is a mutilative operation and should be discouraged. My view is broader: perhaps in such circumstances we should consider not keeping our feline friends as pets at all? If this were the case, we would be deprived, and I think we would deprive our feline charges, of pleasure and, as far as the cats are concerned, a significantly longer and hopefully disease-free life than they would enjoy in the natural environment.

THE FINAL INDIGNITY!
A GINGER TOM FIRING BLANKS!

Are there other disadvantages? Mention was made of the hormonal imbalance that can occur in the queen as a result of continuous calling without a pregnancy. This can lead to anemia and to serious problems affecting the female reproductive system, e.g. pyometra, a uterine discharge. Diseases of the womb and ovaries, and breast cancer, all have been shown to be significantly reduced as a result of early neutering.

In the past, it has been suggested that all female cats should be allowed to have at least one litter of kittens. Scientific investigation however has shown that this is totally unnecessary and carries no benefit whatsoever to the cat. It is for this reason that veterinarians are largely agreed that it is preferable to have the female cat spayed before she reaches sexual maturity. Recent work has shown that this can be done much earlier than previously thought.

In the male, altering has few disadvantages. Concerns are voiced that it leads to obesity and to lazy, characterless cats, no matter whether male or female. This is not borne out by scientific investigation. It can be said that altering does not affect appetite whereas it does affect activity levels so that the altered cat is more home-loving and less liable to wander in search of sexual satisfaction. Both the search and the goal are energy-consuming and thus, with the urge removed, food intake clearly has to be monitored and reduced if necessary. Today, with balanced commercial diets, this is not difficult.

What about lack of character? My personal view is that this is inextricably connected with obesity levels. Experience gained in forty years of clinical practice leads me to believe that the seriously obese cat really only wants to be left alone. My objective view has always been that these unfortunate individuals are no different from cats with other chronic diseases. They do not express their true characters. This I do not blame directly on de-sexing but on malnutrition in the form of excess food consumed.

OPERATION RISKS

In both the male and the female, altering involves major surgery. A general anesthetic is required irrespective of sex. Tremendous strides in feline anaesthesia have been made and, although it would be foolhardy for me to say that the procedure was risk free, nonetheless risks are very minimal and are far outweighed by the advantages already outlined.

Prior to the general anaesthetic and surgery, the kitten or cat must be healthy and the stomach must be empty. Therefore, food but not water is withheld overnight before the operation.

THE OPERATION

In the male, de-sexing involves removal of both testes and this is performed by an incision into the scrotum. In the female, the ovaries and usually, but not always, the uterus (womb) are removed. This is a slightly more involved procedure.

It should be remembered that altering is the most common operation performed by veterinarians. It carries little risk and this is further lessened when the organs involved are themselves immature. Hence, within reason, the younger the animal when the operation is performed, the quicker the recovery.

This used to be offset by the increased risk of anaesthetic in the immature animal. Today, modern anesthetics can be used on very young animals with no increased risk.

It is for this reason that, particularly in North America, there has been a move towards ever earlier neutering of cats. This is of particular advantage for kittens in rescue. Often the queen is taken in pregnant. In the past, in order to minimize the problem of subsequent unwanted litters from her offspring, rescue organizations have offered all sorts of inducements to encourage new owners to seek early neutering. Unfortunately, owners do not always conform. Rescue organizations all have experience of kittens released to ostensibly perfect homes only to have to accept the next generation of unwanted kittens in all too short a time!

Today, with neutering programs in place from as early as 8-10 weeks, these problems have been considerably minimized.

Chapter 24

Breeding
A Litter

If you are thinking of breeding a litter, please don't. There are far too many unwanted cats already, without bringing more into the world. Even if you have good homes lined up, surely these people would be better off with a homeless cat or kitten that is in a shelter?

Every year, thousands of perfectly healthy cats are euthanased simply because there are not enough good homes to go round. If you love cats, please, please, please, don't breed.

If you have a purebred cat, it is best to leave breeding to the experts. It really isn't as simple as choosing a handsome tom of the same breed and letting nature take its course. You can do irreparable damage to a breed by dabbling in things that you do not fully understand. For example, with the Manx breed, mating a tailless cat to a tailless cat can result in very sick kittens, with serious genetic deformities, that will have to be euthanased. The same applies to the Scottish Fold, where cats with folded ears should always be matched to a cat with unfolded ones. Don't experiment with kittens' lives – leave breeding to the experts.

If you want to breed from your cat because you love her and want to continue to have a part of her after she is gone, please reconsider. If you would like to honor your cat, then do the decent thing and get her spayed. Her life will be happier and simpler, she will be healthier and live longer, and you can give a home to a cat that really needs one instead of adding to the cat population problem. And remember – it is a common myth that it is healthier for a cat to be spayed after she has had one litter. (See Chapter Twenty-three.)

If you really want to experience the joy of witnessing a cat birth and of caring for newborn kittens (and it really isn't easy), then why not volunteer your services at your local animal shelter? Foster carers who have the time to cope with a mother and a new litter are in high demand, and your help will be much appreciated, particularly in the summer months when shelters can be overrun in the breeding season.

PLANNING A LITTER

If you are determined to breed a litter, then please talk to the breeder of your own cat. He or she will know your cat's family history and will be able to give you an honest assessment as to whether she should be bred from.

If she is not suitable, then do not breed from her. Breeding should only be done for the future of the breed; only the very best specimens should be used to improve the quality of each generation. Your cat might be the most beautiful creature in the world in your opinion, but if she is not a good example of the breed in the eyes of a show judge, then you could damage the breed by introducing kittens that are far from perfect examples.

If the breeder considers that your queen is suitable, then he or she will recommend a stud that will complement your cat's characteristics. As well as being an experienced stud, from a reputable line that is free of hereditary defects, he should be healthy, fully vaccinated, and have a wonderful temperament (kittens inherit much of their personalities from the dad).

Once you've found a good stud, you must agree the details of the arrangement with his owner. Draw up a contract as to what is agreed – for example, the fee, whether a second mating will be included in the price if the first is unsuccessful, whether the owner requires a pick of the litter, etc. Get it all down on paper, and make sure you both sign. This way, there is no room for confusion or misunderstanding later on.

THE RIGHT TIME

A queen will come into season throughout the year (generally from the end of December to the beginning of September), though, with our rising climate temperatures, this is changing. The queen's seasons are linked to day-length. Her body will come into season to coincide with longer days, thereby avoiding the coldest months of the year which are not ideal for raising kittens. House-cats, exposed to artificial light all year round, can have seasons all year through.

Each season lasts around three weeks. Symptoms include:

- Loud, persistent crying (and I *mean* persistent!)
- Frequent licking of her genitals
- Restless behavior
- Rolling around (usually by the front or back door)
- Erratic moods – oscillating between extreme affection and bad temper (through the frustration of not being allowed out)
- A choir of male cats on your doorstep, probably peeing all outside your house to tempt your queen to them
- Your own female may also urinate, to tell other cats in the neighborhood that she's ready for motherhood!

These symptoms are only guides and there are always exceptions. For example, the Russian Blue is generally not as noisy as the queens of other breeds when in season. If you do not wish to breed from your cat, but have kept her entire, the only way to ensure she cannot become pregnant is to have her spayed. Even if you notice she in season, you will have a terrible job trying to keep her indoors – cats that want sex are extremely cunning, and often get the better of their owners.

CAT COURTSHIP

When your queen is exhibiting the signs that she is in season, contact the owner of the stud to arrange a mating. Often, the owner will keep your cat for several days. Take along your cat's food, together with details of her pedigree and vaccinations.

Your cat is likely to be kept in a specially-designed pen, which has a connecting door to the tom's accommodation. Supervised introductions will take place and the owner will judge when mating should take place according to your queen's reactions. The cats should be kept apart at all other times. Mating can be a vicious business and misjudging the queen's state of readiness can result in two injured cats.

When she is ready to receive the male, the queen will lift her tail high, and raise her hindquarters in the air. The male will sniff her, bite the scruff of the neck and mount her. No flowers, chocolates or poetry – just brutal action. The male grabs the female's neck to make her freeze (page 186). This is because he would otherwise get attacked. Sex is far from enjoyable for a queen – in fact, it is incredibly painful. When the male withdraws, his penile barbs will scrape the female, causing her to cry out and swipe him. It also induces ovulation.

After mating, the female must be kept away from all other males as she is able to be mated again – in fact a litter of kittens can have different fathers. Obviously, in a purebred cat, this situation is not acceptable, as the kittens' parentage would be unknown. With an unsupervised mating (for example, if your queen manages to get out of the house), the males will all fight amongst themselves to defend the queen from other suitors or to get a piece of the action. Injuries can be serious – abscesses and scratches (which can transfer serious diseases) are common.

PREGNANCY

The average gestation time is 63 days, though it can vary from 59 to 71 days. It is not easy to detect if your cat is pregnant until she reaches five to six weeks, at which time her tummy will be slightly larger, and her nipples will become more pink and prominent. Around this time, she will eat more. The best guide is to give her as much food as she wants.

As soon as you suspect your cat is pregnant, you should get her checked over by your veterinarian. He or she will answer any questions you have about the pregnancy and birth, and will also give you details of when the mother should be wormed.

Great care should be taken when handling your cat. You must hold her gently, and support her abdomen if you lift her. No other changes need be made to her lifestyle. Nature will take over and your cat will do as little or as much as she wants.

By the time she is eight to nine weeks pregnant, you will be able to see the kittens moving inside her, and she will be eating around double the amount that she usually consumes.

PREPARATION

Around three weeks before the expected birth, prepare four or five cardboard boxes. The top of the box should be open, and the front should be cut away for your cat to enter her 'nest'. Leave a couple of inches at the bottom of this 'door' side of the box so any subsequent kittens cannot fall out of the box. Mum should be able to step over it with ease. Place some blankets in each box.

Place these boxes in different locations around the house. Choose warm, quiet spots and mum should show a preference for one of these boxes, especially towards the last week of her pregnancy. The other boxes can then be removed. It is important to offer her a suitable location as her nesting place, as otherwise she will choose her own – underneath the bath, in your bed, or even outside. Once she's picked a spot, it can be very difficult to persuade her to change her mind.

Place mum's feeding and water bowls, and litter-tray, in the same room as her chosen box, and, when the birth is imminent, replace the blanket with shredded newspaper. It is absorbent, warm, and easily replaced. Blankets are not recommended. They can easily get messed up, and a kitten can get lost in their folds and may suffocate.

Boil some cotton thread to sterilize it in case it is needed in the birth, and do the same with some sharp scissors. Stock up on newspapers to replace the bedding regularly, and have your vet's number by the phone in case of emergencies.

Once all the preparations are made, it's a case of waiting for nature to take its course.

THE BIRTH

When your cat is about to go into labor, she will appear restless and may scrabble at her bedding to make a suitable nest. A sure-fire sign is that her temperature will drop to 37.8 degrees C. You may be able to see her abdomen contracting, vaginal discharge may be present, and she will probably start purring (cats purr from pain as well as pleasure). Don't panic or fuss around her. Remain calm, stay close by, reassure her – and let her get on with it.

WILD KITS
Wildcats generally have much smaller litters than their domestic counterparts, producing only a couple of kittens each time, rather than the pet cat's four to six kittens per litter.

The first kitten will be born within about half an hour. She should arrive head first, but up to a third of kittens are breech births, meaning they are born feet first. If mum is having trouble getting her out, or if the head gets stuck, you may have to intervene, gently encouraging the kitten out.

As soon as the kitten arrives, give her to mum, who will break the sac in which the kitten is born, lick around the mouth and nose, and then wash the kitten vigorously to encourage the kitten to breathe.

Mum will bite through the umbilical cord too, and will move the kitten to one of her teats to feed. This first milk (known as colostrum) is rich in antibodies that will give early natural protection to the kitten against disease.

KITTENS GALORE
Dusty, a cat from Texas, gave birth to 420 kittens in her lifetime. The last litter was born in 1952, when Dusty was 18 years old.

Mum may eat the afterbirth, which will follow each kitten. This is perfectly natural, giving her lots of nutrients and energy, which she will need – labor is a tiring business. If she eats too many, she may develop an upset tummy, so you might want to remove the afterbirths after she has had a couple.

Keep a count of the afterbirths. They should correspond to the number of kittens born. If they do not, then mum may have retained one or more, and the veterinarian should be contacted to remove them (left inside, they will cause internal infections).

Subsequent kittens will be born every 10 minutes to an hour. If mum is straining for longer than an hour and no kittens appear, then contact your veterinarian, as she may need a Cesarean.

Keep an eye on the kittens to ensure they are all feeding successfully. If a teat does not appear to be working, mum may have an infection, which will need to be treated by a veterinarian.

WHEN TO INTERFERE

If mum doesn't show any interest in the kitten (which is unlikely), you will have to remove the sac around the kitten's face, drying around the mouth and nose. Check the mouth is free of obstruction.

Tie a piece of sterilized cotton (page 184) around the umbilical cord about three inches from the abdomen, and then use the sterilized scissors (page 184) to cut the cord about an inch from the cotton knot (away from the kitten).

Then hold the kitten upside-down and bring your arms down quickly, as if you are dropping the kitten towards the floor. This should release any obstruction in her airways and encourage the kitten to breathe. Then rub her body quite roughly with a dry towel.

If you get into any difficulties, contact your veterinarian at once.

AFTER-CARE

Once all the kittens have been born, and are all feeding successfully, take some food and water to mum. She is unlikely to want to leave the kittens to feed and water herself, and may welcome some refreshment. Do not be concerned if she doesn't want to eat or drink – just take her bowls away and try again a little later. When she is suckling, mum will need to drink plenty of fluids in order to keep up her milk production so do make sure plenty of fresh water is available to her.

It is a good idea to occasionally lift mum out of the box and to take her to the litter-tray nearby, in case she needs to relieve herself. As the kittens grow, mum will become a little more independent and will leave them for short periods to have some food and to use her litter-tray.

Contact your veterinarian once the litter has been born. He or she will need to check the kittens over, discuss worming with you, and give mum a once-over too.

CAT TALES
Tarawood Antigone, a purebred Burmese from Oxfordshire, England, holds the record for producing the largest litter – an eye-watering 19 kittens, born in 1970.

REARING

Mum will pretty much take care of her babies until they are around four weeks old. She will move them by carrying them in her mouth by the scruff of their necks. This is why cats will instinctively freeze if scruffed – in the wild, mum would have moved the kittens away from danger and a struggling kitten would have been in great peril.

Mum will lick their bottoms to encourage them to relieve themselves, and her milk will be all the kittens need in the way of nourishment. During this time, spend time sitting with the litter, talking to them and stroking them. It is important that they get used to the sounds, sights and smells of humans as soon as their senses start working, to help with their socialization.

Make sure the box is clean. Change the shredded newspaper regularly, and replace the box altogether if it is dirty – do keep it in the same location though. Keep an eye on all the kittens to ensure they are all feeding well and growing at the same rate.

When they are about a month old, the kittens should be weaned on to a good-quality kitten food. Mum will gradually allow them to suckle less. If she is very tolerant, and is still letting them suckle at six to seven weeks, discourage them from the teat and point them in the direction of the kitten food.

You should start litter-training the kittens around five weeks of age. They will probably watch mum and take their direction from her. Help by putting the kittens in the tray one at a time and encouraging them to dig.

When the kittens are old enough to move around, play with them as much as you can (as if you need any encouragement!). It is not only enjoyable for you and them, but helps them to learn, and to interact with other cats and humans.

By the time the kittens are eight weeks old, they can cope without mum and can be placed in new homes (although pedigree kittens should not leave until around 12 weeks – see page 52).

HAND-REARING

If there are complications and mum rejects the kittens (or one kitten in particular), or if they are orphaned, then you will have to become their surrogate mum.

Talk to your veterinarian, who will recommend a suitable milk substitute. This will need to be syringe-fed to the kittens every four hours – day and night. Your veterinarian will be able to supply you with a (needle-less) syringe. Kittens are born with an instinct to suck anything that is near to their mouth, so it should be fairly straightforward to get them to feed.

Around two weeks of age, the feeds can be reduced to every six hours, and at three weeks you can start to encourage them to lap the milk from a saucer. This is a very messy time. Some kittens just don't understand the lapping thing, and seem to think that the best way of getting the milk is by rolling in it and then washing it off themselves!

FOSTER CARE
Female cats have fostered many types of orphaned animals – including those that they usually eat! Rabbits, squirrels, rats, mice, and even ducks, have all been adopted by queens.

KITTEN DEVELOPMENT

- *Kittens are quite helpless when they are born – they are blind, deaf, and can barely move more than a couple of inches.*
- *Their eyes will open between five and eight days (though longhairs often need a couple more days). All kittens have sapphire-blue eyes.*
- *By three weeks of age, they will start to smell and hear (their ears will become erect, having previously been flat on the head), and their eye colour will begin to emerge. At this age, their teeth will also start to grow through and they will begin to purr.*
- *Between three and four weeks of age, the kittens will become more mobile – though they will wobble and fall over a lot!*
- *At four to five weeks, their tails will become more animated.*
- *By five weeks, they will be grooming themselves – and each other.*
- *By six to seven weeks old, they will become increasingly playful and adventurous – until, by the time they leave, you will be glad to see the back of them!*

Up to three weeks of age, you should wipe the kittens' tummies and bottoms with moist cotton pads, to encourage them to urinate and defecate. This should be done after every feed.

Because the kittens cannot rely on their natural mother to keep them warm, you should install a heat lamp over their nesting box to keep them warm. Make sure it is not too hot, however, as the kittens will not be able to move away from the heat if they find it uncomfortable.

Heat pads (page 147) or hot-water bottles can also be used, but they should be wrapped well in towels to ensure they cannot burn the kittens.

Hand-reared kittens can develop behavioral problems later in life, so it is worth talking to a behavior counselor for advice.

SEXING

Lift up the kitten's tail and examine the anus and genitals. In a male kitten, the rear looks like a colon (:) two holes above one another. In a female, it looks more like the letter i. The anus and genitals in a male are further apart than in a female (the space in between is where the male's testicles will grow). It is often much easier to identify each sex through comparison with other kittens in the litter. If in doubt, your veterinarian will be able to confirm the sex of each kitten.

FINDING HOMES

If the litter is planned, you should have suitable homes lined up even before the mating. If it is an accidental litter, you should start looking for homes as soon as the pregnancy has been confirmed.

Put the word about to all friends, colleagues and family. Contact your local animal shelter – do they know people who are waiting for a kitten? Advertise in your local paper and/or the cat press.

Once you have found people interested in taking the kittens, you should check them out thoroughly. You are responsible for bringing the kittens into the world, and you should make sure they are going to have the best life possible.

- Where does the person live? Is it a safe area for the cat?
- Do they have experience of looking after cats?
- Why do they want a cat?
- What other pets do they have?
- Do they have very young children?
- Can they afford a cat?
- Will they promise to have the cat neutered?
- If they have had pets before, what veterinary practice have they used? (You should contact the veterinary surgery to take up any references.)

TOP TIP

Remember: mum can become pregnant again four to six weeks after the litter is born (sometimes she is pregnant with a second litter while suckling the first). Keep her indoors so she cannot mate again, and seriously consider having her neutered. If you are adamant that she should remain entire, do not let her breed every season – it is not healthy for her or for her kittens.

- How often do they go away? Who will look after the cat while they are on holiday?
- What are their working hours?
- Always perform a home-check. What is the traffic like in the area? Are the children well behaved? If they have a dog, is it under control? Is it used to cats?

If you have any doubts about someone, do not let them have one of the kittens – you will have to keep it.

When it is time to let the kittens leave, write down everything the new owner will need to know. What food to give, how much and how often, details of worming treatments the kittens have received, any vaccinations they have had, what type of cat-litter you use, etc. Ask the owners to contact you if they have any queries, and make sure you call them to check how the kittens are settling in.

Part 10
Health Care

Chapter 25

Basic
Anatomy

Like humans, cats are mammals. They give birth to live young, which they suckle on milk and care for until the young have learnt to look after themselves. Like most mammals, they have fur.

Cats are predators (meat-eaters), feeding mainly on small mammals and birds if left to fend for themselves. Their bodies are beautifully designed for the purpose of hunting. They have lithe, agile bodies full of grace, which help them to be very successful killers (see Chapter Two).

SKELETAL STRUCTURE AND LOCOMOTION

The skeleton comprises the bones of the body. It supports the body, protects important, delicate organs, and allows movement at specialized areas, through flexible joints.

The main bones that support the body are the spine and the bones of the front and back legs. The pelvis connects the hindlegs to the spine.

Bones that protect organs include:

- The skull, which protects the brain and also houses most of the sensory organs
- The ribs, which form a cage round the heart, lungs and liver
- The vertebrae (the bones that make up the spine) have a channel through them which contains the spinal cord (the bundle of nerves going to various parts of the body)
- The pelvis, which protects organs at the hind end of the abdomen.

Cats have about the same number of bones as humans but they may be very differently shaped (which is why cats do not look like mini-people). They also have the same sort of joints as humans, but, with their very different shape, they have varying amounts of movement within their joints as compared to humans.

Cats have a strong, light skeleton with a very flexible spine which allows for fast movement and agility for climbing and jumping. The joints, as well as allowing

CAT OWNER'S SURVIVAL MANUAL

movement, help the limbs to act as shock absorbers when jumping down from heights. A cat's long tail helps with balance when climbing, jumping and walking along structures such as the garden fence. Cats also use their tails for communicating; being friendly and sticking it straight up in the air, and moving it from side to side when unsure or agitated.

Other important functions of the long bones are the production of blood cells within the bone marrow and to provide a store of minerals, such as calcium and phosphorus.

LOCOMOTION

Locomotion or movement is achieved by having muscles attached to bones across joints so that, when the muscles contract, the bones move relative to one another at the joint. Muscles are often in pairs. For example, in the limbs, contraction of the muscles on one side of the bones leads to flexion of the limb, and contraction of the muscles on the other side leads to extension of the limb.

Muscles do all the work of moving the body; cats are very powerful creatures for their size – consider how high they can jump: much higher than a human could jump relative to size. Much of this power comes from the strong hind limb muscles and the muscles which attach the hind limbs to the pelvis.

THE MAJOR BODY SYSTEMS

THE SKIN

The main function of the skin is one of protection. It protects the other tissues of the body from water loss, infections and damage. A cat's skin is very loosely attached to the underlying tissue, allowing for her flexibility of movement.

Cat skin is covered in fur. It helps to conserve warmth by trapping warm air next to the body. Fur has a defensive role, as cats can erect the hairs of their coats when they are frightened. This makes them look bigger to other animals.

The coat also plays a role in camouflage, allowing cats to creep through undergrowth unseen, keeping them safe from larger animals that might attack them, and enabling them to get near to their prey unseen. The original wild coat color was probably tabby; nowadays through selective breeding by humans we have cats of many different beautiful colors and coat patterns.

There are a number of specialized structures which have developed from skin and or hairs:

- **Claws**: cats have developed sharp claws instead of nails. They are able to retract them (except for cheetahs) so that they can keep them very sharp, and, unlike dogs, do not wear them down when walking. Such sharp, pointed nails make excellent weapons for defense and attack. See also pages 123-124.

- **Feet pads**: the pads on the feet of cats are made of thickened skin. They provide a tough surface to walk on, are spongy so help act as shock absorbers when the cat is jumping, and help the cat to move silently.
- **Whiskers**: the cat's whiskers and the hairs they have above their eyes and on their front legs are long and very sensitive. They help cats find their way around through thick vegetation and in the dark by their sense of touch.
- **Pherephores**: these are glands on the face which produce pheromones (see the section on smell, page 197.)
- **Anal sacs**: there are two anal sacs either side of the anus. They contain glands which produce highly-smelling fluid containing pheromones and used in marking.

THE RESPIRATORY SYSTEM

The respiratory system is responsible for warming, humidifying and filtering air, and transporting it inside the body so that gases can be exchanged. Oxygen is taken from the air for the body's cells to use and carbon dioxide is expelled from the body. The respiratory tract consists of the nostrils, nose, pharynx, larynx, trachea, bronchi, bronchioles and lung alveoli.

- The **lungs** consist of alveoli and the airways and blood vessels which supply them.
- The **nose** functions for smell, to warm and moisten air before it goes down into the body, and to filter out large particles in the air.
- The **pharynx** is where the nose opens into the back of the mouth.
- The **larynx** is the opening to the respiratory airways and contains the vocal cords which make miaowing and purring noises.
- The **trachea** or windpipe is the longest airway; it runs in the neck and the chest where it divides into smaller and smaller airways which end in the alveoli.
- The **alveoli** are where oxygen is taken up and carbon dioxide expelled from the body.

THE CARDIOVASCULAR SYSTEM

The cardiovascular system consists of the heart, arteries, veins and smaller blood vessels. The heart is a four-chambered organ that acts like a large pump to push blood around the body. Arteries are blood vessels carrying blood from the heart to the body organs and tissues. Veins are vessels which carry blood back from the tissues to the heart. Within tissues, arteries branch into very small blood vessels called capillaries which join together again and flow into veins.

Blood is needed by all tissues; some need a larger supply than others. It has several functions: it contains red blood cells which carry oxygen from the lungs to the tissues and white blood cells which detect and fight off diseases. Platelets are involved with blood clotting. Blood carries food molecules and hormones around the body and waste products to the lungs, kidneys or liver. It is also involved in the body's heat control.

THE DIGESTIVE SYSTEM

The digestive system is the part of the body that enables food to be taken in and converted into molecules small enough to be used by the body as energy. It then expels left-over food and some waste products produced by the body.

It consists of the mouth, esophagus, stomach, small and large intestines (bowels) and anus.

Other organs which are closely associated with the digestive system include the salivary glands, the liver and the pancreas.

- The **mouth** contains the tongue which manipulates and swallows food, and the teeth which help with catching food and cutting it up. A cat's teeth are designed for her carnivorous lifestyle. She only has 30 teeth; the incisors are very small and do very little; the canines are large and sharp, and are used for catching, holding and killing prey (also fighting); the premolars and molars are designed for cutting meat into suitable pieces for swallowing.
- The **esophagus** is the tube from the mouth to the stomach.
- The **stomach** is a sac-like structure where food is stored and digestion starts. It produces enzymes and acid which help in the digestion process. The remainder of digestion occurs in the **small intestine**, helped by substances in pancreatic juice and bile. The digested food is then absorbed into the body, also in the small bowel.
- The **large intestine** removes water from the remaining gut contents. They are then stored in the rectum until they are expelled from the body.
- The **pancreas** produces enzymes which help with digestion. (It is also an endocrine organ producing insulin – see page 195.) The **liver** has many functions, including metabolizing drugs, hormones and food molecules into useable forms, and collecting waste products which it expels via bile into the gut.

THE URINARY SYSTEM

The urinary system consists of two kidneys, two ureters, a bladder and urethra. The kidneys control water and salt loss from the body, and excrete waste products (an important one is urea from the breakdown of protein).

Cat kidneys are designed to cope with a lot of urea due to the all-meat feline diet. They also are capable of producing highly concentrated urine so that body water can be conserved. Thus they need to drink relatively little.

The ureters are the tubes that go from the kidneys to the bladder where urine is stored until being expelled.

The urethra is the tube from the bladder to the outside. In male cats, it is long and thin and can easily get blocked with crystals or cellular material. In females, it is shorter and wider.

Cats also use chemicals in their urine to communicate with each other.

THE REPRODUCTIVE SYSTEM

The female reproductive tract consists of two ovaries, which produce eggs and hormones; two fallopian tubes, which carry eggs to the uterus; a uterus, which consists of two long horns which can carry several fetuses at any one time; a cervix, vagina and vulva.

Male cats have two testicles located just below the anus, two vas deferens (tubes from the testicle to the urethra), a small prostate gland and a penis which is small and backward pointing. The penis contains a small bone and is barbed in mature, uncastrated males.

See page 188 on sexing kittens.

THE NERVOUS SYSTEM

The central nervous system comprises the brain and spinal cord, the peripheral nerves which take information (such as sensation and pain) to the brain, and motor nerves which take messages from the brain to the muscles and organs helping in their control. The brain controls all conscious thought and actions, as well as some unconscious body processes and reflexes, such as breathing and body temperature control.

THE ENDOCRINE SYSTEM

The endocrine system is part of the regulatory system of the body. It consists of a number of glands that produce hormones. Hormones act as chemical messengers travelling in the blood from the gland to other tissues or organs and causing them to do something.

- **Thyroid glands**: these two glands, found in the neck, produce thyroxine, which controls metabolic rate and has effects on many different body parts. Hyperthyroidism or an overactive thyroid gland is common in older cats. Hypothyroidism, an under-active thyroid gland is rare in cats.
- **Parathyroid glands**: these are smaller structures found next to the thyroid glands in the neck. They produce parathormone, which helps regulate calcium and phosphorus levels in the body.
- **Pancreas**: this is situated near the liver and next to the first part of the small intestine. It produces insulin, the hormone which controls glucose levels. Insulin ensures that glucose gets into cells where it is the main energy source.
- **Ovaries**: these produce hormones such as estrogen and progesterone that help to control the female reproductive cycle.
- **Testicles**: these produce testosterone which controls the production of sperm and the development of secondary sexual characteristics, such as the thick skin around the neck and wide faces of mature, male cats. They also affect adult male cat behavior, leading to wandering and increased aggression towards other cats, see Chapter Twenty-three.

- **Pituitary gland**: this small gland at the base of the brain produces hormones that control all the other glands mentioned in this section (apart from the pancreas). It tells the glands which hormone to produce and when. It also produces a few hormones that have direct effects on non-glandular tissues.
- **Adrenal glands**: there is an adrenal gland just in front of each kidney. They produce steroid hormones. Glucocorticoids are produced mainly in response to stress and help the body cope. They have effects on many tissues. Mineralocorticoids help with salt balance in the body and maintaining body mass. A small amount of the sex hormones are also produced by the adrenal glands.

THE SENSES

SIGHT

Sight is achieved by the eye and the brain working rather like a camera, on the retina. Light enters through the cornea at the front of the eye. Some light is allowed through the hole in the center of the iris (the pupil) which controls the quantity getting to the back of the eye. Light then passes through the lens which focuses it on to the retina. The retina transforms light into nerve impulses which the brain then interprets.

Cats have eyes that are similar to humans, but there are a few differences:

- Cats' eyes are relatively large, as sight is a very important sense to them, and the eyes are situated at the front of the skull, pointing forward, giving cats excellent binocular vision. This enables cats to judge distances very well – an essential asset for hunting.
- They have a third eyelid (the nictitating membrane) which appears sometimes from the inner corner of the eye. It provides an extra protective layer, and can protrude when cats are unwell.
- The pupil shape in cats is different from humans – it is a vertical ellipse, going down to a slit in bright light.
- There is a reflective layer called the tapetum in the retina. It helps the eye to catch all available light and helps to ensure cats have very good eyesight, particularly at night. This layer is what makes cats' eyes shine in the dark.

HEARING

The ears have two functions: hearing and balance. Cats have large ear pinnae which are very mobile so they can pick up small sounds from many directions. When hunting, they can pinpoint sounds and hear many that are too faint or high-pitched for humans to hear.

The ear pinnae act as a funnel, collecting and channeling sound down the ear canal. At the end of the ear canal is the ear drum, a thin membrane which vibrates with sound. This vibration then moves the three tiny bones within the ear, and their movement in turn stimulates nerves in a structure called the cochlea. The cochlea sends impulses to the brain for it to interpret.

There are also structures called the semi-circular canals, three fluid-filled channels with nerve endings in them, set in three different planes of direction, plus the saccule and utricule. They, along with the brain, are involved with balance.

SMELL

The nose is full of nerve endings which are stimulated by smells and which send messages to the brain. The sense of smell is much more important to cats than humans, and they seem largely to recognize each other by smell rather than sight. Cats also have a much more sensitive sense of smell. They often will not eat well if they cannot smell their food e.g. when they have a blocked nose due to a nasal discharge.

Cats use smells to mark their territory and to communicate with other cats. They have many facial glands which contain pheromones. Cats rub these pheromones on to objects in their homes, making them feel more secure. They also use urine which they spray on to mainly vertical surfaces to mark their territory outside (see pages 107).

TASTE

The tongue is the main structure involved with taste. As with humans, cats' tongues are covered with numerous taste buds that are also found on the palate and in the pharynx. There are four basic tastes that can be detected: sweet, sour, bitter and salty. Cats tend to prefer foods high in animal protein and fat.

TOUCH

Touch is important to cats. They have whiskers, which help them to find their way through dense vegetation and in the dark. They are also used for detecting the precise location of prey when moving in for the kill. (See also page 20.)

Chapter 26

Health Programs

Prevention is always better than cure. Feline preventative health care ranges from general strategies, such as vaccination and the control of internal and external parasites, which all cats require, to specific health concerns. White cats, for example, can sometimes be so sensitive to sunburn that skin cancers can result, particularly affecting the ear tips. Thus, it is sensible preventative health care, if you own a white cat, to ensure that access to strong sunlight is denied as much as possible and it may even be necessary to apply sunblock to the ears and nose.

Preventative health care may also be breed-specific. For example, one-third of longhaired cats worldwide are affected with a condition called polycystic kidney disease (PKD). Therefore, it is good preventative health care to ensure that tests are carried out before breeding a litter from cats at risk.

REGULAR CHECK-UPS

Regular veterinary check-ups are a vital part of preventative health care. Veterinarians world-wide are used to clients presenting a much-loved pet cat and explaining "she has never seen a vet in her life" or, "she only came for her original vaccinations".

This was once considered the sign of a strong constitution and healthy breeding. However, it is quite possible that the very condition for which the cat is now presented could well have been prevented, averted or delayed had regular health checks been carried out. Certain heart problems and chronic kidney failure are examples.

Diagnostic techniques in both human and veterinary medicine are improving all the time. Many are very successfully employed as early warning systems and so are great tools in preventative health care programs, e.g the use of ultrasound for the detection of PKD (polycystic kidney disease).

VACCINATIONS

There are a number of very serious feline diseases that can affect your cat, and some of these diseases can be fatal. Many are of viral origin and there are few drugs that fight viruses in the way that antibiotics fight bacteria. This means that all the vet can do is to treat the symptoms, minimize the suffering, and hope that natural immunity will fight off the infection.

Ensuring that your cat initially completes a course of vaccination and then receives appropriate boosters is a very important part of health care.

When visiting a vet for the first time, you are often asked very searching questions regarding source, lifestyle etc.

- Did you acquire your kitten from a pet shop, a re-homing center, a neighbor?
- Have you seen any fleas or worms?
- Have you noticed any sneezing, diarrhea, lassitude, lack of appetite?

This background is important to the veterinarian. Many pet-shop and rescue animals originate from feral colonies. These are domestic cats that have virtually returned to the wild. The popular belief is that these cats are constitutionally very robust but facts tell a very different story. Viruses such as cat flu, feline immunodeficiency virus (FIV) and feline leukemia virus (FeLV) frequently are rife, and kittens are often infected from an early age. Feline infectious enteritis (FIE), now seldom seen in pet cats in Britain and the US, is also often endemic in feral colonies.

MULTIVALENT (COMBINED) VACCINES

Vaccination of our pets has undergone a radical rethink. Vaccines have been so successful in eradicating very serious feline diseases that, gradually, more and more components have been added to the injections so that some multivalent vaccines now contain components designed to protect against up to seven diseases, all with just one jab.

Combined vaccines became popular because of convenience. One visit to the veterinarian ensures vaccination against up to seven or more separate diseases. This represents less stress for the animal (one instead of multiple jabs), and less cost and inconvenience to the owner. However, reactions may be more prevalent and this appears to be related to the number of boosters (see pages 200-201).

All of the individual antigens contained in a combined vaccine will give protection against separate diseases. Some, however, do not necessarily protect against infection. In other words, the cat may still pick up the causative agent but will not show symptoms.

Some vaccines contain killed components of the causative agent which will stimulate the cat's immunity but cannot cause disease, whereas others contain modified live virus (MLV). The causative virus is modified in such a way that it does not cause the disease, but will stimulate the cat to produce antibodies against the natural virus and so is similarly protected against the disease.

LENGTH OF IMMUNITY

Just as with human vaccines, the length of immunity varies according to the disease and the strength of the immunity. Therefore, the frequency of boosting varies according to the disease involved. Killed vaccines generally require reinoculation (boosting) more frequently than MLV (modified live virus) vaccines.

When live and killed components are all contained within one injection, the question then arises: how often do you re-inject? Historically, and perhaps arbitrarily, this has, until recently, been set annually. Over the last few years, however, it has been realized that certain components can cause reactions and sometimes, in the cat, these can be severe. This has led to a rethink in vaccination policy and a division of feline vaccines into core vaccine and non-core vaccines.

CORE AND NON-CORE VACCINES

The American Association of Feline Practitioners (AAFP) has issued guidelines on feline vaccines, and, as a result, puss's protection program has become more individual. As a result, feline vaccines are no longer routine but tailored to the cat's individual circumstances (e.g. the amount of local infection, and the cat's lifestyle).

Core vaccines are those for which routine vaccination of all cats is recommended in North America, based on the seriousness of the disease or its widescale prevalence.
- Feline panleucopaenia (FPV) – known in the UK as Feline infectious enteritis (FIE)
- Feline herpes virus (FHV)
- Feline calicivirus (FCV)
- Rabies.

In Britain, rabies vaccination is not yet regarded as a core vaccine, but may well become so as mandatory quarantine regulations in the UK are further altered.

Non-core vaccines are those that cannot routinely be justified except when there is a genuine increased risk.
- Feline immunodeficiency virus (FIV)
- Feline leukemia virus (FeLV)
- Feline coronavirus, which causes Feline Infectious Peritonitis (FIP). This vaccine is available in North America but is not licensed in the UK
- Chlamydia and ringworm vaccines are also regarded as non-core.

Cats in catteries where chlamydia infection may be rife, or re-homing centres with a problem with FIV or FeLV would be advised to have components additional to the core vaccines.

CHANGE IN VETERINARY ATTITUDES

Certain tumors have been linked to vaccination reactions in a small percentage of cats. Not all components of the vaccine cocktail are responsible. Inoculation against FeLV and rabies can result in a lump at the injection site. This can develop into a type of cancer called a vaccine-induced sarcoma, which can occur in between 1 in 1,000 and 1 in 10,000 of cats inoculated, according to figures from the States. These reactions have been reported in Britain but considerably less frequently. This may be because FeLV and rabies vaccines have been used in the US for far longer than in Britain. For example, in the UK, rabies inoculation has only routinely been used for cats intended for export; it is only more recently that it became mandatory for cats re-entering Britain under the PETS scheme.

The risks and benefits associated with core and non-core vaccine programs are probably more easily understood in the US where veterinarians often advise keeping cats indoors all the time. Then, only mandatory rabies vaccine, feline infectious enteritis and the flu vaccines are really necessary. Why, you may ask, are these essential? Without the protection of basic vaccination even cats that never go out are vulnerable, whether it be a trip to the vet or contact with infection carried by visitors.

FELINE INFECTIOUS ENTERITIS (FIE)

Also known as panleucopaenia, the vaccine for this disease is common, effective and long-lasting. It protects both against the disease and the infection.

When I first entered practice, this disease was the scourge of all cat owners. Today, the disease is relatively rare in pet cats, both in the US and in Britain. This is so particularly in urban areas where a high proportion of cats are vaccinated. In other words, the immunity it stimulates is so high that even when the cat is infected with the virus, it is swiftly killed.

CAT FLU

Cat flu vaccines are good examples of vaccines which control the disease, but they may not be totally effective against infection. Cat flu, or viral rhinitis, is caused by two main viruses: feline calicivirus (FCV) and feline herpes virus (FHV). These account for approximately 80-85 of all cases of cat flu. Other micro-organisms can also be involved, e.g. certain bacteria and chlamydia organisms, often in combination with FHV and FCV.

An up-to-date combined flu vaccination ensures that the severity of any flu attack is reduced, if not eliminated.

CHLAMYDIA

This disease can also be implicated in the cat flu syndrome. Conjunctivitis is the main sign, with ulcers and discharge from the eyes. It can be devastating in cattery situations, particularly if overcrowded, as can happen in rescue centers. Cats living on their own are at relatively low risk. It is for this reason that it is classified as 'non-core.'

FELINE LEUKEMIA (FeLV)

Discovered in 1964, this has been the cause of death in many young adult cats. Unlike panleucopaenia (FIE), which is very resistant in the environment, FeLV is a fragile virus. It cannot be transmitted on hands, bowls, grooming utensils etc, unlike the FIE virus. It is found in the saliva of infected animals, and so transmission is by direct contact between cats.

To complicate matters, not all cats infected with the virus develop the disease. However, with those that do, it is almost always fatal. Treatment is merely palliative (i.e. it prolongs the cat's life but it is not curative). The disease destroys the cat's defences against other diseases, including fatal cancers, so vaccination is important (especially in feisty/outdoor cats).

RABIES

This is a compulsory vaccine in the US. In the UK, it is compulsory for cats traveling to certain authorised countries and who wish to return to the UK without undergoing quarantine (PETS scheme).

OTHER VACCINES

Other vaccines are available in Europe and the United States, such as feline coronavirus, against feline infectious peritonitis (FIP) and also bordetella which causes coughing and flu-like signs. Feline AIDS, or, more correctly, feline immunodeficiency disease (FIV), like human AIDS, cannot currently be prevented by vaccination. Although FIV is similar to HIV in humans, be assured it cannot cause human AIDS; it is an entirely different virus.

Cats with FIV can often live happily for years, but should be in a single-cat household and should be restricted to the indoors so there is no chance of transmitting the disease to other cats.

ARE BOOSTERS REALLY NECESSARY?

It is now becoming accepted as the result of careful clinical investigation that vaccine-induced immunity may last considerably longer than 12 months for many of the diseases we vaccinate against.

Based on studies at Cornell Veterinary School, the AAFP (American Association of Feline Practitioners) has issued general guidelines on booster frequencies for flu vaccines and panleucopaenia. It is now suggested that immunity against the respiratory viruses can last for at least three years, and in excess of six years against panleucopaenia (FIE).

Current AAFP recommendations are that all kittens should be inoculated against at least the core diseases. Booster vaccinations against flu and feline enteritis may be necessary given after one year and then every three years. More frequent vaccination should be on risk assessment. For example, if you suddenly want to board your cat a year after vaccination, discussion with your veterinarian and a booster may be prudent. If in doubt, manufacturers' recommendations must be followed.

SPECIAL SITUATIONS

Reference has already been made to boarding, but there are other situations where more frequent boosting may be worth considering. For example, if breeding your cat, you should discuss the immune status carefully with your veterinarian. If you are a breeder and have recurrent flu problems in your cattery, then more frequent boosting may be worth considering.

Sometimes so-called 'off-licence' use of vaccines may be advised. This includes inoculating kittens younger than the recommended age and repeating those inoculations more frequently than the manufacturers recommend in order to endeavor to overcome a persistent problem.

The suggestions which may be made in special circumstances by your veterinarian are the result of experience and are made in each case after careful consideration.

PARASITES

Good preventative health care for your cat has to include parasite control. Until relatively recently, this always involved treatment of **ectoparasites** (parasites that live on the body), the most common of which in the cat is the flea, and **endoparasites** (parasites that live inside the body), such as worms. Recently, so called **endectocides** have become available from veterinarians. These will control both fleas and many common worms with one single product.

First, let us look at some of the more common parasites of the cat and their methods of prevention.

ECTOPARASITES

Fleas and ear mites are the most common ectoparasites living on the cat. It is a very lucky cat that does not pick up at least the occasional flea. Some cats can harbor huge flea burdens without concern, whereas others only need a single flea bite to suffer intense irritation. These cats are said to be suffering from **flea allergy dermatitis** (FAD). It is caused by the minute amount of flea 'saliva' injected when the flea bites the cat to obtain blood as nourishment and to complete its life cycle. Rigorous flea control is particularly important should your cat suffer from FAD.

Fleas are not host-specific and can bite humans and dogs as well as cats. Therefore, it is important to maintain preventative flea control even if you only have one cat which never goes out. Fleas can be brought in and they can also live away from their host for long periods.

Once in your home, fleas will lay their eggs upon the host but these usually fall off and the juvenile forms (larvae) hatch in 1-10 days, depending on temperature and humidity.

In the southern states of the US, conditions are often ideal outside and the tiny larvae 2-5 mm ($^1/8 - ^1/5$ ins in length) feed on organic debris in the environment and on adult flea feces. Finally, the larva produces a silk-like cocoon from which the adult flea will ultimately emerge. The outside of the cocoon is sticky and thus can easily be carried into the home with the pre-emerged adult inside.

Pre-emerged adults can survive for 3-4 months or even longer in the cocoon in which they are resistant to insecticides. This is the reason why flea control is complicated and involves repeated applications or residual-action products being used in the home and specific products being used on the pet. Mature adult fleas can also be brought in by visitors particularly if accompanied by a pet, e.g. dog.

Preventative measures in the home include thorough vacuuming to remove any immature fleas. Few insecticides kill larvae, therefore an environmental product with prolonged action should be used to kill adults as they emerge. In addition, the cat has to be treated. Most cats dislike sprays, but they are very effective and some have prolonged action. If aerosol-type sprays are not tolerated, it is worth trying the pump-action type.

For the nervous animal, application of a 'spot-on' preparation is recommended. Modern spot-on flea control products can give protection for up to three months or more and they are effective even if puss gets soaked or is bathed several times between applications.

The action depends on the insecticide spreading through the invisible fat layer covering the skin without actually penetrating the body. It cannot be groomed out once absorbed into the fat layer. The flea has to penetrate this layer when biting to obtain its essential blood meal.

Spot-on applications are safe but they must be correctly applied to the back of the neck so the cat cannot lick the preparation before it has a chance to be absorbed.

There are spot-on preparations which will also control many worms. They are a useful form of prophylaxis against heartworm, a problem in some parts of North America.

Powders, collars, injections and tablets are also available. Some are available over-the-counter without prescription, but, because of the complexity of effective flea control, discussion with your veterinarian is money well spent.

MITES

Otodectes cyanotis, the ear mite, is the most common mite affecting the cat and is probably second only to fleas in the feline ectoparasite league table.

Many preparations are available, some without prescription. A spot-on endectocide is available which is effective against fleas, ear mites and certain worms. This is available only on prescription.

Other mites, such as the harvest mite, *Trombicula autumnalis* and the fur mite, *Cheyletiella blakei*, can cause problems. It is worthwhile consulting your veterinarian if only to establish a correct diagnosis before attempting to use over-the-counter preparations.

OTHER ECTOPARASITES

Ticks can sometimes be a problem in cats that have an outdoor lifestyle. In country areas, coyotes, sheep and fox are the main vectors, but in suburban situations they are frequently carried on racoons or hedgehogs. In some areas, particularly in the United States, ticks can carry Lyme disease.

Most ectoparasite preparations will eradicate ticks which are often identified as small gray or whitish lumps on the skin.

Ringworm (Dermatophytosis) is caused by certain fungi, commonly *Microsporum canis*. It is very contagious and is transmitted by contact with infected hair and scale, and is communicable to susceptible humans, particularly children. Many longhaired (Persian) cats can carry ringworm spores without showing any signs.

Although not life-threatening, it can cause serious irritation, both in people and cats. In exhibition cats, it is particularly serious and any cat showing suspicion of ringworm during veterinary examination at a show will be excluded and tests must be carried out to establish the diagnosis and whether other cats in contact are affected.

There are safe, effective preparations in the form of baths, lotions, ointments and specific oral drugs which will clear up the problem in a few weeks. In the USA, a vaccine is available against Dermatophytosis. Although it does not appear to prevent infection with the fungus, it is useful in controlling the spread of lesions.

ENDOPARASITES

Toxocara species of roundworms (nematode worms) are the most prevalent of all endoparasites of the cat, both in the US and in Britain. Almost a third of all kittens under three months of age and about 10 per cent of adult cats are infested.

They are large worms, up to 15 cm (6 in) long. Kittens can acquire them from the queen while suckling. In heavy infestations, diarrhea, together with a poor, dull coat and an accumulation of gas in the intestines causing a 'pot-bellied' appearance, are the usual signs. In adult cats, signs are usually few, unless a wriggling worm is found in either vomit or feces.

Many effective preparations are available, including an endectocide spot-on preparation which is applied to the back of the neck. This eradicates adult roundworms and also fleas and ear mites.

CAN WE CATCH WORMS FROM OUR CATS?

There is a small risk, particularly in people who are immuno-compromised. The problem is that roundworms undergo a fairly complex migration through the body before they develop into adult worms in the gut. It is this migration in susceptible people that can sometimes cause problems.

The small risk, however, can be reduced even further by regular deworming. Discuss preventative strategies with your vet.

TAPEWORMS

Tapeworms or Cestodes are also important in the house-cat. Most common is *Dipylidium caninum* which also infests dogs. Cats do not become infected directly from dogs since the life cycle involves an intermediate host, which with Dipylidium is a flea, another good reason for regular flea control for your cat.

Other types of feline tapeworms are encountered, but these are usually in outdoor or outdoor/indoor cats that hunt and eat their prey. In some areas, pet-quality, uncooked meat and offal can pose a threat.

Over-the-counter preparations are available, but involve administration of medicine or tablets. If your cat is difficult in this respect, discuss the matter with your veterinarian since there is now a spot-on preparation also available for tapeworm.

OTHER ENDOPARASITES

Lungworms (*Aelurostrongylus*) are not uncommon on both sides of the Atlantic, but are often undiagnosed since signs (coughing and difficulty with breathing) are usually only apparent with really heavy infection. Effective treatment is available from your veterinarian.

Toxoplasma gondii can be a problem, but not usually for your cat. This is a single-celled microscopic organism. Cats are usually infected by eating infected rodents. They rarely show signs themselves unless immuno-suppressed, however once infected they periodically pass microscopic eggs (oocysts), which, after 24 hours, become infective for other animals, including humans. Thus, the disease is zoonotic and the main concern is that it can cause problems in immuno-compromised people and also in pregnant women where it poses a risk to the fetus. However, this risk is small. Most human infections are contracted by eating undercooked infected meat, since, as with the majority of people, food animals can be infected without showing any signs.

Risks from cats can be reduced to negligible proportions provided litter pans are emptied regularly every 24 hours and the contents disposed of safely. If pregnant and fond of gardening, the best advice is to wear gloves and to wash thoroughly afterwards just in case neighbors' cats use your garden as a toilet area.

TREATING YOUR CAT

It couldn't be easier really, could it? Puss is a bit poorly, so you trot off to your friendly, neighborhood vet. After a very thorough examination, you are provided with some pills and asked to return in two or three days. Puss, you are assured, has just got a bit of an infection and he will be fine if he takes the pills. You then find you can't pill puss! You call the vet's office and a friendly voice assures you not to worry, if you bring the tablets back they'll exchange them for liquid medicine. The medicine comes complete with a dropper and precise instructions. You try. Poor puss, so under the weather, summons energies unrealized! Medicine covers the newly decorated walls, little is in the cat.

Medicating even the most placid cat can sometimes be an almost impossible task.

It is, to me, a great consolation that major manufacturers of worm preparations, for example, are now moving towards other forms of medication, such as spot-ons, which are absorbed through the skin. However, it is a lucky cat that does not have to have medication other than for worms throughout her life. How do you approach the task with the best hope of success?

GIVING LIQUID MEDICINES

Many feline medicines are specially formulated to ensure that as small a volume as possible has to be administered at each dose and the taste is as feline-friendly as the manufacturers can make it. If the cat is eating, try first of all mixing the medicine in a small quantity of food.

If that fails, the next attempt has to be direct administration. If it is any comfort, you, as the owner, are probably trusted more by the patient than anyone else. It is important not to destroy this trust. Therefore, attempt as far as possible to ensure that the cat is kept in as natural a position as possible. Try to gain the patient's confidence. If normally a lap cat, make sure she is sitting comfortably on your lap before you begin.

However, cats have four sets of claws and a set of teeth – five separate weapons which they are prepared to use if they consider the situation an emergency. Be prepared! Get everything to hand before you start, including a thick towel or blanket. Wrap this around the cat so that you will not be injured by the front claws. Then, talking gently the whole time, grasp the loose skin at the back of the head and neck (the scruff), and pull the head firmly but gently backwards.

If you have help, you can then get someone to start dropping the pre-measured dose of medicine into the side of the mouth (where there is a gap between the teeth so that the mouth does not have to be opened). Gently stroke the throat and keep the head elevated.

If you do not have a special dropper supplied, special syringe-like gadgets are available from pet outlets or your veterinarian. Before you start, make sure that the medicine is all ready in the dropper.

If your cat is clearly going to put up ever-increasing resistance, do not force the issue, back off and try again later, endeavoring to calm the cat and to handle ever more gently. If this does not work, ask your veterinarian if there is alternative medication, such as tablets.

GIVING TABLETS

Specially formulated palatable preparations are frequently available in tablet form. The question again is whether the cat agrees about the taste. Some tablets are crushable and may be taken in the food. Others are bitter-tasting and are covered in a more palatable coating. These have specific instructions regarding administration without crushing.

In this case, a plastic gizmo called a 'pill popper' is usually a great help. Place the cat in a comfortable position on your lap or on a table or worktop at a suitable height. Again, it is better to endeavor to carry out the procedure in familiar surroundings. In this way, puss is likely to be less tense. As before, wrapping the cat gently in a suitable towel or blanket prevents injury and stress. If placed on your lap, a few layers of blanket, a cushion or a coat between you and the claws is a wise precaution.

Hold the cat's head in your left hand, if you are right-handed, with your thumb on one corner of the jaw and forefinger on the other. In other words, your hand spans the cat's head just behind the eyes. The ears are just under the palm of your hand. Holding the cat this way, you have a firm grip without hurting the patient. Do not grip around the neck – the cat is liable to panic and you could be severely scratched or bitten.

Tip back the cat's head. If you gently tip the head back far enough, the lower jaw will gently sag and the pill popper can be inserted gently and quickly to the back of the throat and the plunger depressed. Then release the hold with your left hand, gently using it to rub the sensitive 'marker pad' area between the ears and the eyes on both sides. With your right hand at the same time ensure that the lower jaw is kept closed, rubbing the throat gently. In this way, the cat swallows and hopefully the tablet is not spat in your face.

If very reluctant to have the head tipped back, some cats will co-operate if they are scruffed, as when giving liquid medicine (above). The loose skin at the back of the neck is firmly grasped and the head pulled back so that the neck is in at least a vertical position. With luck, the lower jaw will begin to open slightly. If you do not have a pill popper and the tablets are reasonably small, you sometimes can drop them at the back of the throat and then follow the rest of the procedure of closing the cat's mouth and gently rubbing the throat. Firmly stroking over the 'marker pads' on top of the head will help to calm her.

Do be warned that cats can carry certain micro-organisms in their mouths that can cause severe infection in people. Do not take risks! Cat bites can be serious. If you are bitten, however small the wound, wash the area with appropriately diluted disinfectant and plenty of running water. Also wash with soap and water several times. Cover the wound and if there is any swelling or soreness consult your doctor without delay.

EAR DROPS

Many cats need ear preparations applied in the form of drops, either to remove excess wax or to eradicate ear mites (*Otodectes cyanotes*). Preparations are usually supplied in a plastic bottle with a specially-designed nozzle and all that is usually necessary is the instillation of one or two drops by squeezing the bottle. If there is resistance from an otherwise placid puss, use a blanket or towel as before.

Try just gently holding the tip of the ear and introducing the nozzle and squeezing in a small amount. Then gently massage just below the ear to make sure the drops are dispersed. Most cats will tolerate this provided you are gentle. As with all feline medication, another pair of hands is a wonderful help.

FLEA SPRAYS

Most cats instinctively dislike sprays. Aerosol sprays are quick and effective provided they are tolerated. They should be applied strictly according to the directions. If the noise is intolerable to the cat, ask if it is possible to obtain the preparation in a pump spray. These are quieter and the preparation is delivered with less force.

Even these are unacceptable to some cats who will subsequently run not only if they see a hair spray in the home but even a laundry spray or plant moistener. Under these circumstances, consult your veterinarian regarding other types of flea control, e.g. spot-on preparations which today can also be employed for routine worming procedures. Oral preparations are also available.

Chapter 27

First Aid

Why is first aid so important that it has a chapter all to itself? Because this is the all-important help that any well-prepared owner can offer to a cat in pain or distress, while veterinary assistance is being sought. In all cases, it will help to relieve suffering. In some cases, it may even save your cat's life.

OBJECTIVES OF FIRST AID
- To prevent further injury and stabilize the patient while veterinary attention is sought
- To alleviate pain and suffering
- To help the recovery process.

THE FIRST-AID KIT
The first essential piece of equipment is a good cat carrier (see page 66). This can provide a ready means of transport at any time, but is especially important in an emergency. Remember, frightened cats can be unpredictable; your normal friendly feline can become an unexpected enemy if she hurts! ALWAYS use a safe carrier when transporting cats – even if she looks quiet as you load her in the car, a panicking cat mid-journey can cause a new crisis.

For the kit itself, find a sturdy box, mark it well, keep it safe and accessible. You may need to find it in a hurry, and you want to keep it away from small hands. Equip it with the following:
- Cotton gauze pads of various sizes
- A few sterile dressings
- Two wide and two narrow cotton-weave bandages
- A 5cm (2.5in) crepe bandage
- Some adhesive strip plaster
- Cotton wool (cotton)
- Blunt-ended scissors

TOP TIP

You can adapt a human first-aid box for your cat. Your veterinarian will be able to provide you with the additional items. Add a notebook to the box, with your veterinarian's phone number, emergency number, taxi numbers and details of previous medical history clearly listed.

- Blunt-ended tweezers
- Thermometer and lubricant, e.g. petroleum jelly (Vaseline)
- Oral dosing syringes, 5ml and 2ml
- A bottle of safe antiseptic e.g. Hibitane
- Two small screw-top jars for feces or vomit samples
- Eye and ear cleaners as approved by the veterinarian.

BASIC FIRST-AID MEASURES

Included below are some of the common ailments you may encounter and advice on how to deal with them. But remember this is first aid. In most cases, once the cat is stabilized, she should be checked by a veterinarian.

ABSCESS

An abscess is a painful, infected swelling which may burst, leaving an unsightly hole. Although a burst abscess can look horrible, the process may bring some relief to the cat.

Action: an abscess is always infected. If discovered, clip the hair around the wound and bathe gently with a safe antiseptic wash or warm salt water (one teaspoonful of salt to one pint of water). Leave it uncovered and seek veterinary attention.

BITES

Often found around the face in aggressive cats and the tail in timid cats! Your first clue may be a dishevelled-looking cat arriving back through the cat flap at speed with clumped or missing fur. Look for deep puncture wounds under clumps of matted hair. Bites on the limb can cause limping. Examine the claws to distinguish fight wounds from road accidents. If the claws appear scuffed, the cat may have been hit by a car and should be checked by a vet for internal injuries. Tufts of fur around the claws tell their own story!

Action: clean the area with a safe antiseptic wash, clipping the surrounding hair if necessary. If bleeding badly, bandage the site (see box). Obtain veterinary advice – even small bite wounds are often infected and need antibiotics.

TOP TIP

BLEEDING LIMB WOUNDS
- *Cover the wound with a pad of absorbent sterile material, e.g. gauze.*
- *Then add a layer of soft dressing, e.g. cotton wool (cotton).*
- *Starting at the paw and including the foot, start to wrap the bandage around the limb, applying gentle pressure and partially overlapping the previous layer with each turn.*
- *Avoid applying too much pressure and causing a 'tourniquet' effect.*
- *Secure with a crepe bandage and a piece of sticking tape.*
- *If the blood starts to seep through this dressing, do not remove the soiled dressing but apply another layer of cotton wool and bandage over the top. This is a serious bleed – seek veterinary advice straight away.*
- *If a wound is too large or awkward to dress in this way, apply a pressure pad to the injury, wrap the whole cat in a clean towel or pillow case, place her in a carrying case and take her to the veterinarian immediately.*
- *Remember, a poorly-applied bandage can do harm. Monitor the dressing carefully and have it checked by a veterinarian at the earliest opportunity.*

BLEEDING

Cats will bleed profusely from areas that are well supplied with small blood vessels e.g. tongue, foot-pad. Although rarely life-threatening, they can look dramatic. Significant bleeding occurs where a larger vessel is involved and may lead to shock or even death.

Action: where possible, clean the wound (just immersion or rinsing with clean water can be helpful), cover with an absorbent pad (gauze, not cotton wool/cotton as the fibers get stuck to the wound) and apply pressure over the area with your fingers. This may staunch the flow after a few minutes. If the wound continues to bleed, apply a pressure bandage (see box, above).

If the cat shows any signs of shock (see page 216), keep her warm and seek veterinary help immediately. In all cases, your veterinarian will advise if the wound needs stitching.

External bleeding is the bleeding you see. Internal bleeding, into the body cavities, is hidden but can be just as dangerous.

For more information, see Road Traffic Accidents, page 216.

BURNS

May be caused by dry heat (e.g. heaters or fire, chemicals, electric current) or hot liquid ('scalding').

Action: chemical burns should be rinsed with lots of water. If the coat is contaminated, wash it with soapy water or baby shampoo and wrap the cat in a towel to prevent further grooming which may burn the tongue and poison the cat. With other burns, apply cold water to the site, cover the area with petroleum jelly, and apply a sterile bandage. Take your cat to the veterinarian straight away. Burns can be very serious injuries and may need intensive care.

TOP TIP

If a cat becomes injured by chewing through an electric cable, switch off the current immediately or use a broom handle to move the live wire away from the cat. If the cat is unconscious, she may need emergency resuscitation, discussed in the next section. Contact your veterinarian immediately for further advice.

FITS

Head trauma, liver and kidney disease and poisons may all result in fits. Sometimes no underlying cause can be discovered. Fits can occur singly or in clusters. They may begin with bizarre behavior and progress through to twitching and convulsive motions, with or without loss of consciousness. They can be very frightening to witness, but in most cases will stop after a few minutes.

Action: don't panic! Do not move the cat while she recovers from the fit. Ensure the cat is safe by covering any hazards, e.g. open fires, stairways. Dim the lights and turn off the radio or TV, as external stimuli (noise, bright light, touch) may make the fit worse. Avoid touching your cat's mouth, as she may bite. A cat rarely, if ever, chokes during a fit. The fit will usually be over within five minutes. Keep the animal indoors in a warm and quiet place while you contact the veterinarian. Even if she appears completely normal after a fit, your cat will still need checking to investigate any underlying cause.

If the fit lasts beyond five minutes, you need to contact your veterinarian urgently, as your cat may need sedation. If you discover that poison was involved, bring a sample or the container so that it can be identified accurately (see Poisons). If no immediate cause for the fit can be discovered, the veterinarian may request that you record any further incidents (e.g. time of onset, duration, feeding history, etc.) to help point to a diagnosis.

FOREIGN BODY IN THE MOUTH

A cat can become frantic if her airway is obstructed. If the cat is able to breathe, it is often safer to place her in a carrier and transport her to the surgery for veterinary treatment. In some cases, it may be possible to remove a foreign body by grasping the cat firmly, opening the jaws, and, if it can be located, removing the object with fine pliers. Never put your fingers in the cat's mouth – you are likely to get bitten. In an emergency, where the airway is blocked and the cat loses consciousness, grasp her firmly by the hindlegs above the hock joints and hold her upside-down to dislodge the foreign body. Only ever do this in an unconscious cat and take great care not to hurt the cat.

FOREIGN BODY IN THE EYE

If there is any sign that the foreign body is penetrating the eye, contact the veterinarian straight away. If the foreign body is floating on the surface, eye drops may help to 'float' it out of the eye, but, if unsuccessful, contact your veterinarian.

FRACTURE

May occur after severe trauma, e.g. road traffic accident (see page 216). Suspect a fracture where the limb looks strange, or where there is abnormal movement or intense pain over an area.

Action: remember, your cat may be in severe pain, so, whatever her normal temperament, approach her cautiously. Do not attempt to splint the body part; this is often painful for the cat and may cause further injury. Instead, securely wrap the whole cat in a blanket, place her gently in a secure box and transport her to the veterinarian for pain relief and treatment.

POISONS

The symptoms of poisoning are variable, and can be mimicked by many diseases, but include salivation, vomiting, diarrhea, weakness, nervous signs, convulsions and coma. External signs may include a sore mouth or contaminated coat.

Action: if you are suspicious that the cat has been poisoned, contact the veterinarian and explain the symptoms to obtain further advice. If the toxin is on the coat, wipe away as much as you can, then wash the coat with a dilute solution of baby shampoo. Never use chemical solvents – they may be more toxic than the original substance. Wrap the cat in a towel to prevent her licking the coat.

If you know that the cat has ingested a toxin, show the veterinarian a sample of the poison and its container for identification. Each poison has a specific treatment and only

TOP TIP

To remove sticky substances such as tar or engine-oil from fur, apply warm vegetable oil or petroleum jelly. Massage it in, then wipe and rinse clean. Cut away any heavily contaminated fur and wrap your cat in a towel to stop further grooming.

TOP TIP

Take care with household cleaning in the presence of cats. Cats will rarely drink disinfectants, due to their unpleasant taste, but if their paws become contaminated as they walk on recently-washed surfaces, they may groom the chemical off. In the case of irritants such as strong bleach this may cause ulceration of the mouth, salivation and possible loss of appetite due to pain. Disinfectants containing phenols (Lysol, TCP, Dettol, etc.) are directly toxic to cats and should be avoided.

general guidelines can be given here. The veterinarian may advise using a salt or mustard solution to make the cat sick, but get specific advice. If the cat has swallowed a caustic substance it is important not to make her sick, as this would burn the mouth and esophagus a second time. Contact your veterinarian for more detailed advice.

CONTACT CONTAMINATION
Cats may come into contact with poison in a number of ways
- They may directly eat a poison, attracted by its taste (e.g. anti-freeze, which tastes sweet), or by its looks (e.g lily-flowers, which look tempting to play with).
- The fastidious cleaning of (most!) cats means that, if their coat becomes contaminated with toxins, they will ingest the poison.
- The hunting lifestyle of cats means that a cat may unwittingly eat poisons used to kill pests e.g. the rat poison Warfarin or equally poisonous slug bait.
- Unfortunately, it is not uncommon for owners to poison their own cats by using human medical products to treat their cat. Never give your cat human medicines – they are very toxic to cats. The common painkillers aspirin and ibuprofen may cause gut bleeding. Paracetemol causes blood toxicity, liver failure and even death.
- Poisons may be inhaled e.g. creosote.

FLEA-TREATMENT OVERDOSE
Flea products containing organophosphates or carbamates are usually the culprits here! Signs of overdose include frothing at the mouth, muscle twitching, excitement and vomiting. There is usually no specific treatment. Supportive care at a veterinary hospital may be necessary in severe cases.

Prevention is better than cure. Always read the instruction labels, never be tempted to use dog products on a cat, and only use one product at a time unless specifically directed otherwise by your veterinarian.

Nowadays, these potentially toxic products can be avoided. Veterinary surgeons are able to provide safe products which target the flea only and have no effect on mammals.

TOP TIP

Road traffic accidents are still the number one cause of injury and death to cats. To help ensure your cat receives prompt medical treatment, add your veterinarian's phone number to her identity tag, in addition to your own. That way, even if you can't be traced, your cat will quickly receive help.

Don't forget microchips! These simple tagging devices are painlessly inserted under the skin by your veterinarian and allow you to be reunited with your cat, even if she has lost her collar.

ROAD TRAFFIC ACCIDENTS

Road traffic accidents may leave the cat shocked or unconscious, but even where the cat appears unharmed it is best to have her checked by a veterinarian, as internal injuries may take some time to manifest. Misshapen limbs or abnormal movement may indicate the presence of a fracture (see page 214). Hemorrhage (see page 212) may be obvious if external, but internal bleeding into the lungs, abdomen or bladder may be less obvious and may only become apparent some time after injury as the cat becomes progressively more shocked. Internal bleeding needs to be assessed by a veterinary surgeon. An X-ray may be required to fully assess the damage. In all cases, the cat should be checked by a veterinarian at the earliest opportunity.

SHOCK

This may occur after a serious accident. The cat feels cold to the touch with shallow breathing and rapid pulse. The cat may appear confused and weak, or become unconscious.

Action: lie the cat on her side. Keep her warm by wrapping her in a blanket or towel without constricting the breathing, or provide warmth in the form of a warm (not too hot) water bottle. Seek veterinary attention without delay.

STINGS

These are rarely serious, but bathing the sting can help to relieve the pain.
- Bee-stings – bathe with an alkaline solution, e.g. bicarbonate of soda.
- Wasp-stings – bathe with an acid solution, e.g. vinegar.

Cats have a large surface area to volume ratio. This means they lose heat quickly and may not be able to compensate when injured or ill. As the core body temperature drops, vital functions fail. Maintaining body warmth is vital to your cat's survival.

SUNBURN

If your cat is predominantly white, the tips of her ears and nose-tip are prone to sunburn. Repeated sunburn can stimulate cancerous skin changes.

Action: apply sun-block to the tips of white-eared cats in summer and keep pale-colored cats indoors in very hot weather. If crusts do appear on the ears or nose, consult your veterinary surgeon.

WOUNDS

Cats are inquisitive creatures with a love of adventure, but this can lead them into scrapes. A minor skin wound with no bleeding should be cleaned with antiseptic and monitored. If the wound is large or is bleeding, wash with antiseptic and apply a bandage while arranging veterinary assistance (see page 212). Applying a smear of clean petroleum jelly over the wound helps to prevent hair from contaminating the wound.

A cat licking at a wound may cause more damage. An 'Elizabethan' or 'lampshade' collar helps allow a wound to heal.

COPING WITH AN EMERGENCY

Prompt action can help to avoid unnecessary suffering and may save the life of a cat. It is easy to panic in an emergency. Following a series of steps makes it easier to remember what to do and how to do it.

1 Organize someone to call the veterinary surgery immediately, while you administer first aid. This ensures that the veterinary center is ready and waiting for the patient when she arrives. Sometimes, helpful advice can be given by phone on stabilizing and transporting the patient. Remember that prompt veterinary attention is a priority – your aim is to stabilize the patient so that she reaches the surgery in one piece. Occasionally, it is appropriate for the veterinarian to attend the emergency, but this may just cause further delay before the cat can receive specialist attention.

2 If the cat is still in danger, move her carefully to a safe area. If she is unconscious or recumbent, place a sheet or board gently beneath her body and lift her from danger.

TOP TIP

- *If the cat is unconscious, remove her collar and lie her on one side.*
- *Open her mouth, and, using a piece of rough cloth or towelling, pull the tongue forward to clear the airway. This may stimulate breathing.*
- *Taking care of your fingers, clear the mouth of mucus with the material.*
- *Then tilt the head downwards so that no fluids are inhaled.*

❸ Next, assess the injury or illness. For anyone who has attended a first-aid course for humans, the essentials will be as familiar as ABC: airway, breathing and circulation.

ASSESSING THE PATIENT

- If necessary, clear the airway and check for conciousness. Gently touch the corner of the cat's eyelid – she will blink if she is at all conscious. Gently pinch the web of skin between the toes – she will pull the leg away if she is conscious. A light touch to the ear flap will result in reflex twitching if the cat is conscious. Note: A cat that is in deep shock may be able to feel the stimulus but be unable to react. Do not persist with the examination longer than is needed.
- Check for breathing. Watch the chest of the cat for movement, and count the number of breaths in one minute. The rate should be 20-30 breaths per minute. If the breathing has stopped, give artificial respiration (see box, below).
- Check the circulation. Feel for a pulse – place your fingers up high on the inside of a hindleg. In a collapsed cat it may be easier to feel for the heartbeat – with the cat on her side, place your fingers gently over the chest behind the elbow and feel for the movement of the heart under the ribs. The rate should be 160-240 beats per minute.
- Check for bleeding. Place a pad (a clean, folded handkerchief or tea-towel will do) and apply enough pressure to staunch any flow. If the flow does not stop, continue applying pressure while the cat is transported to the vet, or apply a pressure bandage as described in the previous section.
- Counter shock. Keep the cat warm with blankets or hot-water bottles.
- Check for fractures. If you suspect a fracture, move the cat by sliding her carefully on to a flat tray or piece of material held tautly which can then be used as a stretcher. Where possible, keep the injured limb uppermost. Gently lower the cat into a secure carrier for transport.

ARTIFICIAL RESPIRATION

This should only be carried out on an unconscious cat where there is no sign of breathing.
- *Place your hands on the chest and, for a count of two, apply gentle pressure over the ribs to expel the air from the lungs.*
- *Then lift your hands, allowing the lungs to refill with fresh air for a count of three.*
- *If the lungs are damaged, they may not refill automatically and you will have to blow into them.*
- *Raise the head, closing the cat's mouth and cup your hand around the nostrils and blow gently for a count of two. You should see the chest area move as you expand the lungs.*
- *Pause for a count of three, then repeat.*
- *Continue with resuscitation until the cat starts to breathe on her own.*

TOP TIP

- *If the heart beat is absent, direct stimulation of the heart may be attempted.*
- *Place your fingers on the chest at the point of the elbow, and press down gently but firmly.*
- *Repeat five or six times at one-second intervals, alternating with artificial respiration and pausing occasionally to look for spontaneous movements of the heart or chest.*
- *If there is no response after five minutes, the procedure is unlikely to be successful and should be abandoned.*

- Wounds should be cleaned of surface dirt where possible, but do not delay transfer of the cat to the surgery if there appear to be more serious injuries or the cat is semi-conscious. Wrap the animal in a clean towel, sheet or pillow case and seek veterinary help immediately.
- Unco-operative cats: if the cat is conscious and moving, approach cautiously and talk reassuringly to her. Move slowly towards the cat until you can cover her in a coat or blanket. Then, using one hand to hold the cat by the scruff through the blanket, quickly but gently use the other hand to wrap the blanket around her to prevent her running off and allow you to move her without further harm. Restraining the cat in this manner will also help to protect you from damage – a frightened cat may be aggressive even to people she knows. It may be advisable to wear thick gloves to protect your hands from bites. Maintain a firm grip on the cat's scruff as you transfer her into a carrier for transportation. Really scared cats are unlikely to allow further treatment, however good your intentions.

Chapter 28

A-Z Of Common Diseases And Disorders

ALLERGIES

Cats are prone to many allergies, including flea bites, atopy (allergies to inhaled particles, such as pollens or house dust), and allergies to substances in their food.

Allergic disease can show in a number of ways: itchy skin (pages 235-236), asthma (page 221), conjunctivitis (page 222), and gut disturbances (pages 225-226).

ANEMIA

Anemia means having low numbers of red blood cells in the blood. Cats with anemia can show the following signs: weakness, decreased eating, decreased activity, increased effort in breathing (particularly when stressed), and pale membranes in the mouth and around the eye. A heart murmur may be heard when the heart is listened to by the veterinarian.

It is diagnosed, and the cause investigated, by doing blood tests; sometimes taking bone marrow will be necessary. Cats can have pale membranes in their mouth and eyes for reasons other than anemia. Feline anemia is usually serious.

Common causes are: blood loss due to bleeding from external or internal injuries, bleeding into the gut, severe flea infestation (particularly in kittens), infections with FeLV or FIV, certain tumors, infection with a blood parasite called *Hemobartonella felis*, many chronic diseases, chronic kidney failure, bone marrow damage.

The treatment and the likely outcome depend on the underlying cause of the problem.

ANOREXIA

Anorexia means not eating. It is a symptom of many diseases and is often one of the first signs of illness that appears in a cat. If your cat has not eaten at all for one day, she needs to be seen by a veterinarian. A history and examination may find the cause, but investigations are often necessary to find out what is wrong.

Treatment will then often be possible. If a rapid return to eating is unlikely, nutritional therapy using a feeding tube is often necessary.

ASCITES

Ascites is the accumulation of fluid within the abdomen. This can lead to the abdomen looking swollen. However, abdominal swelling can be caused by other things. To find the problem, the vet will need to examine your cat and do further tests. Fluid analysis, blood tests and ultrasound are often useful. Although some cats can be treated or cured, most cats with ascites have life-threatening illnesses.

ASTHMA

Feline asthma is caused by cats having an allergy to something they have inhaled (such as house dust, smoke, plant pollens, household sprays, dusty cat litter, flea powders and sprays).

When they come in contact with this initiating substance, the allergic reaction leads to their airways narrowing. There is also inflammation in the lungs and airways that leads to chronic damage and further narrowing.

Signs of asthma include a chronic cough (page 223), and, in severe cases, sudden-onset breathing difficulty (see dyspnoea, page 226), with cats trying to breathe through their mouths. It can be a life-threatening condition.

Cats that have difficulty breathing (e.g. breathing through their mouths) need to be taken immediately to see a vet. These cats are in a critical state and should be handled quietly, calmly and as little as possible.

Long-term treatment usually relies on corticosteroids. Tablets or injections used to be the treatment but now there is a move to use inhalers, as is standard in humans. Oxygen therapy and a stay in the veterinary hospital is often necessary for critically-ill cats. Most cats can be treated relatively easily, but need life-long drugs.

BITE WOUNDS

Bite wounds are very common in cats which go outside. They are usually due to fights with other cats. Punctures of the skin cause holes which are small and quickly close up. Because they are small, they can be difficult to find in the fur. They are commonly found on the head, neck or front legs or at the base of the tail.

When the puncture wounds close, they trap inside bacteria from the cat's mouth. The area around the bite then becomes swollen and painful as the bacteria multiply to cause infection. An abscess forms. These are very painful and often make the cat feel unwell. If left untreated, the abscess will usually burst and pus will drain out. Bites can also cause septicemia (blood poisoning) and consequent serious infections in the chest, abdominal organs, joints and bones.

Abscesses can usually be easily treated by draining out any pus and giving a course of antibiotics.

Occasionally, unusual infections can occur which are harder to treat. FIV is spread by cat bites and thus cats that are often in fights are at a high risk of being infected.

CHLAMYDOPHILA FELIS (CHLAMYDIA)

Chlamydophila (old name: *Chlamydia psittaci*) is a species of bacteria that can infect animals and people. It can cause serious disease and may cause abortions. *Chlamydophila felis* causes a conjunctivitis in cats which can be severe. It can be very similar to infection with the cat flu viruses and sometimes there are infections with both. It has also been linked to reproductive problems in cats. There are now medications which can cure cats of Chlamydophila and there are tests to confirm its presence.

Chlamydophila felis has not been definitely linked with disease in humans but, as other strains have been, it is recommended that pregnant women do not handle cats that have Chlamydophila infections. Wash your hands after handling cats with Chlamydophila.

CONJUNCTIVITIS

Conjunctivitis means inflammation of the conjunctiva, the tissue lining the eyelids including the third eyelid and part of the eyeball.

Signs of conjunctivitis include the eyes watering excessively or being held closed or partially closed, and discharges from the eyes. The conjunctiva may look red, sore and sometimes swollen. Cats may rub their eyes.

Causes include Chlamydophila (above), feline Herpesvirus and feline Calicivirus (the cat flu viruses), Mycoplasma, physical damage by scratches or a foreign body in the eye, and allergies. It can be secondary to other eye disease, such as inturned eyelids or decreased tear production. Bacteria can cause a problem secondary to other diseases. Rare causes are tumors and fungal infections.

Treatment depends on the cause. Chlamydophila and Mycoplasma can be treated with certain antibiotics. Conjunctivitis caused by the cat flu viruses can be very difficult to treat; occasionally it can be impossible to clear for some cats. Allergic conjunctivitis can usually be controlled and conjunctivitis caused by physical damage improves rapidly once the cause is no longer present.

CONSTIPATION

Constipation can be mild or severe. In its mild form, it may be due to the cat eating unsuitable foods. Early signs may be just that the cat is defecating less frequently, then straining and crying may be seen with small fecal pellets being passed. As the problem persists, there may be drooling, vomiting, depression, reduced food intake and then dehydration and collapse.

Causes include: diseases causing long-term dehydration; changes in the salt balance that causes the colon (large bowel) to work abnormally; damage to the nerves that supply the colon (which can be due to an accident or congenital defect); damage to the pelvis that may make defecation painful or there may be a physical blockage from broken bones; masses in the colon or rectum or masses pressing on it from outside may block defecation; and stress which prevents the cat from going in the normal place (e.g. the presence of an aggressive cat). The commonest cause of chronic constipation is a disease called idiopathic megacolon, a progressive disease which is not curable.

X-rays, endoscopy and blood tests may be necessary to make a diagnosis.

Treatments includes laxatives, drugs, enemas, and changes in the diet. We do not recommend giving liquid paraffin, as, if this accidentally goes down into the lungs, it causes a severe pneumonia). Cats with idiopathic megacolon often progress and need life-long treatment. Some need repeated hospitalization with enemas, sometimes under anesthetic. Sometimes, surgery to remove the majority of the colon is recommended. This is major surgery and is not undertaken lightly, but has a good success rate and can be the best option.

COUGHING

Coughing is quite common in cats and can be difficult to tell apart from retching (coughing is often followed by swallowing; retching is associated with vomiting).

Common causes include: feline asthma (above); lungworm infections (hunting cats); foreign bodies stuck in the respiratory tract; masses in the respiratory tract or ones pressing on it from outside; and lung infections with bacteria, fungi or other parasites. Heart disease rarely causes coughing in cats (unlike in dogs).

Treatment depends on the cause, and investigations are necessary to determine this. Common investigations performed are chest X-rays, blood tests, feces tests, endoscopy, and taking samples from the airways for cytology and cultures.

CYSTITIS

See Feline Lower Urinary Tract Disorder.

DENTAL DISEASE

Dental disease is the commonest disease veterinarians see in cats. More than 80 per cent of cats over three years old have periodontal disease. This is a disease of the tissues surrounding the teeth and supporting them.

Periodontal disease progresses from gingivitis (see page 230), with tartar, plaque and calculus building up on the teeth, loosening them and eventually causing them to be lost. Gingivitis is reversible, and, if teeth are cleaned at this stage, they will be saved and kept healthy. Once periodontal disease has occurred, the disease process is irreversible and the teeth will be lost. It is unrelenting and incurable, but it can be controlled by veterinary dental treatment and home dental hygiene. Severe periodontal disease can also lead to bacteria getting into the bloodstream and causing disease inside the body e.g. in the heart, liver, kidneys etc. If this occurs, it can be very serious.

Cats also commonly get holes in their teeth called 'neck lesions' or 'resorptive lesions'. Once present, these continually get bigger and are painful. Dental pain from whatever cause can be generally debilitating.

Broken teeth, particularly the canine teeth, are common. We must assume that they are painful even through cats rarely show signs of pain. They will eventually become infected and lead to a tooth root abscess. Thus, broken teeth need treatment, which nearly always means removal.

Signs of dental disease include: dirty teeth covered with plaque and calculus, red, sore gums, loose or broken teeth, smelly breath, not wanting to eat, or difficulty in eating, and drooling. Pain in cats is often not obvious to owners but it is common for owners to notice a change in the cat's behavior and 'happiness' after dentistry has been performed, indicating there was discomfort beforehand.

Treatment includes: giving the cat an anaesthetic to remove any teeth that are broken or have resorptive lesions. It is not known what causes resorptive lesions; as they get bigger and are painful, current thought is that it is best to remove all affected teeth, apart perhaps from ones showing very early lesions. Dental X-rays should be taken so that the roots of the teeth can be assessed fully. This is very important with resorptive lesions as they often are below the gum line and invisible otherwise. It also enables us to look for root abscesses and root fragments.

Cats manage very well after having teeth removed and are much better off than remaining with painful teeth. Even cats who eat dry cat foods will usually be able to manage these with no problems once their mouths have healed.

The remaining teeth are then totally cleaned using special dental instruments and polished to help smooth the surface which slows calculus build-up again. The teeth are then varnished. Antibiotics are often given and painkillers are also prescribed to ensure the cat is comfortable when she wakes up.

Home dental care is very important and helps prevent plaque and calculus build-up (see page 122). Regular veterinary check-ups will help to catch problems early.

DERMATOPHYTOSIS (Ringworm)

Dermatophytosis is a fairly common skin condition. It commonly spreads to people and is quite common in dogs. While it is not a fatal disease, it can be difficult to get rid of completely from cats, especially in a multi-cat household.

Ringworm is the infection of the hair, and sometimes the skin or claws, by one of a group of fungi. In cats, it is almost always one called *Microsporum canis*. This fungus is carried in the coat of about 2 per cent of all cats but about 20 per cent of longhaired cats. The fungus survives as spores in the environment, which may live for years in carpet, woodwork, bedding etc. The spores are also very difficult to kill.

Animals develop immunity against the fungus and so most animals will have a skin disease that lasts for a few months and then gets better, or they will develop immunity without clinical signs. Kittens are most likely to get clinical signs and animals that are immunosuppressed may get a more severe disease. Despite it being a disease that resolves itself, in most cases we advise treatment to clear it faster so as to decrease the chance of human infections. Some cats, especially longhaired ones, can have disease that has been present for years or which takes many months of treatment to eliminate.

The classic dermatophytosis lesion is an area of hair loss with scale; it is usually not very itchy and is most often on the head and front legs. However, dermatophytosis can mimic any skin disease. Diagnosis is made by culturing the fungus. This can take up to three weeks. Other tests are less reliable.

Treatment needs to be performed on all susceptible in-contact cats and the house needs to be treated thoroughly. This can be very difficult, time-consuming and expensive. Cats may have one or more of several treatments, including shampoos, clipping affected areas, and tablets. Affected cats should be isolated and owners need to take care to avoid catching it. Houses can be cleaned by vacuuming, and washable surfaces can be cleaned with a 1:10 bleach solution or by steam-cleaning.

DIABETES MELLITUS

This is characterized by an inability to regulate blood sugar levels due to a problem with the hormone insulin. A lack of, or an inability to respond to, insulin causes the body to metabolize other energy stores, such as fat or muscle, resulting in weight loss. Despite high blood sugar levels, cells are unable to utilize this important energy source.

Two forms of the disease are recognized, either insulin dependent (i.e. cats that need injections of insulin) or non-insulin dependent (i.e. cats that still produce some insulin but the tissues respond poorly). About 20 per cent of diabetic cats are non-insulin dependent – they are often older, obese cats, who show signs intermittently, especially during periods of stress. If untreated, these cats can become insulin dependent. Most cats are insulin dependent and if they are left untreated, have a tendency to develop a condition called ketoacidosis, which is life-threatening.

Signs seen with diabetes include weight loss, increased drinking and urination, and sometimes an increased appetite. If ketoacidosis develops, the cats become very ill and depressed and can show vomiting, anorexia, dehydration and collapse.

Other conditions can produce similar signs (see weight loss – page 238, polydipsia – page 235). The diagnosis is made from urine and blood tests. Treatment for non-insulin dependent cases involves tablets and often weight reduction and special diets. Most cats require insulin injections, usually for the rest of their lives and often twice daily. They will need a lot of monitoring by the veterinarian, with blood and urine tests, particularly until their disease is stable. Cats with severe signs and ketoacidosis will need hospitalization and intensive treatment to get them better.

DIARRHEA

Diarrhea is an increase in the water content of feces. There are many causes of diarrhea in cats. To narrow down the possibilities, we first decide if the problem is acute or chronic. Acute diarrhoea is when it has been happening for less than three weeks.

Chronic is when it has been longer.

Common causes of acute diarrhea are dietary changes, certain viral and bacterial infections, and gut parasites.

Common causes of chronic diarrhea are inflammatory bowel disease (see page 232), tumors, parasites, FIV infection (see page 227), food allergies or intolerances, and other systemic diseases, such as hyperthyroidism (see page 232).

Because there are so many causes, a good history and clinical examination are important. If it is an acute problem, then supportive treatment and special diets may be tried. If the problem is more chronic, it is very likely that diagnostic tests will be necessary. These may include blood and fecal tests, and often endoscopy with biopsies (samples of the gut) being taken. Occasionally X-rays or surgery of the abdomen, with other organ samples being taken, may be needed.

The treatment and outcome depends on the cause (see the specific disease headings).

DYSPNOEA

Dyspnoea is defined as 'difficult breathing'. If a cat is showing signs of having difficulty breathing and/or breathing through her mouth, she may well be in a critical condition and needs to be taken to the vet quickly and quietly.

There are a number of causes and the veterinarian will have to balance doing investigations with emergency treatment, as these cats are often critically ill. Most cats will need hospitalization and intensive care. Tests may include blood tests, chest drainage and X-rays, analysis of fluid or samples from masses, and ultrasound.

The commonest causes are heart failure, asthma, and fluid build-up in the chest due to infections, trauma or tumors. Other causes are airway obstruction, pneumonia, heart worm disease (in endemic areas), tumors in the lungs, FIP, and anemia. The outlook depends on the cause, but many of these cats are seriously ill.

EAR DISEASE

Ear disease is common in cats of all ages. Common symptoms are: scratching the ears, shaking the head, holding the head or an ear in an odd position, and a discharge or smell from the ear.

The commonest cause is the common ear mite *Otodectes cyanotis*. It causes irritation and a discharge which is usually black and waxy. Mites can be seen in samples looked at under the microscope. Both ears will always be affected.

Treatment used to be with ear drops for several weeks, but now there are drop-on skin preparations that are easy to use and very effective. Mites can easily be spread to in-contact cats, dogs and ferrets.

Other causes are polyps (non-cancerous, inflammatory growths), which can be removed with surgery; tumors, some of which can be cured with surgery, or, if a cure is not possible, it may be possible to make the cat more comfortable for a time; skin allergies, and occasionally other mites. Bacterial infections, which are common in some breeds of dog, are generally rare in cats.

FELINE IMMUNODEFICIENCY VIRUS

Feline immunodeficiency virus (FIV) is similar to HIV in humans but is not the same virus and transmission to humans has never been recorded. The prevalence is higher in sick cats than healthy cats. It is also more prevalent among unneutered males and free-roaming cats. Infection is uncommon in cats under one year old and rises steadily to a peak at 6 to 10 years.

Biting is the main route of spread. Thus cats most at risk are those which roam freely and fight with other cats. There are different stages of the disease: a few weeks after infection, some cats show a high temperature and enlarged lymph nodes. Most cats then go through a phase of having no symptoms at all, and this may last for months or years. The later stage of disease is characterized by immuno-deficiency.

There is great individual variation in the signs seen but the commonest are: lethargy, weight loss, inflammation of the mouth, chronic respiration infections, enlarged lymph glands, nerve problems, high temperature, chronic diarrhea, eye disease and the growth of tumors.

Some of these signs are due to the virus directly affecting the body and some are due to secondary infections of bacteria, parasites or fungi. Some of these secondary infections can be a risk to immunosuppressed humans, e.g. people on chemotherapy or immunosuppressive drugs, humans with major illnesses or HIV, and very young babies.

At present, there is no totally effective treatment for the virus. Treatment of the secondary infections are often effective, especially early in the disease. In the future, there may be a vaccine and more effective treatments.

Recommendations for FIV-positive cats include: keeping cats indoors to decrease the likelihood of picking up secondary infections and to stop them from passing FIV to other cats; feeding high-quality food; worming regularly; and keeping them free of parasites.

We recommend continuing to vaccinate infected cats but always with dead vaccines. There is some evidence that essential fatty acid supplements are helpful.

FELINE INFECTIOUS ENTERITIS

This is also called feline parvovirus, panleucopaenia and cat distemper. It causes severe disease in vulnerable cats and is very contagious (easily spread). It can cause devastation in rescue centers if cats are unvaccinated. It is also a very resistant virus in the environment.

In very young kittens, it can cause sudden death; in older kittens and cats, it causes a severe disease with depression, vomiting and diarrhea, and is life-threatening. A few cats may recover. The vaccines are very effective at preventing disease.

FELINE INFECTIOUS PERITONITIS

Feline infectious peritonitis (FIP) is a major viral disease of cats and it is almost invariably fatal. FIP is commoner in larger multi-cat households, thus it is seen more in pedigree cats than non-pedigree. There is a group of coronaviruses which includes FIP virus (FIPV) and feline enteric coronavirus (FECV). FECV infection appears to be very common, but it rarely causes significant disease. The exact relationship between these viruses is not clear yet, but FIPV is probably a mutant version of FECV.

Observations have led to the belief that asymptomatic carrier cats may be involved with the spread of the disease. The carrier cats may remain carriers for months to years, releasing the virus to infect susceptible cats but not having symptoms themselves. It may be that, in each case, the cats were infected with FECV which then mutated to the FIPV which caused disease. Whether a cat resists getting FIP depends on several factors including the virulence of the virus and the cat's immune response to the virus.

FIP often starts with vague signs, then, after time, more specific signs develop. The disease is usually either an 'effusive' or 'non-effusive' disease. In effusive FIP, a protein-rich fluid accumulates leading to ascites (see page 221), or, if occurring in the chest, breathing problems (see dyspnoea, page 235). In non-effusive FIP, there is little or no accumulation of fluid but inflammation occurs in the eyes, brain, kidneys, liver and gut. Because inflammation can occur in a wide variety of organs, the symptoms can be very variable and can mimic other diseases.

There are various tests to try to diagnose FIP, but great care has to be taken in their interpretation and the only totally reliable test is to have tissue samples looked at (though they may be difficult to obtain depending on the organs involved). There is no effective treatment at present but one may appear in the future. There is a vaccine in the USA, but its efficacy is questionable.

Control of FIP in multi-cat households can be difficult and current recommendations include: isolating any cats with symptoms suggestive of FIP; good hygiene measures for cleaning litter-trays and feeding bowls; one litter-tray per two cats in an easily cleanable area (FIPV is susceptible to most disinfectants); a decreased density and stress on the cats. If FIP has been diagnosed, no new cats should enter the home for six months and none should be rehomed. All breeding should be stopped for at least six months after the last case of FIP. These are by no means fool-proof measures but present the best advice with the current understanding.

FELINE LEUKEMIA VIRUS

Feline leukemia virus (FeLV) used to be common in pedigree cats but has now largely been eliminated from breeding catteries and is now more common in cats from a 'poor' background. Persistent infection with the virus results in immunosuppression, anemia and/or the development of tumors, all of which are life-threatening.

The virus is passed mainly in saliva and usually to cats that are in close contact with an infected cat; occasionally it is spread by biting or from a queen to her kittens. Not all cats exposed to the virus develop persistent infections and some that pick up the virus get rid of it quickly. Cats with persistent infections invariably go on to get problems, though it is thought that even short infections can lead to the development of certain cancers later in life.

There are various blood and other tests to diagnose FeLV infection, but care needs to be taken in interpreting the results. There is no specific treatment to get rid of the virus. Some of the diseases caused by it can be helped for a time, but more than 80 per cent of cats persistently infected die within 3.5 years of being diagnosed.

The signs seen are not specific for FeLV infections and can include lethargy, chronic infections, anemia (see page 220), development of tumors, weight loss, and chronic gut, skin or respiratory disease.

There are vaccines to prevent it (see pages 201-202). Nowadays, good cat breeders and rescue centers check their cats are free from the disease with a blood test.

FELINE LOWER URINARY TRACT DISORDER

This term describes the common problems seen in cats with signs of disease in the bladder or urethra. Affected cats usually show some of the following signs: frequent urinations with small amounts or no urine produced; crying when trying to pass urine; urination in unusual places; blood in the urine; and licking their back-end more than usual. If the urethra becomes blocked, they can quickly become very ill and may collapse. Blockage is much more common in males than females.

Cats with a blockage need urgent treatment. Cats without a blockage have discomfort but the condition is not life-threatening. The causes include inflammation of the bladder of unknown cause (idiopathic cystitis); stones in the urinary tract; bacterial infections (these are uncommon); tumors (which are rare) or congenital (present at birth) abnormalities.

Finding the cause involves doing urine tests and possibly X-rays or ultrasound of the bladder. There are some special diets that will help with some types of stones, but many need to be removed surgically. Idiopathic cystitis can be a frustrating disease to treat but now there are various drugs that can help in most cases. Stress is thought to play an important role, so measures to decrease stress can help. Some cats are on life-long treatment or on frequent courses of treatment as the disorder recurs. Bacterial infections respond well to courses of antibiotics, but often have an underlying cause.

FELINE UPPER RESPIRATORY TRACT DISEASE

This disease is usually known as 'cat flu'. It is caused by one of three agents or sometimes a mixture. About 40 per cent are caused by feline herpesvirus which causes feline viral rhinotracheitis, 40 per cent are caused by feline calicivirus and 15 per cent are caused by *Chlamydophila felis* (*Chlamydia psittaci var. felis*) – see page 222.

Cat flu occurs most commonly in kittens under six months old, particularly from multi-cat households, cat colonies and rescue centers. It is not usually a fatal disease but can be, especially in young kittens. It is usually transmitted directly from a diseased or carrier cat to a susceptible cat; occasionally it is spread on food bowls, bedding etc.

The diseases caused by herpesvirus and calicivirus are similar; the only way to tell which a cat has is to perform a culture. Signs include sneezing, red eyes with a discharge, runny nose, blocked nose, sticky eyes and open-mouth breathing, mouth ulcers and excessive drooling, inappetence, occasionally a cough, loss of voice, or pneumonia. Chlamydophila tends to affect the eyes more than the nose. Herpesvirus infection during pregnancy may cause abortion or result in fatal diseases in new-born kittens. Calicivirus may cause a shifting lameness.

The acute infection is usually better after about two weeks. After this, most cats carry the viruses for a period of time. The herpesvirus carrier status persists for life; the cats shed virus for about two weeks after being stressed and provide an important source of infection for susceptible kittens. The stresses that may set off shedding include moving, introducing new cats, illness, surgery and pregnancy/lactation. Calicivirus carriers persist for months or years but they shed the virus continuously. These carriers may look normal or they may have gingivitis (see below), or runny eyes or noses.

Treatment for the acute infections includes nursing care, cleaning the eyes and nose, keeping cats warm, isolating affected cats, and ensuring they are eating and drinking enough. Antibiotics are used to prevent secondary bacterial infections. There is no treatment to kill the viruses or to prevent carrier status. Prevention of disease is by vaccination.

GINGIVITIS-STOMATITIS COMPLEX

Gingivitis is inflammation of the gums, stomatitis is inflammation of the mouth. This complex is a chronic problem which may be mild or severe enough to stop the cat from eating. It can be very frustrating to treat.

Causes are dental disease (see pages 223-224), calicivirus infection particularly with chronic carriers of the virus (see above), infection with FeLV or FIV (see pages 227-228), tumors, gingivitis of unknown cause (idiopathic gingivitis or lymphocytic-plasmacytic gingivitis/stomatitis), kidney failure or immune-related diseases. Idiopathic gingivitis and gingivitis related to dental disease are the commonest causes. Diagnosis can involve blood tests and swabs for the viruses, biopsy of the gum tissue, and trial dental treatment (see dental disease, pages 223-224).

Treatment involves regular dentistry, good home dental care, and treatment for underlying causes. Treatment of idiopathic gingivitis may involve repeated dental cleaning with antibiotics and oral antiseptics, trials with corticosteroids, and other immunosuppressive drugs. Extraction of teeth may be necessary and some cats need all their teeth removed. Some cats do not respond to any of these treatments.

HEART DISEASE

Heart disease is not the same as heart failure. A heart which has a disease can often cope, especially to start with, and can continue to pump the blood efficiently because of various compensatory mechanisms. When it starts to be unable to cope, signs of illness will appear – this is heart failure.

Heart disease may only show when a cat develops heart failure. The cat has difficulty breathing because of fluid build-up in the lungs. This can appear very rapidly (see dyspnoea, page 226). It is also common for us to detect heart disease when we check over a kitten or cat that an owner thinks is normal and we hear a heart murmur or an odd rhythm. Some cats develop blood clots (thromboemboli) in arteries and present with paralysis of the hindlegs. Some just show general signs of ill health with heart failure. Thus we usually find heart disease in either cats that appear normal or cats that are very ill.

One common cause is hypertrophic cardiomyopathy, a disease of unknown cause, though it may be hereditary in certain breeds (such as Persians, Maine Coons and British Shorthairs). It is seen in young to middle-aged cats and is commoner in males. Hyperthyroidism and hypertension are also common causes of heart disease. Other causes are congenital problems (i.e. abnormalities with the heart formation that are present from birth) and other forms of cardiomyopathy.

Investigation of heart disease includes listening with a stethoscope and careful examination of the cat, chest X-rays, ultrasound, electrocardiogram (electrical recording of the heart), blood tests, and blood pressure measurement. Very ill cats will need emergency treatment before being well enough to have some of the tests performed.

Treatment will be life-long unless the underlying cause can be eliminated, and is based on life-long tablets. Hyperthyroidism can be cured, and hypertension can be treated. Occasionally, cats with a congenital problem can have this surgically corrected, otherwise treatment involves dealing with the heart failure if it occurs. Thromboemboli are very serious – they cause very painful disease which is difficult to treat and many cats with these symptoms will die or need to be put to sleep.

HEARTWORM

This is best managed by prevention. Discuss the matter with your own veterinarian, who will know if treatment is necessary in your own geographical area. See also Chapter Twenty-six for worming advice.

HYPERTENSION

Hypertension means elevation of blood pressure above the level generally considered normal. It is only recently that we have been able to measure blood pressure easily in cats and thus only recently that the importance of this disease has been recognized.

Common problems it can cause are: acute blindness due to bleeding in the eye and/or detachment of the retina, kidney failure, heart failure, and bleeding in the brain (leading to symptoms such as fits, dementia or signs like strokes).

Hypertension in cats is usually secondary to another disease – the common two are chronic kidney disease and hyperthyroidism. Many veterinary surgeons now have equipment to measure blood pressure. To control hypertension, the underlying disease must be treated, drugs prescribed, and a low-salt diet advised.

HYPERTHYROIDISM

Hyperthyroidism is a very common diseases in older cats. It is caused by an overactive thyroid gland producing too much thyroid hormone. Thyroid hormone controls metabolic rate, so, if it is in excess, it leads to the symptoms described. Hyperthyroidism is a slowly progressive disease and, if left untreated, will be fatal.

Signs include weight loss, often despite a good or increased appetite, and increased thirst. Sometimes there is vomiting and diarrhea, and occasionally, if advanced, the cat goes into heart failure. A poor coat and behavioral changes are often seen. When a vet examines a cat with hyperthyroidism, enlarged thyroid glands may be detected and the heart rate may be elevated. It is confirmed with blood tests.

Treatments are radioactive iodine treatment at specialized centers (this is curative and safe); surgery to remove the thyroid tissue (which is curative in most cats); or life-long control with tablets.

INAPPETENCE

This means loss of appetite. See anorexia, page 220.

INFLAMMATORY BOWEL DISEASE

This disease is probably the commonest cause of chronic vomiting and diarrhea. It may be intermittent initially and with more long-standing cases can also cause weight loss. It can be mild through to severe.

There are different causes. The disease is suggestive of an immune reaction to something in the gut and it is probably an abnormality of the cat's immune system. Some cats have been shown to have a food allergy.

As there are other causes of vomiting and diarrhea (see pages 225-226, 238), in order to make a diagnosis, a range of tests must be performed. Inflammatory bowel disease is diagnosed by examination of the gut and biopsies, and this procedure also rules out tumors of the gut which may produce very similar signs. Biopsies are taken by endoscopy or surgery.

The following treatments may be tried: hypoallergenic diets, corticosteroids, certain antibiotics and antiparasitic drugs, and other immunosuppressive drugs. Some cats respond and relapse and can be difficult to control; other cats may come off treatment after months or years.

INHERITED DISORDERS

There are many inherited disorders, most of which are rare and there is not room to cover them all in this text. The most clinically significant are hypertrophic cardiomyopathy (see heart disease, page 231); polycystic kidney disease (see kidney disease, below); amyloidosis (seen in Siamese and Abyssinians where amyloid is deposited in various organs leading to organ failure); cryptorchism (failure for one or both testicles to descend into the scrotum properly); deafness in white cats; congenital heart defects; and undershot and overshot jaws.

Affected cats should never be bred from. Unfortunately, some of these problems do not show signs until later in life. It should be remembered that many cat breeds have been developed by humans specifically breeding in abnormal genes, e.g. the Manx.

JAUNDICE

Jaundice is the yellowing of the skin, mouth and the whites of the eyes. It is a symptom of certain anemias, liver disease or a blockage of the biliary system (see liver disease, page 234, and anemia, page 220).

KIDNEY DISEASE

Kidney disease is a common condition of older cats, but may be seen at any age. The signs are: increased drinking (polydipsia), increased urination (polyuria), weight loss, depression, vomiting, inappetence, dehydration and hypertension. These signs are vague and can mimic many other conditions so tests, particularly blood and urine tests, are needed to confirm the presence of kidney failure. X-rays, ultrasound, urine cultures and kidney biopsies may be necessary to find the underlying cause.

Causes of kidney disease and subsequent failure include: chronic interstitial nephritis (the commonest cause), tumors (not very common except lymphomas), amyloidosis (see inherited disorders, above), drug and toxin damage, bacterial infections, FIP, glomerulonephritis, polycystic disease (see inherited disorders) and blockage of the urinary system. Older cats with kidney failure and small kidneys usually have chronic interstitial nephritis.

Treatment depends on how ill the cat is. Very ill, dehydrated cats need intensive treatment, hospitalization and being on a drip. If they can be stabilized, they can then be tried on treatments for long-term help for kidney failure. These include diets that are restricted in phosphate and protein. Research has shown that cats with kidney failure eating these diets live two to three times longer than cats eating ordinary foods.

Affected cats should always have free access to water. Other drugs can help with the secondary problems of chronic kidney failure, such as feeling sick, inappetence, hypertension and anemia. Potassium supplements may be necessary in the foods. Cats with evidence of infections will need courses of antibiotics and some types of tumor can respond well to drugs.

There is much that can now be done for cats with chronic kidney failure, but they need regular monitoring by the veterinarian. These cats can live happy lives for a number of years with this disease, so treatment is often very worthwhile.

LIVER DISEASE

Signs of liver disease are often vague – loss of appetite, depression, weight loss, vomiting and increased drinking. Jaundice may occur especially in more severely affected cats. Liver disease is not one single condition so, before treatment, we must try to find the cause.

A diagnosis is made using blood tests, X-rays, ultrasound and biopsy of the liver. Common causes of liver disease are chlongiohepatitis (where bacteria move up the bile ducts from the gut into the liver); lymphocytic cholangitis (a disease of unknown cause); hepatic lipidosis (fatty damage to the liver, seen much more in USA than Europe – possibly due to the increased incidence of obesity in the USA); tumors (especially lymphoma and carcinomas); FIP; and toxic damage.

Treatment is usually medical. Some severely ill cats may need hospitalization, fluids and nutritional support. Tablets may be necessary for months or for life. Sometimes tumors can be surgically removed, but most are not treatable.

MURMURS

Heart murmurs are abnormal sounds that the veterinary surgeon may hear when listening to a cat's heart. They often indicate that heart disease is present, though occasionally they are innocent or due to other problems, such as anemia (page 220) or hypertension (page 231-232).

NASAL DISCHARGES/SNEEZING

The commonest cause of sneezing or nasal discharge is feline upper respiratory tract disease complex (see page 229); other causes are tumors, a foreign body in the nose e.g. a piece of grass, polyps (inflammatory masses especially seen in young cats), trauma, fungal infections, and allergies to dust and pollen.

Tests may need to be performed when there is a need for urgent treatment, such as to remove a foreign body, or in the case of a chronic problem that has not responded to treatment. Tests include: examination under anaesthetic with an endoscope, X-rays, blood tests, nasal biopsies and doing cultures for cat flu viruses, fungi and bacteria.

Treatment depends on the cause. The commonest cause of chronic nasal discharge is chronic cat flu damage; these cats cannot be cured, but can be helped with long-term antibiotic treatments and other drugs.

Polyps can be removed but may recur; tumors often have a poor outlook, except lymphoma which can respond to treatments. Fungal infections need long courses of treatment.

OBESITY

Obesity is having excess body fat. Being overweight is a common problem in cats and it affects their life-expectancy, their health and their enjoyment of life. The most common cause is eating more calories than are needed for the cat's daily activities. In fact, the popular belief that cats only eat what they need and that they moderate their intake is by no means true and cats will often overeat if given the opportunity. Overeating may result from overfeeding, greediness or boredom. It is rare for a medical problem to cause obesity in cats.

The problems obesity can cause or make worse probably include heart disease, joint disease, hypertension, breathing problems, and liver disease. It increases the risks of surgery and anesthetics, and increases the likelihood of labor problems in queens. It may lower the resistance to infections. Overweight cats have problems grooming.

Veterinary surgeons and veterinary nurses can help with weight reduction programs, along with lower calorie foods, stopping neighbors or members of the family feeding cats, and being strong-willed when those big eyes look at you.

POLYDIPSIA/ POLYURIA

Polydipsia is excessive drinking and polyuria is excessive urination. They often go together, and are nearly always indicative of a serious disease going on. Often owners do not know how much their cats drink, but if you see a change in your cat's drinking habits, it is worth taking note, especially if you have noticed any other changes. Common causes of polydipsia and polyuria are kidney disease, diabetes and hyperthyroidism, but there are many less common causes which can be investigated.

RINGWORM

See dermatophytosis, page 224-225.

ROAD TRAFFIC ACCIDENTS

This is the commonest cause of trauma and death in cats. The injuries can vary from none to instant death, or to medical and surgical problems that may cost a lot to fix. It is a risk we take if we allow our cats to roam outside freely. See Chapter Eighteen.

SKIN ALLERGIES

Allergies are the commonest cause of skin disease. There are four common ways in which the allergies show: miliary dermatitis (small bumps over the body especially along the back); hair loss; eosinophilic granuloma complex (upper lip ulcers or raised bald, reddened areas of skin) and excoriation (hair is scratched out by the cat and the skin becomes raw). A hallmark of allergies is itchy skin, but cats often lick rather than scratch. Often they overgroom in private so owners never see it, but just see the damaged skin.

FLEA ALLERGY

The vast majority of allergies are due to flea bite reactions. When fleas bite, some flea saliva enters the cat. In some individuals, this leads to an allergic reaction. Treatment should be thorough anti-flea treatment of the affected cat, other cats and dogs, and the home. It will recur if fleas are not prevented.

FOOD ALLERGY

This is usually an allergy against a type of protein in the food e.g. beef, fish, chicken etc. To diagnose a food allergy, a food trial with a special diet, decided on by your veterinarian, will be necessary. The special diet will avoid proteins that your cat has been known to eat; if she improves on the diet, then the old food is reintroduced to see if the symptoms return. Performing a good food trial can be difficult as it takes weeks and your cat must not be able to eat anything other than the new diet. Treatment is to avoid the allergy-producing substance. This may be difficult.

ATOPY

This is an allergy to inhaled particles, such as the housedust mite, pollen and moulds, and can be diagnosed by blood and/or skin tests. It is often impossible to avoid the substances that the cat is allergic to; occasionally hyposensitization is tried with a course of injections, but often drugs are needed to control the itching.

Drugs may also be necessary to control a food allergy or while treatment for fleas is taking place.

SNEEZING

See feline upper respiratory tract disease (see page 234) and nasal discharges (see pages 229-230).

TUMORS

It is beyond the scope of this book to discuss all possible tumors that cats can get, so we will talk about three common ones. Any lumps or bumps should be investigated, as the only way to make a diagnosis is to have an experienced person look at the cells under the microscope.

LYMPHOMA

Lymphoma is a solid tumor made up of white blood cells. If the cells are mainly in the bloodstream rather than a solid lump, it is called leukemia. Lymphomas can be found anywhere in the body but common sites are the chest (in younger cats), the kidneys, or the gut. A malignant tumor damages the organs where it is growing and will spread to other tissues. It is commonly associated with infection with FeLV, though not all cats have the virus at the time of having the tumor.

The outlook for cats with lymphoma is variable. Sometimes they respond very well to drug treatment (chemotherapy) so this can be well worth trying. There are, however, a number of things to consider when deciding whether to try treatment. Your cat will need repeated veterinary visits, so how well does she tolerate this? How ill is she? What tissues are affected? Does she have FeLV? Can you afford it? Not all veterinary practices undertake treatment for cancer and you may need to visit a specialist center. It is important to keep side effects from the treatment to a minimum so that the patient can enjoy a reasonable quality of life.

MAMMARY TUMORS

Cats have two strips of mammary tissue running along their chest and abdomen, and they can get tumors anywhere in this tissue. Unfortunately, nearly all mammary lumps in cats are malignant tumors. The smaller the lump is and the sooner it is discovered, the better the outlook. Unfortunately, they seem to spread early on, so the outlook for many cats is poor.

Surgical removal is the best treatment at present and removing all the mammary tissue on the affected side is recommended. Chemotherapy has been tried a little, but there is no good evidence at present that it is of considerable help.

SQUAMOUS CELL CARCINOMA

This is seen especially in cats with pink skin on the ears, nose and face, and is caused by UV light damage from the sun. It is a malignant skin cancer which spreads locally, damaging tissues in the surrounding area. If caught early, surgery can remove it. To start with, they can look like scratches or scabs that don't go away. At-risk cats should be protected by keeping them in, especially during the hottest hours of the day and on sunny days, and/or using a high-factor sun protection cream on the vulnerable areas (though most cats quickly remove the cream through grooming).

TOXICOSES

It is beyond the scope of this book to discuss all possible things that are toxic to cats. Cats are prone to toxicoses because they tend to metabolize chemicals differently to other animals.

Common causes of toxicity are: anti-flea and anti-insect products (new, more expensive products available from vets tend to be safer); many drugs including acetaminophen (paracetamol), and other human medications; some plants; household chemicals, especially products that may get on paws or the coat and be licked off; products to kill slugs, snails or vermin that cats may then eat; car anti-freeze (more common in colder climates).

Prevention is always better than cure, so do not ever give your cat any human medications or products not designed for cats. Never use multiple medications on your cat without seeking veterinary advice, and always read labels carefully. Keep household cleaners away from cats and rinse surfaces after their use.

If you think your cat has ingested something she shouldn't have, talk to your veterinarian immediately and try to show him or her any packaging.

See also pages 214-215.

VOMITING

Vomiting is a bodily reflex which is controlled by the brain. Causes of vomiting include: disease, distension or irritation of the stomach or intestines (e.g. inflammatory bowel disease, tumors, foreign bodies, infections); disease or inflammation of other areas of the abdomen (e.g. pancreatitis or peritonitis); blood-borne substances affecting the brain (e.g. drugs or toxin build-up due to kidney failure); stimulation of the balance canals (e.g. motion sickness); psychological causes (due to fear, stress or excitement); and increased pressure in the brain.

Because there are many causes, investigations are necessary for a chronic problem. Blood and urine tests, X-rays, endoscopy, with biopsies and sometimes ultrasound or surgery, will usually diagnose the cause. Treatment depends on the cause.

WEIGHT LOSS

There are many causes of weight loss, particularly in older cats, and it is often accompanied by other signs. If a cat is losing weight, even if she is eating well, it should be investigated.

ZOONOSES

Zoonoses are animal infections which can be passed on to humans. Zoonotic cat infections include: Pasteurella and cat scratch fever from cat bites and scratches; roundworms (mainly a risk to young children); Toxoplasma (mainly a risk for pregnant women as it can damage the unborn baby); dermatophytosis; cowpox; Salmonella; Campylobacter and tuberculosis. This is not an exhaustive list.

Those most vulnerable are: people who work with cats; people whose immune system is compromised (such as very young babies); those on immunosuppressive drugs or chemotherapy; and those with immunosuppressive illnesses, such as AIDS.

Chapter 29

Alternative Therapies

Alternative medicine and complementary medicine are all-embracing titles, which imply many separate disciplines, usually involving two common themes: natural medicines and holistic principles.

There are three major 'systems' of medicine included under this heading: homeopathy, Chinese medicine (incorporating acupuncture), and herbal medicine; and two supportive therapies: chiropractic and physiotherapy/massage. An overview of these will be provided in very brief detail below.

Broadly speaking, homeopathy and acupuncture act as stimulants or triggers to the body's healing powers. Herbal medicine, the true forebear of modern conventional medicine, is a holistically-based therapy which uses blends of natural substances directly to alter the body's way of operating. Other therapies, such as Bach flowers, radionics, color therapy, tissue salts, anthroposophy, osteopathy, etc. are not described here but do attach themselves to the 'alternative medicine' tag.

Physiotherapy, a worthwhile system of helping the body to rehabilitate after, for instance, injury, is not a system of medicine in its own right, neither stimulating healing nor directly altering biochemistry. While it has little 'stand-alone' therapeutic value in disease, it is a very useful and often invaluable support to any system of medicine.

HEALTHY EATING

A study of nutrition and the necessary understanding to formulate natural diets, which are wholesome, as free as possible from pollution with modern chemicals, and which are compatible with the special evolved needs of each species, is a fundamental requirement of any medicine which purports to be holistic. For instance, it is folly to feed vegetarian diets to cats. They need to chew bones and raw flesh in order to maintain gum and teeth health. This is one of the disease areas least well prevented in our modern management. I prefer to feed fresh food to cats, rather than the processed canned or bagged foods, in the same way that I consider it wiser for humans to eat fresh food. Diet is a common thread through all the 'systems' of natural medicine, and is vitally important to health and to healing.

VETERINARY HOMEOPATHY

Veterinary homeopathy is based on the same principles as its human medical counterpart, i.e. the principles discovered and worked out by Samuel Hahnemann in Germany in 1790.

Homeopathy is the science of medicine based on the principle 'similia similibus curentur' (let likes be cured by likes). Samuel Hahnemann discovered that Peruvian Bark (or cinchona which gives us the drug quinine) was able to produce signs and symptoms in a healthy body quite indistinguishable from those of malaria, a disease which it is singularly well able to cure. This apparently paradoxical effect he named 'homeopathy', which is Greek for 'similar to the suffering'.

An analogous phenomenon is observable for an infinite variety of substances, whether plant, animal or mineral in origin. In other words, in order to cure a disease syndrome, we must select a substance most able to produce similar signs and symptoms in a healthy body. The substances used are commonly known as remedies. Their properties are listed in books called *Homeopathic Materia Medica*.

HOW DOES HOMEOPATHY WORK?

Hahnemann found, in addition to this startling discovery, that if he serially diluted his curative substances (and succussed or violently agitated the solution at each stage), they were less and less able to produce any harmful effects and became (paradoxically again) more and more powerful curatively.

We now know, from molecular and atomic physics, that his common dilutions were beyond the point at which we would mathematically expect the last molecule or atom to remain. This 'sub-molecular' nature of the remedies means that we are using energy, not drug material, as a curative force. This rules out any chance of 'side effects' and hence rules out any damage that ensues from such side effects.

The dilutions are called 'potencies'. The level of potency is denoted by a number, written after the remedy name, and representing the number and scale of dilution undergone by the solution (e.g. 30c denotes a dilution of one-in-one-hundred, repeated thirty times, i.e. 10^{-60}).

Homeopathy treats the animal as an 'energetic whole', not as a collection of symptoms with a specific 'scientific' disease name. Since we are treating the animal itself, not the disease, we need to know a great deal of information about the patient and about its medical history, its background and its home environment. This entails asking seemingly strange questions, which appear often to be quite unrelated to the specific problem for which the animal is presented. To achieve good health, we also need to identify and remove those factors, in the life of the patient, which may impede healing.

Homeopathy is a force for good in the animal world, since it is able to treat so many diseases, ranging from simple to serious and acute to chronic, quite without the risk of side effects and without the need for laboratory animal experimentation. Humans have already volunteered as 'guinea pigs' and have done the work of determining the effects of the substances in healthy bodies!

Since the prescription is so 'individualized' for any named disease, many different homeopathic medicines may be required for different patients. Conversely, a single homeopathic medicine may be able to treat many different diseases, if the symptom-picture in a particular patient fits that of the remedy. This apparent paradox is not easily comprehended by the conventionally-trained mind.

Homeopathy works by stimulating the body's own powers of healing. The final outcome of treatment by homeopathy depends both upon the prescriber's ability to select the correct remedy and upon the animal's ability to respond. We do not necessarily need to know the 'name' of the disease and, in many cases, diseases may be undiagnosable, in a conventional sense. If no mechanism exists in the body to heal the disease effects, then necessarily no cure can result (e.g. in kidney degeneration). The best we can hope for in such diseases is an improvement in the animal's quality of life, cessation of the degenerative process and a stimulation of remaining healthy tissue to function better. Nevertheless, many so-called 'incurable' diseases can respond.

WHAT CAN HOMEOPATHY TREAT?

The range of diseases which can respond to homeopathy is very wide but it is particularly useful in:

- Skin disorders
- Allergies
- Digestive disturbances
- Viral diseases (for which conventional medicine has no answer)
- Behavioral disorders (since we are treating mind and body together)
- Inappropriate urination behavior
- Cardiac support
- Acute conditions such as injuries.

Patients suffering cancer are also presented regularly. There are opportunities of success, but only if the disease has not gone too far, if the body has sufficient ability to fight the disease (with help), and if diet and other external factors can be optimized. While individual successes are wonderful news, the overall success rate is not high.

VETERINARY ACUPUNCTURE

Veterinary acupuncture is based on the ancient Chinese art of acupuncture in humans, which started to evolve anything up to 4,000 years ago. It is part of Traditional Chinese Medicine (TCM), which also includes Chinese herbal medicine, dietary wisdom, and moxibustion (below).

Acupuncture, properly applied, treats the animal as an 'energetic whole', rather than as a body presenting with a specific named disease. As such it constitutes much more than a method of pain relief. This is especially true when it is used as originally intended, along with diet work and internal medicine. Many of the disappointments of modern veterinary acupuncture are probably attributable to the modern tendency to short cuts, needling without the full dietary and medical support which is part of the tradition.

Disease is considered to be a result of disordered energy flow in the body. The normal energy patterns in humans were charted in China, several thousand years ago, in the shape of meridians or channels, of which there are 26 major ones. Health depends upon the regular rhythmic flow of energy within these channels and upon the balance between Yin and Yang, 'the eternal opposites'. When the energy flow is interrupted, disturbed or wrongly distributed, symptoms of disease are seen.

Cure of the disease depends upon rebalancing the disturbance and this is done by the stimulation of precisely identified points on the body surface. These points can be stimulated in various ways, e.g. needles, finger massage, heat (moxibustion), laser, electrical impulse, implant or injection. Herbs and diet are also brought to bear, by the wise practitioner, to aid return to a proper energetic balance.

QI: THE LIFE ENERGY

The mechanisms involved in the working of acupuncture, based as it is on oriental philosophy, are obscure to modern Western minds, which use linear thinking. Each living creature is thought to be endowed at birth with life energy (Qi or ch'i). This energy is consumed by the body in the business of living and is replenished by eating and breathing. Imbalance in the flow of this energy through the meridians is caused by internal or external factors (pernicious influences, which the good practitioner must identify and minimize), and is the fundamental process of disease.

The acupuncturist will attempt to correct this imbalance by stimulation of specific points. These points are often far removed from the site of apparent trouble, since points are found, relating to various organs and functions, over the whole body.

The primary purpose of acupuncture treatment is to stimulate the body's own healing powers and its own ability to maintain the equilibrium of its internal environment. The acupuncturist is therefore less concerned with the specific 'scientific' name of the disease from which the animal is suffering than he is with the nature of the general energy imbalance caused and the causative factors themselves.

WHAT CAN ACUPUNCTURE TREAT?

Diseases which can respond are not merely painful conditions, such as injury, lameness (arthritis), or back problems, but also many internal diseases. The success depends upon the body's stimulated ability to heal, and therefore upon whether or not mechanisms exist within the body which, if appropriately stimulated, can resolve the problem. There are therefore many spectacular successes, some major disappointments, and a proportion of cases in which temporary relief only is achieved. A notable area of consistent success is in the treatment of nerve dysfunction or paralysis.

WHAT DOES TREATMENT ENTAIL?

Treatment is generally non-painful. Some sensation, transitional between pain and pleasure, can be felt by humans at the site of needling, so it is reasonable to assume that animals feel a similar effect. There is often a relaxing effect during treatment and an immense sleepiness for 24 hours following treatment. Treatment lasts for varying periods from 5 to 30 minutes usually, generally averaging 15 to 20 minutes. We usually repeat the treatment at between 2- to 14-day intervals and, if no response is seen after 3 or 4 such treatments, the likelihood of a response is much reduced.

Cats tolerate acupuncture well. I have even had a feline patient continue to eat, with seven needles sticking out of her face.

VETERINARY HERBAL MEDICINE

Herbal medicine is as old as human civilization itself. Records go back as far as the oldest medical text books known, some 4,000 years ago, according to some sources.

All cultures have deep traditions of herbal medicine and a study of those in different civilizations makes not only for fascinating reading but also for a wealth of medical lore. African tribes, Amazonian Indians, Native North Americans, Middle Eastern and Near Eastern cultures, the Indian subcontinent, the Far East, including, of course, China, Australian Aborigines, Maoris and many others, all show understanding of the wisdom of herbal medicine. They have a rich and diverse plant medicine culture, deeply integrated within their societies. Only the poor Eskimo would have had difficulty in building up a large herbal pharmacopœia – so widespread and varied are the botanical gifts bestowed upon us by nature! It is hard to imagine anyone in Britain living more than 100 yards from at least one plant species with known medical properties, even in urban centers.

It is not surprising that our forefathers mingled religion, mystique, folklore and superstition with their medicine. Shamanism and its counterparts were very much linked with reputed medical knowledge, and witch doctors, druids, tribal medicine men and, later, in medieval Europe, the Christian church, took on the role of traditional medical continuity.

LOST KNOWLEDGE

Astrology also became entangled with herbal medicine, a tradition epitomized by Nicholas Culpeper in the mid-17th century. Herbal medicine, however, still holds its validity without the strong mystical and religious connotations handed down to us from ancient works. Sadly, many traditions of herbal medicine were unwritten and many formulas, which were enshrined in oral tradition, will have been lost over the centuries, as a result of the conquest of civilizations and the destruction of cultures. Many of these will inevitably ever remain hidden to our modern world.

Even when records were properly made, wars and clashes of culture often combined to destroy them. For instance 700,000 or more books, amassed in the medical school in Alexandria (incorporating information from conquered territories such as India and the Middle East), were destroyed by Christian fanatics in 391 AD. The pictogram records of the Aztecs, encoding great culture and lore, were destroyed by the Conquistadors, in an act of mindless vandalism so often enacted by conquering armies throughout history. Victory brings on a form of intoxication, fuelled by adrenaline and by the perceived need to subjugate by destruction of culture.

Even in modern times, systematic efforts at eliminating herbal competitors to the modern drug industry have been seen. The massive profits to be obtained from drugs, so often directly derived from the very plant medicine the industry professes to despise, are a powerful magnet and anesthetic to conscience.

WESTERN HERBAL MEDICINE

Our western herbal medicine culture dates back to Greek and Roman traditions, oversown with lore from Saxon and medieval scholars from all over Europe. Names, such as Hippocrates, Pliny, Dioscorides, Galen, Paracelsus, Gerard and Culpeper, crop up again and again in writings. The rationale behind herbal medicine has changed and evolved through these times, astrological and religious beliefs being intertwined with medical experience.

However, one recurring theme which dates back to Paracelsus and probably much earlier, is the Doctrine of Signatures, or the Cosmic Principle of Signatures. According to this principle, a plant could give a clue to its medical uses via its habit, habitat, morphology and appearance. Chelidonium (the Greater Celandine), for instance, is a remarkable remedy for jaundice. It led ancient prescribers to this idea via its bright yellow sap, which turns skin a bright orangey-yellow color, exactly as if the person were suffering jaundice. Turmeric was similarly adopted in the ancient East, showing this 'theory' to be widespread among independent peoples.

Nowadays, however, herbal medicines are selected more according to their known medical action, which is mediated via their analyzed ingredients. Active chemicals in plants, in unique combinations, have known medical effects which are supported by modern science, e.g. alkaloids, glycosides, saponins, flavones. Herbs can also be grouped according to their general action, e.g. alteratives, aperients, astringents, bitters, demulcents, diuretics, expectorants, nervines, vulneraries.

In fact, a surprisingly large proportion of modern conventional drug medicines are either prepared from herbal material or owe their origins to herbs. For example, vincristine started from the Madagascar periwinkle, aspirin (salicylic acid) from willow or meadowsweet, digoxin from the foxglove, morphine derivatives from the opium poppy and so on. Many other drugs have originated from fungi, for example penicillin from moulds, ivermectin (a powerful modern anthelmintic and parasiticide) from a Japanese soil fungus.

One major difference between modern chemical medicine and properly applied traditional herbalism, however, is the holistic principle. This is applied both to the patient (i.e. treating the patient as a whole rather than just trying to counteract the symptoms), and to the medicine (using the whole plant with its 'drugs' and many essential natural synergists, as opposed to a single supposed 'active ingredient'). Also, herbs can be combined in a formula, which is tailored to the individual, in order to achieve a balancing effect within the body. It is these properties which render herbal medicine so safe, when properly applied by adequately qualified people, avoiding harmful side effects.

WHAT CAN BE TREATED?

Herbal remedies have proved useful for the majority of disease conditions from which animals suffer, either on their own or co-ordinated and integrated with other therapies, such as homeopathy or acupuncture. Nutrition is also vital. Lung allergies, rheumatism and arthritis, hyperexcitability, digestive problems and many others respond well.

Treatment with herbs is safe and without side effects, as long as it is used carefully, with due regard to formulas and doses. It can be given in fresh form, chopped leaves, dried form, capsules, powders, tablets, tinctures, infusions, oils, creams, ointments, etc., but instructions must always be carefully followed. All species of animals respond to this most natural of therapies.

It is as well, however, to watch out for products with inadequate labeling and those formulated by manufacturers who may not have the appropriate tradition, knowledge or understanding of the subject. The marketing of such products owes more to commercial intentions than to good or safe medicine. Off-the-shelf formulas show no pretence at individualization for a given patient, so stand little chance of being ideal and some chance of being downright dangerous. The naming of such products often contains a cunningly worded and quasi-legal allusion to a specific disease syndrome, in order to encourage sales.

CHIROPRACTIC

Meaning, literally, done by hand, this is a form of manipulative therapy. The McTimoney training for animal chiropractors teaches very gentle techniques. Some other forms of chiropractic can be a little 'heroic', in my opinion.

Since the innervation for the organs and muscles of the body (whether conscious or autonomic) comes from the spine, it stands to reason that body function can be directly affected by spinal alignment. Many feline patients show some degree of misalignment, correction of which produces immediate evidence of relaxation and comfort. There is particularly an effect on the jumping ability and co-ordination of hind limb movement by pelvic misalignment, which many cats show.

It is recommended that only suitably qualified animal chiropractors are visited, unless your veterinary surgeon has the necessary skills. They can only operate on your veterinarian's recommendation and under your veterinarian's supervision.

PHYSIOTHERAPY AND MASSAGE

As mentioned before, this is not a 'stand-alone' therapy, but a means of health maintenance or of encouraging healing, by gentle massage and active movement. It has great wellbeing benefits, if gently and sympathetically performed. Correct movement provides the body with the necessary challenge, for correct healing of locomotor structures. If the cat does not like it, then it is not being done correctly for that patient.

There is a plethora of technological instruments, designed to enhance the capability of the practitioner. These have advantages and disadvantages, and their safety or efficacy depends greatly upon the skills and sensitivity of the practitioner.

As with chiropractic, physiotherapists can only operate on your veterinarian's recommendation and under your vet's supervision.

SUMMARY

There is a huge wealth of knowledge and understanding, accumulated over many centuries of human civilization, which can be brought to the aid of ailing or disabled animals. This lore is supported by some good modern research work and by a continuous thread of clinical reports and experiences, leading down the ages to the present day. There are also training courses for veterinarians in the major therapies. The safety of natural medicine, in the right hands, is unrivalled, having been tested 'in the field' for so long. The quality of natural medicines, if purchased from properly-licensed manufacturers, is on a par with the best that modern pharmacies can offer.

Pet insurance companies are acknowledging the benefit of natural therapies, and are covering fees on their pet policies. If natural medicine help is needed for an animal, then it is best to seek out those organizations which can provide a list of properly trained veterinary surgeons. Those veterinarians will be able either to provide the best possible care or to refer the patient to a colleague who is well-versed in the appropriate techniques. In both the UK and the USA, it is illegal for any medicines to be prescribed or acupuncture to be given to animals, except by a qualified veterinarian; manipulation therapies alone are permitted for non-veterinarians.

I: Useful Addresses

SHOWING

CAT FANCIERS' ASSOCIATION (CFA)
PO Box 1005, Manasquan,
NJ 08736-0805, USA
Tel: 732 528 9797
Fax: 732 528 7391
Email: cfa@cfainc.org
Web: www.cfa.inc.org

THE INTERNATIONAL CAT
ASSOCIATION (TICA)
PO Box 2684, Harlingen
TX 78551, USA
Tel: 956 428 8046
Fax: 956 428 8047
Email: ticaeo@xanadu2.net
Web: www.tica.org

GOVERNING COUNCIL OF THE CAT
FANCY (GCCF)
4-6 Penel Orlieu, Bridgwater
Somerset, TA6 3PG, UK
Tel: 01278 427575
Email: GCCF_CATS@compuserve. com
Web: www.gccfcats.org

CAT PRESS

CATS AND KITTENS MAGAZINE
Pet Publishing, Inc.
7-L Dundas Circle, Greensboro,
NC 27407
USA
Tel: 336 292 4047
Fax: 336 292 4272
Email: info@petpublishing.com
Web: www.catsand kittens.com

YOUR CAT MAGAZINE
Roebuck House, 33 Broad Street, Stamford
Lincolnshire, PE9 1RB, UK
Tel: 01780 766199
Fax: 01780 766416
Email: various email addresses according to
the query – see the webpage.
Web: www.yourcat.co.uk

OUR CATS
This is for show enthusiasts, and is the official
journal of the GCCF.
5 James Leigh Street, Manchester
M1 5NF, UK
Tel: 0161 236 6966
Fax: 0161 236 5534
Email: accounts@ourdogs.co.uk
Web: www.ourcats.co.uk

SHELTERS/CHARITIES

AMERICAN SOCIETY FOR THE
PREVENTION OF CRUELTY TO
ANIMALS (ASPCA)
424 East 92nd Street, New York,

NY 10128, USA
Tel: 212 876 7700
Email: website@aspca.org
Web: www.aspca.org

THE HUMANE SOCIETY OF THE
UNITED STATES (HSUS)
2100 L Street, NW, Washington
DC 20037, USA
Tel: 202 452 1100
Email: via website
Web: www.hsus.org

CATS' PROTECTION
17 Kings Road, Horsham, West Sussex
RH13 5PN, UK
Tel: 01403 221900
Fax: 01403 218 414
Email: cpl@cats.org.uk
Web: www.cats.org.uk

BLUE CROSS
Shilton Road, Burford, Oxfordshire
OX18 4PF, UK
Tel: 01993 822651
Fax: 01993 823083
Email: info@bluecross.org.uk
Web: www.bluecross.org.uk

FERAL SUPPORT

FERAL CAT COALITION
9528 Miramar Road, PMB 160, San Diego
CA 92126, USA
Tel: 619 497 1599 (local only)
Email: rsavage@feralcat.com
Web: www.feralcat.com

ALLEY CAT ALLIES
1801 Belmont Road NW, Suite 201
Washington, DC20009, USA
Tel: 202 667 3630
Fax: 202 667 3640
Email: alleycat@alleycat.org
Web: www.alleycat.org

THE ORIGINAL CAT ACTION TRUST
PO Box 2202, Bishops Stortford,
Hertfordshire, CM23 2SW, UK
Tel: 01279 757184
Fax: 0208 660 6011
Email: info@o-cat.freeserve.co.uk
Web: o-cat.freeserve.co.uk

LOW-COST NEUTERING

SPAY USA
North Shore Animal League International
14 Vanderventer Avenue, Suite L-1
Port Washington, NY 10050, USA
Tel: 800 248 SPAY
Email: via website
Web: www.spayusa.org

LOVE THAT CAT
The website, which can be found at
www.lovethatcat.com/spayneuter.html, also has
a state-by-state listing of low-cost neutering
programs.

CELIA HAMMOND ANIMAL TRUST
The Trust also has a rescue shelter.
The Celia Hammond Animal Trust Head
Office
The High Street, Wadhurst, East Sussex
TN5 6AG, UK
Tel: 01892 783820
Fax: 01892 784882
Email: info@celiahammond.org
Web: www.celiahammond.org

PEOPLE'S DISPENSARY FOR SICK
ANIMALS (PDSA)
Free/subsidized veterinary care to those who
are unable to afford it.
Whitechapel Way, Priorslee, Telford
Shropshire, TF2 9PQ, UK
Tel: 01952 290999
Fax: 01952 291035
Email: via website
Web: www.pdsa.org.uk

BEHAVIOR COUNSELING

Your veterinarian will refer you to a counselor.

ASSOCIATION OF PET BEHAVIOR COUNSELING (APBC)
PO Box 46, Worcester, WR8 9YS, UK
Tel: 01386 751151
Email: apbc@petbcent.demon.co.uk
Web: www.apbc.org.uk

GENERAL ADVICE

FELINE ADVISORY BUREAU (FAB)
FAB publishes leaflets on a host of subjects, and the website is invaluable to all cat owners – check it out!
FAB
Taeselbury, High Street, Tisbury
Wiltshire, SP3 6LD, UK
Tel: 01747 871872
Fax: 01747 871 873
Email: fabcats@fabcats.org
Web: www.fabcats.org

VETERINARY BODIES

THE ROYAL COLLEGE OF VETERINARY SURGEONS (RCVS)
Belgravia House, 62-64, Horseferry Road
London, SW1P 2AF, UK
Tel: 020 7222 2001

AMERICAN ASSOCIATION OF VETERINARY STATE BOARDS
3100 Main Street, Suite 208, Kansas City, MO 64111, USA
Tel: 816 931 1504
Email: info@aavsb.org
Website: www.aavsb.org

THERAPY CATS

As a cat owner you will experience numerous psychological, emotional and physical benefits from contact with your pet. To spread the benefits to those who are unable to have a pet (in hospitals, residential homes, hospices etc.), why not inquire about therapy-cat work, where well-behaved, friendly cats visit those in need of a good cat cuddle?

NET PETS
PO Box 563, N. Myrtle Beach,
SC 28597, USA
Tel: 842 249 5262
Email: info@netpets.com
Web: www.netpets.com

PETS AS THERAPY
4 New Road, Ditton, Maidstone
Kent, ME20 6AD, UK
Tel: 01732 872222
Fax: 01732 842175
Email: info@pat-prodog.org.uk
Web: www.pat-prodog.org.uk

PET LOSS

PET LOSS SUPPORT
Fantastic site, with lots of advice and support.
www.petloss.com

ASSOCIATION FOR PET LOSS AND BEREAVEMENT
PO Box 106, Brooklyn,
New York 11230, USA
Tel: 718 382 0690
Email: aplb@aplb.org
Web: www.aplb.org

SOCIETY OF COMPANION ANIMAL STUDIES (SCAS)
Organizes a befriender service, where people can talk to a trained pet loss counselor.
10b Leny Road, Callander, FK17 8BA, Scotland, UK
Tel: 0800 096 6606
Email: via website
Web: www.scas.org.uk/pbss.htm

II: Cat Breed Groupings

Appendices

CAT FANCIERS' ASSOCIATION (CFA) GROUPINGS, USA

CHAMPIONSHIP CLASS

Abyssinian
American Curl
American Shorthair
American Wirehair
Balinese
Birman
Bombay
British Shorthair
Burmese
Chartreux
Colorpoint Shorthair
Cornish Rex
Devon Rex
Egyptian Mau
Exotic
Havana Brown
Japanese Bobtail
Javanese
Korat
Maine Coon
Manx
Norwegian Forest Cat
Ocicat
Oriental
Persian (including Himalayan)
Ragdoll
Russian Blue
Scottish Fold
Selkirk Rex
Siamese
Singapura
Somali
Tonkinese
Turkish Angora
Turkish Van

PROVISIONAL CLASS

European Burmese (N.B. The European Burmese is
eligible for Championship Competition in the
International Division of shows only. At all other
times, it remains in the Provisional Class).

MISCELLANEOUS CLASS

American Bobtail
Laperm
Siberian
Sphynx

GOVERNING COUNCIL OF THE CAT FANCY (GCCF) GROUPINGS, UK

LONGHAIR (PERSIAN)

Bi-colour
Cameo
Chinchilla
Colourpoint
Exotic (Shorthaired, Persian type)
Golden
Pewter
Self
Shaded
Smoke
Tabby, including Tortie Tabby (Classic)
Tortie, including Tortie & White

SEMI-LONGHAIR
Birman
Maine Coon
Norwegian Forest Cat
Ragdoll
Somali
Turkish Van

BRITISH SHORTHAIR
Bi-colour
Colourpointed
Manx
Self
Smoke
Tabby, including Tortie Tabby (Classic, Mackerel, Spotted)
Tipped
Tortie, including Tortie & White

FOREIGN
Abyssinian
Asian, including Bombay and Burmilla
Tiffanie (Longhaired Asian)
Bengal
Cornish Rex
Devon Rex
Korat
Ocicat
Russian
Singapura
Tonkinese

ORIENTAL
Angora (Longhaired Oriental)
Oriental Selfs, including Havana and Foreign White
Shaded
Smoke
Tabby, including Tortie Tabby (Classic, Spotted, Mackerel, Ticked)
Tortie

BURMESE
Self
Tortie

SIAMESE
Self-pointed
Tabby-pointed, including Tortie Tabby
Tortie-pointed
Balinese (Longhaired Siamese).

THE INTERNATIONAL CAT ASSOCIATION (TICA) GROUPINGS

CHAMPIONSHIP CLASS
Abyssinian
American Shorthair
American Wirehair
Bengal
Birman
British Shorthair
Burmese
Chartreux
Cornish Rex
Cymric
Devon Rex
Exotic Shorthair
Havan
Himalayan
Maine Coon
Manx
Norwegian Forest Cat
Ocicat
Oriental Shorthair
Persian
Pixiebob
Ragdoll
Russian Blue
Scottish Fold
Selkirk Rex
Siamese
Siberian
Singapura
Snowshoe
Somali
Sphynx
Tonkinese
Turkish Van

HOUSEHOLD PETS CLASS
New Breeds or Colours (not yet registered as Championship)
American Bobtail
British Longhair
Munchkin
Peterbald

BREEDS REGISTERED ONLY WITH TICA
Serengeti
Safari
Chausie

III: Glossary

Appendices

Acinonyx: big cats that cannot retract their claws.

Bastet: the Egyptian goddess of fertility, life and death.

Bi-color: used to describe a coat which has one color, combined with white.

Breed Standard: a written blueprint outlining the ideal physical and temperamental characteristics of each cat breed.

Calico: tortoiseshell and white.

Castration: the removal of a cat's testicles, rendering him infertile.

Catnip: *Nepata cataria*, a herb that was used to make tea by the Victorians. It produces a slightly hallucinogenic effect in some cats, but is safe and non-addictive.

Chocolate: a pale brown, lighter than the Brown coat variety, which is usually darker.

Cobby: short and compact body.

Colorpoint: where a cat's extremities are shaded darker than the rest of the body, notably on the legs/feet, face/ears and tail.

Complete foods: those that contain everything the cat needs to maintain good growth and health – they are nutritionally complete.

Crepuscular: most active during the times of dawn and dusk.

Declawing: the barbaric practice of removing a cat's claws, in addition to associated muscles, ligaments, nerves and tendons.

Entire: a cat whose reproductive system has been left intact, unaltered by neutering.

Euthanasia: humanely putting an animal to sleep through an injection of barbiturates.

Felis: small wildcats.

Feral: 'domestic' cats that have turned wild, or have been born in the wild.

Fingerbrush: a textured piece of rubber that fits snugly over the finger, used for brushing a cat's teeth.

Gloves: white hair on the back of the feet.

Guard hairs: the harsher, long hairs that form the weatherproof topcoat.

House-cat: a cat that never goes outside – she is confined to the house.

Inbreeding: the breeding of close relations to each other (e.g. father to daughter).

Lilac: a pinkish-gray coat color.

Mackerel: a striped tabby pattern, similar to a fish skeleton.

Mask: a darker-colored face that makes it look as if the cat is wearing a mask.

Miacids: a group of animals dating back 60 million years ago, from whom the cat originated.

Microchipping: permanently identifying the cat by inserting a microchip in between the shoulder blades. When scanned with a special reader, this microchip reveals a unique number which corresponds to the owner's contact details.

Middening: when a cat leaves uncovered feces in prominent places to mark her territory.

Mittens: white hairs on the front feet.

Mixed-breed: a non-purebred cat; of mixed parentage.

Moggie: a mixed-breed/non-purebred.

Muzzle: the cat's nose and mouth.

Neutering: sterilizing a cat, so he or she cannot reproduce.

Odd eyes: where a cat's eyes are two different colors.

Osiris: the Egyptian god of agriculture.

Outcrossing: breeding to an unrelated cat, often of a different breed altogether.

Panthera: big cats, such as the lion and tiger.

Part-colored: two coat colors, combined with white.

Pointed/Points: see Colorpoint.

Pedigree: a cat's family tree, showing ancestors over several generations.

Purebred: a cat of a recognized breed whose ancestors can be traced for at least four generations.

Queen: an entire, unneutered female cat.

Ruff: a cat's 'mane' – more abundant hair around the neck.

Seal: dark brown coat color.

Season: the period during which a female cat becomes able to conceive.

Self color: see Solid color.

Shaded: used to describe a tipped coat, where hair is shaded more than in a Shell coat, but less than a Smoke one. See also Tipped.

Shell: where hair is shaded only at the very tip. See also Shaded, Smoke, and Tipped.

Smoke: a tipped coat that has the most depth of shading up the hair shaft. See also Shaded, Shell, and Tipped.

Socialization: exposure to life experiences.

Solid color: where a cat's coat is just one color.

Spaying: the surgical removal of a female cat's reproductive system.

Spraying: this is different to urination. The cat will not squat, but will stand, lift her tail and squirt out hormone-rich, very smelly urine as a form of marking her territory.

Tipped: where hair is shaded at the tip. See also Shell, Shaded and Smoke.

Ticked: hair that has bands of color on it.

Tom: an entire/unneutered male cat.

Topcoat: the outercoat, consisting of hard guard hairs.

Tortoiseshell: a coat pattern consisting of dark and light orange/red with black. The majority of torties are females; males are the result of a genetic abnormality and are usually sterile.

Undercoat: the cat's insulation – a layer of soft down beneath the top coat. It is usually lighter in color than the topcoat.

Van: a coat pattern where the top of the head and ears, and the tail, are colored – as in the Turkish Van breed.

Whole color: see Solid color.

IV: Index